The Making of Asian America through Political Participation

The Making of Asian America through Political Participation

PEI-TE LIEN

TEMPLE UNIVERSITY PRESS
Philadelphia

Temple University Press, Philadelphia 19122
Copyright © 2001 by Temple University
All rights reserved
Published 2001
Printed in the United States of America

Library of Congress Cataloging-in-Publication Data

Lien, Pei-te, 1957–
    The making of Asian America through political participation/Pei-te Lien.
      p. cm.
    Includes bibliographical references (p.) and index.
    ISBN 1-56639-894-0 (cloth : alk paper) — ISBN 1-56639-895-9 (pbk : alk paper)
    1. Asian Americans—Politics and government. 2. Asian Americans—Social conditions. 3. Political participation—Social aspects—United States. 4. United States—Race relations—Political aspects. I. Title.

E184.O6 L53 2001
305.895073—dc21   00-066679

Contents

List of Abbreviations

Organizations or Groups

AAFCFR	Asian Americans for Campaign Finance Reform
AAICS	Asian American Institute of Congressional Studies
AALDEF	Asian American Legal Defense and Education Fund
AAS	Asian American Studies
ACJ	American Citizens for Justice
AFL	American Federation of Labor
AIWA	Asian Immigrant Women Advocates
ALC	Asian Law Caucus
APALA	Asian Pacific American Labor Alliance
APALC	Asian Pacific American Legal Center of Southern California
APIAHF	Asian Pacific Islander America Health Forum
APSU	Asian Pacific Student Union
AWIU	Agricultural Workers Industrial Union
AWOC	Agricultural Workers Organizing Committee
BTS	Break the Silence Coalition
CAAAV	Committee Against Anti-Asian Violence
CACA	Chinese American Citizens Alliance
CAPAFR	Coalition of Asian Pacific Americans for Fair Re-apportionment
CARES	Coalition Against Racial and Ethnic Stereotyping
CAUSE	Chinese Americans United for Self Empowerment
CAWIU	Cannery and Agricultural Workers Industrial Union
CCBA	Chinese Consolidated Benevolent Association or the Chinese Six Companies
CERL	Chinese Equal Rights League
CHAMP	Coalition for Harmony in Monterey Park
CHLA	Chinese Hand Laundry Alliance
DNC	Democratic National Committee
ECASU	East Coast Asian Student Union

FilCRA	Filipino Civil Rights Advocates
FLU	Filipino Labor Union
HERE	Hotel Employees and Restaurant Employees Union
HSPA	Hawaii Sugar Plantation Association
IACPA	India Abroad Center for Political Awareness
ICPSR	Inter-university Consortium for Political and Social Research
ILWU	International Longshoremen's and Warehousemen's Union
JAA	Japanese Association of America
JACL	Japanese American Citizens League
JMLA	Japanese-Mexican Labor Association
KAC	Korean American Coalition
KIWA	Korean Immigrant Workers Advocates
KNA	Korean National Association
LULAC	League of United Latin American Citizens
MASU	Midwest Asian Student Union
NAAAP	National Association of Asian American Professionals
NAACP	National Association for the Advancement of Colored People
NAKA	National Association of Korean Americans
NAKASEC	National Korean American Service and Education Consortium
NAPABA	National Asian Pacific American Bar Association
NAPALC	National Asian Pacific American Legal Consortium
NAVASA	National Alliance of Vietnamese American Service Agencies
NCAPA	National Council of Asian Pacific Americans
NCPRR	National Congress for Puerto Rican Rights
NFFAA	National Federation of Filipino American Associations
NFIA	National Federation of Indian-American Associations in North America
NMU	National Maritime Union
NNAAV	National Network Against Anti-Asian Violence
NYTWA	New York Taxi Workers Alliance
OCA	Organization of Chinese Americans
RCPOR	Roper Center of Public Opinion Research
SEARAC	Southeast Asian Refugee Action Center

UCAPAWA	United Cannery, Agricultural, Packing, and Allied Workers of America
UFW	United Farm Workers
USPAACC	U.S. Pan-Asian American Chamber of Commerce

Survey Datasets

CPS	Current Population Survey Voter Supplement Files
GSS	General Social Survey
LATP, 1992–97	*Los Angeles Times* Poll of Asian Ethnic Groups in Southern California
LATP-CA	*Los Angeles Times* Poll, California General Election
LATP-SC	*Los Angeles Times* Poll, Study #318, Asians in Southern California, 1993
LATP-LAC	*Los Angeles Times* Poll, Study #395, City of Los Angeles Survey, Fifth Anniversary of the Rodney King Riots, April 1997
LASUI	Multi-City Study of Urban Inequality, 1992–1994: Los Angeles, Household Survey
MCSUI	Multi-City Study of Urban Inequality, 1992–1994
NES	American National Election Study
Race Poll	*Washington Post*/Kaiser Foundation/Harvard University Poll, 1995
VNS	Voter News Service
VNS-CA	Voter News Service, California state file

Introduction

WHEN I began research for this book five years ago, I had a somewhat different purpose in mind. I was to focus on developing a theory of political behavior that can help explain the apparent disparity between Asian American economic and political accomplishments observed in the census data. I was to move quickly from a brief review of the general history of Asians in America and rely heavily on statistical analysis of survey data to interpret the meanings of being Asian American as compared to other American groups. And I was not to question assumptions of their relative passivity and complacency, but to take them as a given. This approach soon crumbled as I tried to reconstruct the group's history of community formation in the new land. I could not help but be drawn in by the sophisticated and audacious means the men and women who came before me used to adapt to and to fight the system. The stories of how these unsung heroes and heroines negotiated with both a repressive system and with other racial and ethnic groups have loomed larger in this project than I have planned. It is impossible to try to present a more comprehensive profile of the political participation of Asian Americans without paying proper attention to these decisions and actions. It has been a luxury and an awesome experience to share their stories and learn about myself, my community, and my adopted country.

What is America? Part of any speculation about the future of America depends on developing a more accurate picture of the past and present status of its major racial and ethnic groups. Although Asian immigrants have resided in the United States since at least the mid-1800s and they were the nation's fastest growing minority group in the 1990s, their stories of exclusion, adaptation, and participation have been largely missing from scholarly discussions on such vital issues as race and diversity. This book aims to fill that void by offering an interdisciplinary interpretation of the political experience of Asians in America that bridges research in Political Science and Asian American Studies.

It will unravel stereotypes and misconceptions about the supposedly monotonous, conformist, and uniformly inconsequential character of Asian American participation in U.S. politics and explore the meanings of political participation by Asians in multiracial/multicultural America and in both historical and contemporary settings.[1]

The last fifteen years have seen the emergence of excellent single-authored historical accounts in Asian American Studies (e.g., Daniels 1988; Ichioka 1988; Jensen 1988; Takaki 1989; Chan 1991; Yu 1992; Wei 1993; Friday 1994; Okihiro 1991, 1994; Yung 1995; Takahashi 1997; Tchen 1999). But formal, quantitative analyses of the sociopolitical status of Asian Americans have been scarce. This book attempts to strike a balance between the two approaches. It opens with an overview of the multifaceted and multiethnic group history of political participation prior to 1965 and follows with an examination of issues at both organizational and mass political levels that relate to the creation of a distinct, socially constructed race and a transnational and multiethnic community in contemporary America. To compare the patterns of political attitudes and behavior between Asians and those of non-Hispanic whites, Blacks, and Latinos,[2] I analyze an extensive set of archival data on American public opinion collected in the 1990s that contains a significant number of Asians in the sample. To account for the increasing diversity in the ethnic and national origin of Asian Americans, I make comparisons between populations of, for example, Chinese and Filipinos, and Chinese and Koreans and Vietnamese. I also pay special attention to the remarkable progress of Asian American women and the lingering barriers they face compared to Asian men and other groups of men and women in becoming equal partners in U.S. society and polity. The results of this project should provide not only benchmark data on the political participation of Asian Americans but also a more comprehensive understanding of the continuity and change in the status of Asian Americans and their relationships with other American groups in multiracial/multicultural America than has been available to date.

One thesis of the project is that, contrary to a triangulated group image of cultural docility, socioeconomic success, and political complacency, peoples of Asian descent have always been able to interact with a transpacific system of multiple forms of repression to bargain for their best possible space in American society and polity. Rather than being passive objects of social forces, Asian American men and women have been pragmatic and calculating actors who have adopted a multifaceted style of politics to maximize their chances of survival and their interests. Prior to the eras of modern civil rights and electoral politics, they manifested a variety of political strategies ranging from active resistance to accommodation, of tactics ranging from protest to litigation, and of styles encompassing both the left and the right ends of the political spectrum. Their explicit forms of political expression reflected the confluence of a complex dynamic between internal community structure and external legal, social, political, and international context. Their participation not only earned them a rightful place to survive and thrive in America but helped transform the identity of both the foreign- and the U.S.-born generations into one that is both ethnic and American.

Based primarily on theories of racial formation and panethnicization, I argue in Chapter 2 that it takes a strand of coalition-building movements for liberation, justice, and empowerment at the organizational level in the post-1965 era to transform the ethnic-specific group identity into one that is panethnic in nature. The chapter depicts the onerous birth and growth of the pan–Asian American community and identity after 1965, in arenas moving from the margins to the mainstreams of American politics as well as from ethnic-specific group politics to panethnic and transnational politics. These transformations were made possible by the drastic expansion of the community population base since the passage of the 1965 U.S. Immigration Act, but they were also made more difficult by the subsequent rise in the diversification and fragmentation of the population. Nevertheless, concurrent changes in the domestic sociopolitical and global economic context threatening the primary identity and interests of the localized community created organizing momentum for a more coherent community, which demography alone does not predict.

The fallacy of the cultural deficiency hypothesis in predicting Asian American political behavior is further attacked in Chapter 3 by examining the situation of Hawaiian Asians in mainstream electoral politics. The goal of the chapter, however, is to illustrate another thesis of the book: Political participation by Asian Americans matters, either as immigrants or citizens, men or women, leaders or followers of organized community, student, and labor groups, or as governing elites, voters, or other participants in the formal electoral process. Both the Asia-born and the U.S.-born protested immigration exclusion and other discriminatory legislative and administrative actions and contributed to the establishment of important precedents in civil rights litigation. Participation in community-based and social movement organizations helped construct and reconstruct ethnic identity in America. In this chapter, I argue that, whereas the presence of Asians in Congress was highly significant to the uplifting of Asian American political efficacy, the more important role of these men and women sent to Congress from the Pacific states has been their contribution to constructing a more viable political community for Asian Americans nationwide. Acting as more than a reflection of constituency opinions, many took it upon themselves to advocate for justice and rights for Asians and other communities of color. Their participation in government, in turn, helped mobilize mass participation in the electoral process.

Evidence of support for the second thesis can be found in the remaining chapters. Both organizational- and mass-level results demonstrate, among other findings, that given proper social and political context and equal access to resources, political participation can help forge a larger sense of community beyond racial, ethnic, class, and gender boundaries for Asians as well as for other groups of Americans. Key to transcending primordial boundaries is the presence of bridging institutions such as interethnic or interracial couples and multiethnic or integrated organizations. These institutions have facilitated the forging of cross-ethnic and -racial coalitions in both historical and contemporary times based either on common class status, anti-racist ideology, shared neighborhoods, economic interest, or friendship and marital ties. I also find that becoming U.S. citizens and voters or getting integrated into the political system can help reduce the racial, ethnic, and gender gaps in political opinions between Asians and others as well as among Asian subgroups. Last but not least, I emphasize in Chapter 6 that, like Asian American men (whose presence dominated the majority of the group's history), Asian American women engaged in numerous incidences of individual and collective political action to fight against repression based on ethnicity, race, class, and gender and for democracy and freedom in both the United States and their ancestral homelands. They were essential in preserving and transmitting ethnic cultures and enabling social and political mobility of the community in America.

Nevertheless, for reasons arising from societies of both the East and the West, the political experience of Asian Americans has been mostly an uphill battle against multiple forms of oppression in race, ethnicity, class, and gender. Outside of Hawaii, there is a severe case of Asian underrepresentation in the American political system, even though the extent of political incorporation varies greatly from one locality to another and it does not necessarily correspond to Asian population share or size in each community. This reflects, in part, the lack of citizenship and voting registration of individual Asians. More importantly, it implies the reality of the American racial and class systems and the paradoxical and ambivalent racial status of Asian Americans as simultaneously superachievers in education and income, underachievers in politics and participation, and constant outsiders to mainstream culture and institutions. The participation potential of Asian Americans has been suppressed by discriminatory legislation regarding immigration, citizenship, education, and other social and economic rights throughout history. The divide-and-conquer policy has prevented Asians from forming partnerships with one another. In the post-1965 era, the transformations of community population structure as well as the political and economic restructuring on both sides of the Pacific have presented new opportunities for, but also challenges to, the conception of community identity and citizenship as well as the efficacy of panethnic-based empowerment strategy.

Braving the confluence of these forces, how have Asian American men and women of various ethnicity, class, nativity, and other backgrounds been able to express themselves politically and cooperate with men and women of other racial and ethnic origins? The quantitative part of this project strives to provide a more accurate and sophisticated understanding of the contours of Asian American political attitudes and behavior than currently exists. I present in the tables summary statistics of behavior domains that are as diversified as data permit. I also discuss results of multivariate regression analysis to help distinguish or specify the unique influence of race, ethnicity, class, and gender and their interrelationships. However, because of the lack of nationally representative data and the multitude of methodological issues associated with the surveying of Asian American political opinion (as discussed in the Appendix), the answers provided in the statistical analyses can only be tentative, and readers are asked to exercise extreme caution when interpreting results.

This research was assisted by a fellowship from the International

Migration Program of the Social Science Research Council with funds provided by the Andrew W. Mellon Foundation. I also wish to acknowledge support by the Ethnic Studies Program at the University of Utah, which gave me a one-course release in Fall 1999. My most sincere appreciation goes to Jennifer Hochschild for being extraordinarily helpful in providing comments for writing and revision. I also thank Andrew Aoki, Ling-chi Wang, Michael Omi, Karen Leong, Him Mark Lai, Tony Affigne, Okiyoshi Takeda, Ron Schmidt, Don Nakanishi, Lily Lee Chen, and M. Margaret Conway, as well as my colleagues Susan Olson and Haruko Moriyasu at the University of Utah, for their generosity in providing invaluable comments and encouragement. I appreciate as well the editorial assistance from Doris Braendel and Janet Francendese from Temple University Press, Kathleen Hom of Salt Lake City, Don Reisman of Washington, D.C., and Melanie Wiggins and Tricia Stuart of Graphic Composition, Inc. Last but not least, I thank Karen Narasaki of the National Asian Pacific American Legal Consortium, Margaret Fung of the Asian American Legal Defense and Education Fund, and Kathay Feng of the Asian Pacific American Law Center for sharing information on community exit polls.

1   Charting a Hidden Terrain: Historical Struggles for Inclusion and Justice Prior to the Era of Civil Rights and Electoral Politics

"We, therefore, appeal for an equal chance in the race of life in this our adopted home—a large number of us have spent almost all our lives in this country and claimed no other but this as ours."
—Chinese Equal Rights League (1892)

ANY ATTEMPT to characterize the evolution of Asian America is similar to the impossible task of painting a Chinese dragon. Each artist may come up with a version, depending on his or her own vantage view, but none will be able to provide a full and authentic account of the mysterious creature. For no one can claim to have seen it all, head to tail. Yet, unlike the fabled dragon, the very real and prolonged existence of the Asian community in America cannot be questioned. It exists in historical research, literature, folklore, artifacts, archaeological sites, trading accounts, personal journals, newspaper articles, government documents, and other writings. To what extent and in what ways have Asians in America been able to participate in politics? The answer depends not the least on where one begins the story and how one defines the concept of political participation. If the concept is defined solely in terms of contemporary electoral politics, Asian Americans as a racialized group have lagged behind all other major socially constructed groups in voting participation and political representation (Lien 1997a). However, if one expands the conception to include all types of political action adopted in the group's pursuit for immigration, citizenship, and social and economic justice throughout its history, scholars in the disciplines of history, law, sociology, and ethnic studies have suggested that Asian Americans were hyperactive and sophisticated in their attempts to influence government decisions as well as those of the labor bosses and the American public prior to the 1960s.

Curiously, mentions of this level of political sophistication and involvement by a nonwhite immigrant population have been sorely absent from the American political science literature. What follows is an interdisciplinary and preliminary survey of a vast but underdeveloped terrain of American politics. The primary purpose is to unravel stereotypes of passivity and monotony.[1] Rather than perceiving Asian Americans as voiceless or docile recipients of racial oppression, this chapter attempts to portray Asians as pragmatic and calculating people capable of adopting a wide array of political strategies and styles encompassing both the left and the right ends of the political spectrum. Their purpose of action was to maximize both their chances of survival and their interests within the given constraints of the ethnic community structure as well as the social, economic, legal, and political conditions in both the United States and Asia. The chapter begins with a brief introduction of the immigration history of Asian Americans and the racial treatment they received. It then discusses the formation of umbrella organizations as a chief means of response among the immigrant population, followed by a discussion of political organizing among the U.S.-born. To illustrate the multifaceted and, at times, controversial style of participation used by groups of Asian Americans before 1965, the balance of the chapter examines a parade of participation spheres such as labor protests, pursuit of immigration and naturalization, the search for economic and social justice, involvement in homeland politics, and wartime patriotism and dissent.

COMING TO AMERICA

Although the precise origins of the Asian presence in America cannot be firmly attributed,[2] the Filipino villages found along the coast of today's Louisiana were built by sailors from Manila in 1763 and are considered the oldest continuous Asian settlements in America (Espina 1988). However, significant Asian migration to America began with the arrival of the Chinese during the California Gold Rush in 1849. In 1870, the Chinese were 0.16 percent of the U.S. population, but 8.8 percent of California's population, and 25 percent of the state's workforce (Bonacich 1984; Takaki 1989). Before the passage of the Chinese Exclusion Act in 1882, nearly 300,000 Chinese male laborers had arrived in the continental United States—even though about half of them eventually returned to China (Sandmeyer 1973; Takaki 1989).

Welcomed for their industriousness, dependability, mobility, and low costs, these sojourners toiled in the gold mines long after others abandoned the field. They helped connect the Pacific and Atlantic ends of the transcontinental railroad at Promontory Point, Utah, and reclaimed thousands of acres of tule swamps in the Sacramento-San Joaquin Delta and turned them into agrarian fields. Chinese men filled in for female service workers on the frontier and established themselves as operators of hand laundries and restaurants in America (Chinn, Lai, and Choy 1969; Lee 1978; Tsai 1986). They contributed at least as much to the development of the American West as their Irish, Italian, German, Greek, Portuguese, and Polish counterparts (Fuchs 1990). Yet, their presence was considered too visible, too sudden, too strange; they had the dubious distinction of being both meek and menacing to the predominantly Anglo society. More importantly, many perceived their inclusion in the developing American workforce as detrimental to the joint interests of the Democratic party politicians and trade union leaders (Saxton 1971). Vilifying Chinese labor provided a cheap panacea to the multiple social and economic problems generated out of the massive industrial upheavals of the 1870s (Gyory 1998). Subsequently, only Chinese of merchant and diplomat classes and their families as well as students, teachers, ministers, and travelers were permitted to enter during the period of Chinese exclusion, 1882–1943 (Tsai 1986).[3]

The exclusion legislation of 1882 inaugurated a unique part of the Asian American experience that was both qualitatively and quantitatively different from the Americanization experience of all other immigrant groups. Although neither the experience of the Chinese nor that of other peoples of color can be understood without invoking simultaneously such concepts as racism, nativism, sexism, and labor exploitation, the exclusion legislation significantly curtailed the size and future growth of the Chinese immigrant community and helped secure the dominance of the merchant elite in the predominantly male society. To capitalist America, the termination of the inflow of cheap Chinese labor meant it needed to recruit other Asian labor for replacement. Henceforth, Japanese workers began to arrive in Hawaii and on the mainland in substantial numbers after the mid-1880s. They were followed by a small number of Korean and Asian Indian immigrant workers in the beginning of the twentieth century. The first major wave of Filipino labor migration occurred in the 1920s, in the wake of the exclusion of

Japanese laborers in the 1908 Gentlemen's Agreement, of Japanese women in the 1924 Immigration Act, and of Asian Indians in the 1917 Asiatic Zone Act (Bonacich 1984).[4]

Together, these Asian immigrants from parts of China, Japan, Korea, India, and the Philippines constituted Asian America prior to the liberalization of the U.S. immigration policy in 1965. Regardless of differences in the country of origin and time of immigration, each of the other early Asian American groups shared a degree of similarity with the Chinese in the conditions of entry and the problems of exclusion and alienation. For the Japanese and Korean men and women, this period fell roughly between 1910 and 1952; for Asian Indians, it spanned from 1917 to 1946; for Filipinos, whose Asian homeland became a U.S. territory in 1898, immigration was reduced to an annual quota of no more than fifty between 1934 and 1946 (Melendy 1977; Hing 1993; Kim 1994; Kitano and Daniels 1995). It was not until 1943, in the midst of the United States' war with Japan, that Congress began to loosen the immigration and naturalization barriers for its wartime allies—first for China, then later for India and the Philippines. However, for Japanese Americans, World War II (WWII) brought about a severe encroachment of their civil liberties and rights. Executive Order 9066 enabled the U.S. army to relocate to internment camps some 112,000 persons of Japanese descent living in Washington, Oregon, California, and the southern half of Arizona (about 90 percent of the Japanese population in the continental United States), without appeal or due process of law (Weglyn 1976).[5] It was not until the Korean War that the McCarran-Walter Act of 1952 made Asians of Japanese and Korean ancestry eligible for naturalization and immigration based on a token number of national quotas.

AGAINST A CONTEXT OF RACIAL ANTAGONISM

Part of the reason for the mistreatment of early Asian immigrants was that they came to an America that was plagued with racism and nativism. They arrived in a country where dispossession of American Indians, enslavement of Africans, conquest of Mexicans, and opposition to foreign (Irish, Italian, and German) immigration were endorsed by nearly all of the white Anglo-Saxon Protestant Americans (Daniels 1988; Fuchs 1990; Saxon 1990; Jacobson 1998). They arrived in an America whose supreme legal documents contained not only liberal, democratic values, but also inegalitarian, ascriptive ideology (Kim 1994; Smith 1997). Even before their entry into the United States, the Chinese were victims of racist thoughts found in the accounts of traders, diplomats, and missionaries and were often exploited by the popular penny press (Miller 1969). Once they had landed in America, Asian immigrants almost immediately faced violent attacks because of their perceived threat to the nation's racial, cultural, sexual, political, and class structures.

Between 1849 and 1910, fifty-five anti-Chinese incidents were reported in nine Western territories and states (Tsai 1986). The most egregious ones occurred in Los Angeles (1871), San Francisco (1877), Denver (1880), Rock Springs, Wyoming (1885), Tacoma and Seattle (1885–86), and Snake River, Idaho (1887). Other Asian workers who came after the Chinese were also the subjects of assaults. The more notorious incidents included the forceful removal of Asian Indians from Bellingham and Everett, Washington, in 1907 and from Live Oak, California, in 1908 (Jensen 1988). They also include the expulsion of the Japanese between 1921 and 1924 from various California sites and from Toledo, Oregon, in 1925 (Ichioka 1988) as well as the expulsion of Koreans arriving at Hemet, California, in 1913. Major anti-Filipino riots were reported in Stockton and Dinuba, California, in 1926, and in Exeter and Watsonville, California, in 1929–30 (De Witt 1976; Chan 1991a; Lee 1996).

Lesiglative actions politicized and institutionalized the anti-Asian sentiment previously expressed through mob violence. When Chinese first arrived in California, no national immigration policy existed; the legal and administrative jurisdiction over immigration was mostly in the hands of local governments. Prior to 1882, Congress stepped in only when the health and safety of passengers on ships carrying foreigners were in question (Kim 1994). Nevertheless, the first and foremost national policy detrimental to Asians was established before they entered in large numbers. The 1790 Nationality Act forbade the naturalization of nonwhite immigrants and the enslaved.[6] Although the omission by the drafters of this bill to specify Asians as a nonwhite group subject to exclusion had created inconsistent legal interpretations and openings for the naturalization of some Asians, their successors in Congress had little trouble extending its application to the Chinese.[7] A provision in the Chinese Exclusion Act specifically prohibited the naturalization of Chinese immigrants; the U.S. Supreme Court in the cases of *Ozawa* (1922) and *Thind* (1923)[8] decided the ineligibility of other

Asian immigrants for naturalization. Earlier, the immigration of Chinese women was practically banned by the alleged charges of prostitution in the Page Act of 1875.[9] The Cable Act (enacted between 1922 and 1931) could deprive American-born women of citizenship if they married aliens (Chan 1991a).

At the state level, a reenacted foreign miner's license tax formerly used to drive out Mexicans was levied against the Chinese in 1852.[10] During the same year, a fifty-dollar head tax was imposed on each Chinese passenger who arrived by ship. In 1854, the California Supreme Court ruled that, similar to the case of Blacks, mixed-blood individuals, and American Indians, no Chinese could testify against whites in state courts.[11] The enactment of alien land laws and anti-miscegenation laws in California and many other western and southern states abridged the right of Asians to own property and to form families (Hing 1993). In addition, local statutes such as the laundry ordinances, the cubic air ordinance, and the queue ordinance in San Francisco imposed heavy economic, psychological, and legal burdens on Chinese immigrant workers and businesses (McClain and McClain 1991; Ancheta 1998). The establishment of "Oriental Schools" in San Francisco and the application of segregation laws to Mamie Tape and Martha Lum in Mississippi[12] instituted educational segregation for Chinese and other Asian students (Loewen 1971; Low 1982).

THE NATURE OF ASIAN AMERICAN POLITICAL EXPERIENCE AND PARTICIPATION

Victimhood, nevertheless, is hardly the only or the most appropriate term to describe the historical Asian American political experience. For, as shall be revealed in the following sections, Asian Americans were not merely passive recipients of mistreatment. Many wrestled with every possible means to secure their rightful place in America. Their behavior consisted of both activism for accommodation and resistance against oppression and was seen in both blatant and latent forms. Even if the majority reaction appeared to be compliance or nonresistance, this did not mean that Asian Americans were unaware of their deprived political status or that they would abandon the use of protest in the future. Their behavior may simply be approached in a more circumspect or strategic fashion. For instance, a concentration on economic productivity and financial security among new immigrants may be deemed a necessary step to establishing themselves before they accumulate sufficient resources for political changes (Sowell 1983, 1994). Because of the perceived symbiotic relationship between the native and the adopted homelands, an interest in homeland political affairs could be considered an indirect avenue to raising the political status of overseas Asians (Kwong 1979; Yu 1992). Furthermore, to scholars of immigrant labor such as Lal (1993) and Friday (1994; 1995) or to many who studied Japanese American wartime behavior (e.g., Hosakawa 1982; Daniels 1988; Takezawa 1995; Takahashi 1997), even a response of accommodation might have modified and transformed the nature and impact of oppression. For the first U.S.-born generation of Japanese (Nisei) leaders both on the left and right of the political scale, the strategy of "constructive cooperation" was a temporary measure in exchange for the greater vision of securing their constitutional rights in the long run (Takahashi 1997). Last but not least, Asians were also the beneficiaries of individual friendships and support from other Americans—both white and nonwhite—who chose not to participate in racism and discrimination and helped their fellow Americans obtain justice and equality (Foner and Rosenberg 1993).

Although we may never be able to ascertain the precise amount of political activism within each early Asian American community, what we know shows that an unusually high number of individuals and groups demonstrated their keen interest in and knowledge of the inner workings of the U.S. governmental institutions and the democratic principles—legalism, federalism, separation of power, and checks and balances—from the early days of their immigration (Chan 1991a; McClain 1994; Salyer 1995; Ancheta 1998). Instead of accepting the status quo, they learned to lobby the federal- and state-elected and appointed officials and to challenge within the judicial system the constitutionality of laws made against them. Asian Americans contributed to the establishment of important precedents in civil rights litigation such as the application of the Fourteenth Amendment protection to noncitizens (McClain and McClain 1991) and laid the foundations of modern U.S. immigration law (Salyer 1995). Long before the celebration of nonviolent direct action strategies in the civil rights movement of the 1960s, Asians resisted with boycotts, noncompliance, and filling jailhouses to protest discriminatory city ordinances (Daniels 1988; McClain and McClain 1991). Other tactics of political participation developed before the era of electoral politics included the formation of umbrella organizations in ethnic enclaves, labor organizing and strikes, the waging of diplomatic and public campaigns to sway American public opinion, and the making of political donations for international and domestic causes.

In sum, not unlike other American ethnic groups, Asian immigrants used whatever devices were available to them to participate in the political process. Each group had its own issues, timing, tactics, and rationales for action. Their campaigns for inclusion and protests against injustice cannot be characterized with a single political strategy or style. Instead, the groups adopted a hybridity of actions. Their choice of a participation strategy that ranged somewhere between accommodation and resistance, using either passive or active styles, reflected their own resources, inherited group norms and practices, and faith in the ideals of the American democratic system. Also, it was shaped by the prevailing forms of political expression as well as by the racial, economic, political, and international orders at the time when political action was required. Where resources were available, their participation often began with the conservative approach, by working through the legal and political system. The strategy then escalated to the more diversified and confrontational action plans when accommodation failed or was beyond reach. The working class practiced collective action activities long before the formation of labor union organizations. The spheres of activities highlighted in this chapter include the pursuit of immigration and naturalization rights, economic and social justice, workers' rights, homeland independence, reform, and survival, as well as wartime patriotism and dissent. Generally, ethnic organizations, rather than individuals, led and organized the campaigns; these community organizations provided a vital basis for ethnic political actions (Parrillo 1982; Sayler 1995).

The Basis of Community Response: Immigrant Political Organizations

An unintended consequence of the early anti-Chinese movement was the strengthening of the ethnic community through the forced concentration of population in urban centers. Here, immigrant workers found not only the means of survival in laundry shops, restaurants, grocery stores, and other urban service businesses but also a complex network of community organizations (Lyman 1974). Based on their ties to the homeland, the Chinese relied on *huiguans* (district associations) and clans (family associations) for mutual support and protection. Out of the need to present a united front to the host society, and at the encouragement of the Chinese consul general in San Francisco, a powerful confederation was formed at the peak of the anti-Chinese movement called the Chinese Consolidated Benevolent Association (CCBA) or the Chinese Six Companies, for it began with six district associations. In addition to providing critical aid including language, housing, employment, and medical assistance to the bachelor society, the CCBA also helped settle disputes, finance litigation, and advocate community concerns over the exclusion of immigrants from white America. Unfortunately, it also exerted tight social control through its semi-government status by being able to demand payment of fees and deny "exit permits" to those sojourners desiring to return to China who had not paid off their debts. *Tongs*, or secret societies, developed in opposition to the establishment class, the most infamous being the Zhigongtang. While it often operated in the gray area between political opposition and crimes involving drug trafficking, gambling, and prostitution, Zhigontang contributed significantly to the homeland liberation movement by providing critical financial support to Dr. Sun Yat-Sen's revolutionary party (Chan 1991a; Kitano and Daniels 1995).

The closest analogy to the CCBA in other early Asian American communities was the Japanese Association of America (JAA), a loosely coordinated organization composed of four central bodies in San Francisco, Los Angeles, Seattle, and Oregon and dozens of local affiliates. Formed at the height of the anti-Japanese movement in 1908, JAA not only fought the exclusion movement but, as part of the process for implementing the Gentlemen's Agreement, it also enjoyed a semi-government status by being able to issue certificates of registration and entry and reentry permits and control the immigration and travel of Japanese to America. Between 1917 and 1923, it was also involved in a number of lawsuits testing naturalization and alien land laws. The central bodies coordinated policies and the hiring of attorneys, whereas local associations were assigned to raise the designated amount of money for the court expenses. Theoretically all Japanese in America had to belong to the association, but in reality JAA never enrolled more than a third of the Japanese adult male population. This was in part because many had already spent their limited resources on dues to ethnic trade associations (Chan 1991a).

The Korean and Asian Indian communities were much smaller in size and showed much more concern about the political development in the colonized homeland in Asia than the status of the ethnic community in America. Because of their relative lack of community resources, they were more open to the use of militant actions to achieve their goals. Unlike the ruling elite in the Chinese and Japanese communities (such as successful merchants or farmers who not only maintained close ties with the homeland government but possessed significant economic resources in the new world), spokespersons for Koreans and Asian Indians were often expatriate intellectuals and political activists (Chan 1991b). Nevertheless, many in the communities also understood the interconnectedness of experiences in the Asian homeland and the adopted land and made efforts to promote the welfare of immigrants in America.

The Korean National Association (KNA) was launched in 1909 in San Francisco by the merger of the Korean Consolidated Association in Hawaii, the Korean Mutual Assistance Society in California, and other mainland organizations in a collective effort to protect the lives of two Korean immigrants accused of assassinating an American foreign affairs advisor who openly defended the Japanese occupation of the Korean peninsula in 1905 (Lyu 1977; Melendy 1977; Choy 1979). The KNA organized mass rallies, directed diplomatic and propaganda campaigns, and raised funds for attorneys and other expenses related to Korean independence. Besides playing a leading role in the political movement, KNA set up language schools for the children, prepared textbooks, and published a newsletter. Homeland politics were also a major concern among Korean religious institutions, particularly Protestant churches, which were the most important community institutions and provided not only religious services, social support, and cultural maintenance but also significant aid to the homeland independence movement.

To promote Indian independence, Taraknath Das and Har Dayal, two individuals with different class and ideological backgrounds, formed the Ghadar Party in Seattle in 1913 under the auspices of two organizations serving Bengali Hindus and Punjabi Sikhs, respectively (Lee 1996). The formation of this political organization represented the possibility of a coalescence among Asian Indians despite profound differences within the population. The party generally advocated a strategy of direct action and spontaneous mass uprising in India. Its call for revolution became more appealing to the Indian community after the *Komagata Maru* standoff in May–July 1914: Canadian officials refused the landing attempt of a ship carrying almost 400 Punjabis and a crew of 40 Japanese and 165 Sikhs from Hong Kong to Vancouver, and the refusal mobilized virtually the entire Asian Indian population on the West Coast (Jensen 1988). However, plagued by the arrest, persecution, and deportation of its leaders by both the American and the British governments, as well as personal feuds, the party lost its appeal to the community in 1918 after the assassination of its remaining founder (Hess 1974). In addition to the Ghadar Party, a number of political and social groups in California, Oregon, and Washington and on the East Coast also rallied around the issue of Indian homeland liberation despite their separate religious and political affiliations. An organization perhaps more representative of the opinion of the majority of Indian nationalists at home and in America was the India Home Rule League of America, which advocated a more moderate approach to educate the American public about India's status (Hess 1974). To compensate for the Ghadar Party's obliviousness to the economic and social problems of the Indian American workers, a number of organizations such as the Indian League of America and the India Welfare League also fought discriminatory immigration and naturalization laws in the United States (Helweg and Helweg 1990). The divisiveness in religion, race, class, and ideology among the small and dispersed population probably impeded the emergence of a lasting umbrella organization for Asian Indians.

The organizational life of Filipinos was equally diverse and aligned itself along fraternal, homeland political, geographical, kinship, linguistic, religious, and community interests (Chan 1991a; Parrillo 1982). In virtually every area of the American West where Filipinos labored in large numbers, the predominantly male workers established strong and lasting organizations. However, few seemed able to extend their reach beyond regional boundaries. Being U.S. nationals who entered Hawaii and the mainland in large numbers between 1907 and late 1920s to fill the labor shortage created by the exclusion of other Asians, Filipino Americans were less concerned about issues of immigration and naturalization than about labor rights and, to a lesser extent, homeland independence. In Hawaii, they faced a segregated system where workers were stratified by race and paid different wages for the same work. Their colonial status guaranteed little representation either in the Philippines or in Washington, D.C., and little protection from exploitation. On the West Coast, their belated arrival to a region already infested with various anti-Asian and anti-alien regulations also precluded their chances of owning land and climbing the agricultural ladder of success. Instead, the majority toiled in the fields as migrant workers and sought to better their lives through labor activism (Chan 1991a; Espiritu 1995).

In general, umbrella organizations in Chinese, Japanese, and Korean immigrant communities were formed in reaction to the escalation of anti-Asian sentiment. Their major functions were to protest mistreatment and advocate the interests of the immigrant community by working within the American political system. A much less structured organizational network consisting primarily of fraternal and self-help societies could be found among Asian Indians and Filipinos. However, because of differences in immigration history and restriction, community size and make-up, settlement patterns, and homeland political and economic conditions, no other communities developed an umbrella organization for the foreign-born that equalled the clout and control enjoyed by the Chinese. Each ethnic community developed its own type of leadership and style as well as sphere of participation based on the community's structure and primary concerns. For the Chinese, the merchant class acquired political leadership because of its early arrival, economic resources, communication skills, and a privileged exemption status during the era of exclusion. Leadership in the Japanese immigrant community also belonged to those who either had close ties with the homeland government or possessed significant economic resources, such as successful farmers. Elites in the early Korean and Asian Indian communities were expatriate intellectuals and political activists. Although intellectuals also spoke for the Filipinos, labor contractors controlled the lives of the majority members of the farmworker community (Chan 1991b).

POLITICAL ORGANIZATIONS AMONG THE U.S.-BORN AND NATURALIZED CITIZENS

Although the Chinese American population during the major part of the exclusion era was predominantly foreign-born, that percentage declined in each subsequent census taken after 1900 and fell below the 50th percentile mark for the first time in 1940 (see table 1.1).[13] This transformation of the demographic makeup is another effect of immigration exclusion when the source of population growth depended more on births in the United States than on international migration. However, given the scarcity of women at the turn of the twentieth century, the Americanization of the Chinese community took much longer than that of the Japanese community. Because of the Gentlemen's Agreement, which cut off the immigration of Japanese men in 1908, but not of Japanese women until 1924, the Japanese population had a much more balanced gender ratio than the Chinese. As a result, the Japanese community in the continental United States shifted from a majority foreign-born to a majority native-born population on the eve of the WWII. In addition, although the Chinese female population was always more native- than foreign-born in the first half of the century, the Japanese female population in the contiguous United States quickly turned from majority foreign-born in 1920 to majority native-born within the next decade.

Growth in the size and importance of the native-born population in the Chinese community was accompanied by increased awareness of its marginal political status. Chinese American citizens realized that their fate was intricately linked to the alien status of their foreign-born counterparts in both the United States and China. They formed political organizations to seek equality and justice for themselves and for fellow Chinese living elsewhere. One such organization was the Chinese Equal Rights League (CERL) of New York, which was perhaps the first Asian American civil rights organization in the United States. It was founded in the wake of the 1892 Geary Act, which not only renewed the Chinese Exclusion Act of 1882 but also made it far more stringent by requiring Chinese in the United States to register for certificates of residence and imposing heavy penalties on violators. The League was to obtain representation and recognition in American politics, but its constituency was a very small group of Chinese naturalized before 1882 whose rights were not recognized by the U.S. government. These naturalized U.S. citizens found that they were not only ineligible for U.S. passports, diplomatic protection from U.S. consulates in foreign countries, and employment in professions requiring citizenship (such as attorneys and legal counselors), but also were not exempt from the restrictions set by Chinese exclusion laws (Zhang 1998).

TABLE 1.1 Chinese and Japanese Population by Sex and Nativity, 1900–1950

	Chinese				Japanese			
	Total	Male	Female	% Female	Total	Male	Female	% Female
1900	89,863	85,341	4,522	5.0	24,326	23,341	985	4.0
U.S.-born	9,010	6,657	2,353	26.1	269	156	113	42.0
Foreign-born	80,853	78,684	2,169	2.7	24,057	23,185	872	3.6
Percent Foreign-born	90.0	92.2	48.0		98.9	99.3	88.5	
1910	71,531	66,858	4,675	6.5	72,157	63,070	9,087	14.4
U.S.-born	14,935	11,921	3,014	20.2	4,502	2,340	2,162	48.0
Foreign-born	56,596	54,935	1,661	2.9	67,655	60,730	6,925	10.2
Percent Foreign-born	79.1	82.2	35.5		93.8	96.3	76.2	
1920	61,639	59,891	7,748	12.6	111,010	72,707	38,303	34.5
U.S.-born	18,532	13,318	5,214	28.1	29,672	15,494	14,178	47.8
Foreign-born	43,107	40,573	2,534	5.9	81,338	57,213	24,125	29.7
Percent Foreign-born	69.9	75.3	32.7		73.3	78.7	63.0	
1930	74,954	59,802	15,152	20.2	138,834	81,771	57,063	41.1
U.S.-born	30,868	20,693	10,175	33.0	68,357	35,874	32,483	47.5
Foreign-born	44,086	39,109	4,977	11.3	70,477	45,897	24,580	34.9
Percent Foreign-born	58.8	65.4	32.8		50.8	56.1	43.1	
1940	77,504	57,389	20,115	25.9	126,947	71,967	54,980	43.3
U.S.-born	40,262	25,702	14,560	36.2	79,642	42,316	37,326	46.9
Foreign-born	37,242	31,687	5,555	14.9	47,305	29,651	17,654	37.3
Percent Foreign-born	48.1	55.2	27.6		37.3	41.2	32.1	
1950	117,140	76,725	40,415	34.5	141,365	76,447	64,918	45.9
U.S.-born	62,090	36,256	25,834	41.6	102,926	53,473	49,453	48.0
Foreign-born	55,050	40,469	14,581	26.5	38,439	22,974	15,465	40.2
Percent Foreign-born	47.0	52.7	36.1		27.2	30.1	23.8	

Source: U.S. Bureau of the Census (1943, Table 4; 1953, Tables 4, 5).
Note: Figures are for contiguous United States only.

Prior to its founding, the chief CERL organizer, Wong Chin Foo, toured eastern cities such as Boston, New York, and Philadelphia as well as Midwestern cities such as Chicago to correct American public misunderstanding about the Chinese culture and people (Tchen 1999). He also published several articles in mainstream magazines to acquaint Americans with Chinese traditions and culture. In order to promote mutual understanding between Chinese Americans and the American public, he published the first Chinese bilingual newspaper on the East Coast, entitled *Chinese American (Hua Mei Xin Bao)*, in 1883. This may have been the first attempt by Chinese to identify themselves as Americans of Chinese descent. At its founding, CERL published the pamphlet *Appeal of the Chinese Equal Rights League to the People of the United States for Equality of Manhood*. CERL organized a mass meeting some three weeks after its founding in which 1,000 supporters who were not Chinese joined 200 Chinese merchants to protest against the Geary Act. In its pursuit for franchise, the League was able to persuade a member of the U.S. House of Representatives from Illinois, George W. Smith, to introduce a bill to permit Chinese naturalization. CERL also sponsored a test case, spearheaded by the CCBA, questioning the constitutionality of the Geary Act. The League's plea for the franchise was rejected by the Supreme Court in *Fong Yue Ting v. United States* (1893), which stated that Chinese persons not born in the country were not recognized as citizens of the United States, nor authorized to become such under the naturalization laws.

Initially named the Native Sons of the Golden State, the Chinese American Citizens Alliance (CACA) was established in 1895. It was formed to protest the ineffectiveness of the CCBA's handling of the 1892 Geary Act, whose renewal and expansion was considered a violation of their birthrights as American citizens (Chung 1998). The group was also inspired by the activities of the CERL in New York. The stated goals of the Alliance were to elevate their position within the Chinese community, to end racial discrimination, and to accelerate the process of assimilation into American society. The early leaders were usually professionals or white-collar workers whose proficiency with the Chinese language decreased with each passing decade. After overcoming internal strife over participation strategies, the organization was revived by the adverse developments in perpetuating Chinese exclusion following the Chinese government's refusal to renew the 1894

Gresham-Yang Treaty in 1904. They participated in the transpacific anti-American boycott in 1905 and gained respect from the immigrant community for speaking out against the exclusion acts.

Members of the Alliance used their rights as citizens to try to redress many of the discriminatory policies and acts by lobbying Congress and appealing to government officials and agencies on behalf of Chinese Americans and their families. One of the early but failed efforts was the attempt to repeal the Act of March 2, 1907, which required any American woman married to a foreigner to take on the nationality of her husband. The Alliance gained prestige in 1913 by successfully blocking a proposal by California Senator Anthony Caminetti to disenfranchise Chinese Americans. Alliance members wrote to and testified before Congress against the 1924 Immigration Act and succeeded in amending the Act to permit alien wives married before the Act's passage to enter the United States. They also assisted individuals in their cases regarding immigration exclusion by hiring an attorney for each applicant and contributing money to defray the legal fees. According to its official historian, members were involved formally or informally in practically every piece of national legislation affecting the Chinese American and other minority communities. The Alliance encouraged its members to vote and to persuade others in the Chinese American community to vote (Chung 1998). However, the majority of the adult Chinese population were denied franchise until 1943, and despite the efforts of the Alliance the concept and concerns of a citizen-only association remained remote and effectively inconsequential.

A different situation befell the leading native-born organization of the Japanese population. Compared to its Chinese counterpart, the Japanese American Citizens League (JACL) had grown to become a powerful political organization because of its organizational ideology and strategy as well as the demographic composition and wartime treatment of the population. However, it did not secure its leadership position until the incarceration of Issei (foreign-born) leaders in WWII. Formed by a group of Nisei (first U.S.-born generation) professionals in 1930, the San Francisco-based organization was the outgrowth of several regional organizations, the most significant being the American Loyalty League. Similar to many American-born or naturalized Chinese, these Nisei were incensed by the social, economic, and legal discrimination against the Japanese in America. They were "rebels" motivated to improve the lot for themselves and other Japanese Americans (Hosakawa 1982). Many in the organization believed that the only way to gain acceptance in the United States was to become 100 percent American and to discourage anything that might cast doubt upon their loyalty. Their preference for accommodation over confrontation was influenced by their social skills, knowledge of and faith in the American democratic system, and the tenor of nonconfrontational political expression of the time (Hosakawa 1982). Although it helped finance the repeal of the Cable Act and the acquisition of citizenship for Issei World War I (WWI) veterans, the League's emphasis on loyalty, patriotism, and Americanization amidst Japanese exclusion was in direct conflict with the primary concerns of the immigrant community. Conceivably, the JACL was far from a major part of Japanese America when Pearl Harbor was bombed in 1941 (Daniels 1988). Nevertheless, JACL membership nearly tripled after the war broke out (Hosakawa 1982).

When the internment order came, the League not only urged compliance but tried to stifle all dissent within the community.[14] Members in general "sincerely believed that enthusiastic cooperation with their own oppressing government was the best way to ensure decent treatment during the relocation. Even more important, they believed it was the way to get better treatment after the war. To this end they not only obeyed orders and helped to execute those orders, but also . . . went so far as to send gifts of fruit and vegetables throughout the war to high government officials . . . " (Daniels 1988, 239). Many JACL leaders were among the first to volunteer for military service, when that privilege was restored to Japanese Americans in 1943 through voluntary induction. Chosen by the federal government to be the liaison between the Japanese community and the military, the collaboration of JACL members had earned contempt and even physical violence from other Japanese Americans at relocation centers. However, it can be argued that those Japanese Americans who collaborated with the Wartime Relocation Authority and helped supervise the camps were in a process that eventually led to freedom for most of their people and that through accommodation they might have changed the course of oppression in a positive way (Daniels 1988).

In the postwar era, the JACL triumphed with the passage of the Japanese American Evacuation Claims Act of 1948 and the naturalization (but not Title II of the Internal Security) provisions of the McCarran-Walter

Immigration Act of 1952. It achieved these partial successes by building a civil rights coalition with African Americans and white liberals— through actively participating in the National Leadership Conference on Civil Rights, providing support for the passages of fair housing, anti-lynching, and antipoll tax bills, and by filing amicus curiae briefs in a chain of civil rights cases leading up to *Brown v. Board of Education* (Daniels 1988). In return, it gained support for the Reparations Act, which was "a partial vindication of the accommondationist strategy and tactics of the JACL" (Daniels 1988, 298), even though in reality the Act delivered little of the promised payment for property loss due to the internment. Also in 1948, an anti-Asian ballot measure in California that would have made land ownership less accessible for Japanese Americans was defeated in the general election. This victory was a historic first and represented a dramatic change in public opinion from four years prior when a study showed that three out of four respondents had favored a constitutional amendment to deport all Japanese and ban all further immigration from Japan (Daniels 1988).

It would be tempting to conclude that the organizational life of Asian Americans prior to 1965 fell into two camps: those that were concerned about immigrants' rights and those that were concerned with citizens' rights. For example, the foreign-born belonged to organizations aiming to address the needs for mutual-aid, self-protection, and preservation of social and political order inherited from the Asian homeland, whereas organizations seeking social justice and equal franchise were more appealing to the native-born. These alignments may appear correct but only to a limited extent; for the most part, the experiences of the foreign-born and the native-born were deeply interrelated. This dynamic was most obvious in, but not limited to, the experiences of the tiny group of naturalized citizens. These Asian American populations were additionally concerned with both the welfare of people back in the Asian homeland and that of the working class on the domestic front. Moreover, the international and class dimensions often intersected with the ethnic, gender, and generational dimensions of the Asian American experience. Because of differences in immigration history, treatment, and demographic makeup, each ethnic group also had a unique sphere of participation. Generally, the Chinese fought against exclusion and for economic justice. The Japanese sought to protect property rights and strove for accommodation. Koreans' and Asian Indians' participation centered around activities for homeland independence. Filipinos' political experience was dominated by the struggles for labor rights. Based on the resources accessible to work the system, some groups (Chinese and Japanese) adopted a more conservative approach or style of participation than others. Nevertheless, Chinese and Japanese workers also figured prominently in numerous labor protest movements. The remainder of the chapter is an attempt to synthesize the participation experiences of early Asian groups by highlighting certain actions that fall into these spheres of activism.

LABOR PROTEST AND UNION ORGANIZING

Although leaders in the American Federation of Labor (AFL) understood early on that Asian workers were capable of being organized and demanding better treatment, they chose to exclude Asian immigrant workers from labor unions for not only economic and cultural reasons but political, ideological, and moral reasons (Foner 1947; Saxton 1971). Union leaders believed that Asian American labor would be used to lower wages and break strikes and that they could neither be assimilated nor organized (Wong 1994). The exclusion of Chinese in the latter half of the nineteenth century was perceived by AFL leaders as a necessary step in building a closer cooperation between white labor and capital in the face of technological transformation. Yet, as early as 1867, thousands of Chinese railroad workers in the High Sierras went on strike againt the Central Pacific to demand better pay and treatment (Chinn, Lai, and Choy 1969). Whereas most of the actions failed to achieve their purposes, Asian American workers staged their own strikes and engaged in other forms of resistance and activism such as mass protest, litigation, and, on occasion, violence against exploitative employers and labor contractors, white or Asian, long before their admittance into the American labor union movement (Lee 1996).

For instance, Chinese railroad and plantation workers in several southern states and Japanese railroad workers in the Pacific Northwest stopped work and either filed suit against the company for breach of contract, seized the company property to demand payment, armed themselves with sticks and knives to protest fatal abuse, or negotiated directly with the companies for better wages (Cohen 1984; Murayama 1984). In the 1870s and 1880s, Chinese workers participated in many strikes against white manufacturers and their Chinese merchant allies. In San Francisco, a brief but violent uprising occurred in 1876 when fifty shoemakers attacked the trading company of Yee Chung and Co. for contracting 750 Chinese workers to white firms that then segregated them in quarters known to be dangerously crowded and poorly ventilated (Franks 1993). Even those who were hired as strikebreakers in North Adams, Massachusetts, and Belleville, New Jersey, engaged in strikes themselves (Lee 1996).

In Hawaii, Japanese immigrant workers participated in numerous spontaneous work stoppages throughout the 1880s and 1890s, usually to protest brutality or substandard living environments (Yoneda 1971; Ariyoshi 1976; Chan 1991a). At the turn of the century, when the contract labor system ended, many workers participated in unorganized strikes to demand higher wages and obtain promised benefits. For example, 7,000 Japanese workers went on strike against a major plantation on Oahu for four months in 1909. They were subsidized by workers on other islands who continued to work so as to send in contributions. Although the small business and professional associations supported their actions, the Japanese consul general and other members of the establishment within the ethnic community opposed the militant approach. The Hawaii Sugar Plantation Association (HSPA) was able to exploit the internal divisiveness of the Japanese community and defeat the strike. After the mid-1920s, Filipinos became the main Asian group in Hawaii to engage in labor militancy, and they did so under threats of criminal charges. A most violent incident occurred in 1924 when 16 Filipino workers were killed and 161 arrested (Chan 1991a).

On the mainland, the Japanese section of the Agricultural Workers Industrial Union (AWIU) conducted more than twenty strikes, which involved over 5,000 Japanese and tens of thousands of Filipino, Mexican, Black, and white workers in the early 1930s (Yoneda 1971). Meanwhile, Filipino workers, reacting to the hostile social environment embodied in the anti-Filipino riots in northern California in and around 1930, began to support labor union ideas (DeWitt 1980). The lettuce pickers in Salinas Valley of California formed a Filipino Labor Union (FLU) in 1933, after the AFL refused to organize a union on their behalf. Although leaders of the Filipino Federation of America as well as most of the local Filipino fraternal organizations disapproved of the militant approach, the formation of FLU laid to rest most of the suspicion against

Asian (and Chicano) labor as being anti-American and pro-Communist and it contributed to breaking the chains of indentured servitude during the Great Depression (De Witt 1980). Since 1941, the Filipino Agricultural Laborers Association has won a number of asparagus strikes. In 1959, an AFL-CIO organization known as the Agricultural Workers Organizing Committee (AWOC) was formed, thus permitting the Filipino labor organization to receive the benefits of a major labor organization. However, it was not until the 1960s that the full force of Filipino attitudes and ideas were recognized in California. In 1965, Filipino members of the AWOC, led by Vera Cruz, started a strike against grape growers in Delano, which Cesar Chavez and the National Farm Workers Association soon joined. One year later, the biracial coalition became the United Farm Workers Union. As a result of the experience of Filipino unionization, the political impulse of Filipino Americans became stronger than ever. Many realized that only the development of a united front and a strong political push could end racial discrimination and second-class citizenship (De Witt 1980).

Inside the salmon cannery industry, a significant number of Chinese workers took advantage of the seasonal work culture and pushed for changes in the system with ad hoc work stoppages and violence in the last quarter of the nineteenth century (Friday 1994). Their targets included not only distant owners or contractors but also Chinese foremen. In 1881 and 1901, Chinese cannery workers in British Columbia stopped work to protest the introduction of machine soldering, which would displace skilled tinsmiths. From the late 1870s to mid-1930s, the recruitment and management of Asian labor was in the hands of a small corps of Asian contractors. Filipinos in Seattle and a few progressive Japanese and Chinese leaders in San Francisco began to push independently for more inclusive unionization in the early 1930s. Their formation of a pan-Asian coalition and eventual success demonstrated their ability to " 'play' the larger structures to their advantage" (Friday 1994, 150) and capitalize on the convergence of changing company strategies, international politics, and interventionist federal agencies.

During the Great Depression of the 1930s, many Chinese laundrymen, seamen, restaurant workers, and the unemployed in New York banded together in their first organized attempt to join the mainstream of the U.S. labor movement (Kwong 1979). The laundrymen formed the Chinese Hand Laundry Alliance (CHLA) in a self-help effort to stop a discriminatory city ordinance intended to drive Chinese laundries out of business. The organization was considered a threat to the traditional authority in the Chinese community and suffered oppression by the leading association of CCBA. Its very demise suggests how difficult it was for the Chinese working class to be integrated into the industrialized U.S. labor force. By contrast, a special group of Chinese workers, the seamen (who were preferred over the U.S.-born for cost and labor dispute concerns), were more successful in gaining support and approval from the National Maritime Union (NMU), a mainstream labor organization. In 1936, about 3,000 Chinese sailors participated in a strike organized by the NMU. In return, the Union came out in support of China's war of resistance, joining Chinese seamen in refusing to ship scrap iron to Japan. Significantly, the Union's identification with China's cause came much earlier than that of U.S. public opinion (Kwong 1979).

FIGHTING AGAINST IMMIGRATION EXCLUSION BY MANEUVERING THE LEGAL SYSTEM AND BEYOND

From early on, Asian immigrants relied on judicial federalism to frustrate the impulses of American racism. They mounted cases affecting immigration, naturalization, and economic and social rights in the nation's municipal, district, and appellate courts and the U.S. Supreme Court. Prior to 1882, more than 100 Chinese cases were heard in the Supreme Court of California and other western territories. They were able to void many of the discriminatory measures enacted by state and local governments by invoking the due-process, equal-protection clauses of the Fourteenth Amendment, Section 16 of the Civil Rights Act of 1870, and Article VI of the Burlingame Treaty (McClain 1994). During the era of Chinese exclusion, more than 1,100 cases involving Chinese plaintiffs or defendants were processed in the nation's lower federal courts, and approximately 170 more cases were heard by the U.S. Supreme Court (Chan 1991a). Although more than eight out of ten Chinese who filed writs of habeas corpus were successful in gaining admission by a judge or the commissioner of immigration, they failed to overturn the legality of various exclusion acts (e.g., *Chae Chan Ping v. United States* 1889 and *Fong Yue Ting v. United States* 1893).

The astonishingly high number of Chinese cases heard by the federal and state courts may have represented less than a tenth of the total number of all the cases filed. Among the Japanese, close to 100 federal cases were recorded prior to WWII. Approximately forty cases involving Asian Indians were reported in the *Federal Reporter* and the *U. S. Reports;* there were also a small number of cases filed by Koreans and Filipinos. As a whole, it is not an exaggeration to suggest that tens of thousands of Asian immigrants sought justice through the legal system (Chan 1991a). The relative scarcity or absence of ethnicities other than the Chinese in litigation may be attributed to interethnic differences in the time of entry, legal context, group legal status, class status, group size, and the strength of supporting ethnic organizations. These indicators of group resources and political context may have influenced a group's choice of viable political strategies (McAdam 1983). In the second half of the nineteenth century, Chinese were able to bring their claims before the courts, and, on balance, had more gains than losses because they had the resources (large sums from the relatively prosperous merchant class and small but compulsory donations from each member of the labor class), were a part of a community highly controlled by the business elite who worked closely with a largely protective minister and consulate sent by the Beijing government, had a competent American legal counsel,[15] and operated within a legal climate of Jacksonian constitutionalism and administrative sovereignty (McClain 1994).

Over 90 percent of Chinese cases involved immigration exclusion, which was a galvanizing issue of survival for both admitted individuals and those in the process of being admitted. Litigation was pivotal, but it was not the only weapon adopted by the Chinese to fight discrimination. Sensing the imminence of exclusion, the Six Companies sent a letter to President Ulysses S. Grant in 1876 asking him to take leadership and protect the rights of the Chinese in America guaranteed by treaties between United States and China. In 1877, in the wake of rising anti-Chinese sentiment, the Six Companies published its own pamphlet, *Memorial of the Chinese Six Companies to the Congress of the United States,* and commissioned the publication of books written by Americans who were friendly to the Chinese. When the 1882 Exclusion Act was renewed, Chinese Americans responded to the stringent registration requirement specified in the Geary Act of 1892 with a multipronged strategy. Under the auspices of the CCBA, they exercised noncompliance in communities all over the nation and tested the constitutionality of the Geary Act in court. An estimated total of $60,000 was raised for the legal defense fund, the majority of the money donated by working-class immigrants. They also appealed to diplomats from China to push for a delayed implementation and an expedited proceeding of cases challenging the legality of the Act. After the arrest of Fong Yue Ting and two other Chinese (who were selected in advance by the Six Companies) for failing to produce certificates of residence, it took only two days before the three cases were heard by the U.S. Supreme Court (McClain 1994). When the traditional ruling organization was considered ineffective to deal with the crisis, members of the second generation and the naturalized immigrants formed new organizations. Similar to the traditional organizations, they staged mass meetings and flooded Congress with petitions.

Of all the tactics, the Chinese boycott of 1905 provides the most striking illustration of how Asian immigrants developed concrete and powerful strategies to confront the exclusion laws (Salyer 1995). The boycott was in response to the U.S. government's request to renew the 1894 Gresham-Yang Treaty in 1904 and to a growing nationalism and anti-imperialism in China (Tsai 1983; McKee 1986). Convinced that they were on the verge of being expelled from the United States because of the ever harsher exclusion policies and their enforcement by an abusive Bureau of Immigration, Chinese Americans pleaded with merchants in China for help. They were able to take advantage of their unique position at the center of the rivalry for financial aid and other forms of assistance from three Chinese Parties—the Peking government, the Reform Party, and the Revolutionary Party—and helped engineer a boycott of American goods in China (McKee 1986). They used the threat of trade restrictions on the United States to obtain a more liberal immigration policy. Their spokesman, Ng Poon-Chew, went on a speaking tour to expound about Chinese American grievances on behalf of the San Francisco Six Companies and others. He was able to address the U.S. House of Representatives and meet with President Theodore Roosevelt in the White House (Hoexter 1976). In San Francisco, the Chinese formed a Resist Treaty Committee to raise money for boycott leaders. Although the boycott was short-lived, suffered from internal strife, and failed to pass any reform laws, it was successful in halting the momentum to expel Chinese and in obtaining improved treatment from the immigration administration (McKee 1986).

Immigration exclusion was also an issue, albeit not the most salient one, in the early Japanese American community. Every now and then, a Japanese immigrant who was refused entry would somehow find the ways and means to take her or his plight to court—sometimes all the way to the U.S. Supreme Court. Almost from the beginning, they were assisted by a number of Christian missionary organizations as well as by academics such as the presidents of Stanford University and Clare-mont College and other social elites. A Japanese woman, Ekiu Nishimura, became the first Japanese to have her case decided by the U.S. Supreme Court. After her petition to stay was denied based on a 1891 congressional act that could exclude a person considered likely to become a public charge,[16] she was ordered to leave. Between 1908 and 1925, there were eight reported federal litigations involving exclusion, all of which originally came to court on petitions for writs of habeas corpus. Six were granted admission. During the same period, there were twenty reported cases of deportation proceedings involving Japanese aliens; all the orders of deportation were upheld except two. During the 1920s and 1930s, as the Japanese faced an increasing number of immigration and deportation proceedings, Japanese immigrants developed a habit of retaining attorneys to represent them (Chuman 1976). Although there were twenty-eight cases taken to the federal courts of appeals in the sixteen years after 1908, there were approximately sixty cases of appeals reported during the ten-year period after 1924. Like the Chinese, many more might have retained attorneys and taken their cases to the courts if they had not been disposed of at the administrative level (Chuman 1976).

Petition for Naturalization

Asian immigrants were categorically banned from seeking U.S. citizenship because of a series of racially exclusive naturalization statutes instituted between 1790 and 1901, particularly Section 2169 of Title 30 of the Revised Federal Statutes of 1875, which granted eligibility for naturalization to only those aliens of white and Black descent (Ichioka 1988). Any questions raised by the 1906 and 1918 revision of the statutes regarding the eligibility for naturalization of persons of Asian descent who served in the military were settled when the U.S. Supreme Court maintained that only whites or persons of African nativity and descent were entitled to citizenship.[17] However, prior to 1882, the year when the Chinese were expressly denied naturalization, a number of Chinese in New York were able to take advantage of a loophole in the revised statute and gained naturalization between December 31, 1873, and February 18, 1875 (Chan 1991a). The Chinese in Hawaii, in the wake of the U.S. annexation in 1898, sent petitions to Congress demanding U.S. citizenship. In response, Congress passed an act extending citizenship to Chinese who were citizens of the Republic of Hawaii at the time of annexation (Zhang 1998). Because of the ambiguities, inconsistencies, and irrationalities in defining "whites," the ineligibility of other Asian immigrants was not a foregone conclusion. Prior to the landmark decisions denying the eligibility of citizenship to Japanese and Asian Indian immigrants in the early 1920s, some lower federal courts issued naturalization papers to persons of Asian nativity (Haney Lopez 1996). Yet, the acquisition and retention of U.S. citizenship through naturalization became an important issue of litigation for early Japanese, Asian Indian, and Korean immigrants.

Japanese immigrant leaders did not persistently advocate the acquisition of naturalization rights until after the 1913 California Alien Land Law (Ichioka 1988). Until then, some were concerned that naturalization would be an act that reflected a lack of Japanese patriotism. They had considered alternative ways to obtain the right, either through diplomatic channels, asking the Foreign Ministry of the Japanese government to convene with the American government, or lobbying for direct congressional legislation, but eventually settled upon the litigation approach. A council that represented a higher coordinating organ of the Japanese Association was formed, and it identified the case of Takao Ozawa, who had been contesting the denial of his petition on his own, as an ideal test case for an assimilated Japanese immigrant. In 1922, the U.S. Supreme Court ruled with no ambiguity that Japanese immigrants were ineligible to acquire U.S. citizenship. The case of *Ozawa v. United States* (1922) remained a landmark decision until 1952 (Ichioka 1988). However, special legislation was enacted in 1935, through the efforts of JACL and a particular WWI hero, Master Sergeant Tokutaro Slocum, to grant citizenship to about 500 WWI veterans of Asian ancestry, mostly Japanese (Chuman 1976; Hosakawa 1982).[18]

Race was also a hotly debated and unresolved issue in a number of naturalization cases concerning Asian Indians until the *Thind* case.

However, prior to 1923, more than seventy Asian Indians were granted citizenship by a number of district courts. In a landmark decision, the U.S. Supreme Court ruled that Bhagat Singh Thind's claim of citizenship approved by an Oregon court could not stand, for Asian Indians were not "white" and therefore ineligible for citizenship. Following this decision, the U.S. Immigration and Naturalization Service sought to cancel the citizenship of all Asian Indians. Although forty-three were denaturalized by the end of September 1926 and the cases of another dozen were pending, the momentum of denaturalization was rocked by the congressional lobbying efforts of highly active community members such as Taraknath Das and Sailendra Nath Ghose and curbed by the skillful legal challenge presented by California attorney Sakharam G. Pandit (Melendy 1977).

Section 2169 of Revised Federal Statutes of 1875 also was used to deny naturalized citizenship to Koreans and Filipinos. Two Korean immigrants who served in the U.S. Army were denied naturalization in Missouri and California because they were "admittedly of the Mongol family" (Melendy 1977, 136).[19] After Korea regained independence from Japan following WWII, Korean immigrants, especially those from Hawaii, lobbied hard in Congress for the right to citizenship; but success did not come until 1952. Filipinos—although they were U.S. nationals between 1898 and 1934, who were free to enter the United States and able to carry the U.S. passports when traveling beyond the territorial limits of the United States—saw their petitions for citizenship denied except in California, where a federal district court judge ruled favorably in the Bautista case (Melendy 1977; Chan 1991a).[20] Filipinos who served in the U.S. Armed Forces during WWI could not become eligible for citizenship until 1919 when the Armed Forces Naturalization Law was changed to redefine an "alien" as "a person of foreign birth" (Lesser 1985–86, 89).

Seeking Economic and Social Justice

In addition to fighting against immigration exclusion and for naturalization, another major sphere of activism was the pursuit of economic and social justice. In fact, the first encounter of Asian immigrants with the American legal system as well as the first Asian case heard by the U.S. Supreme Court both dealt with disputes over economic rights. For example, Chinese went to court to retrieve stolen gold dust as early as

1852 (Chan 1991a). In 1866, Sun Cheong-Kee went to court to contest the charge of an unpaid debt of $1,240 (Kim 1992).[21] Chinese, however, quickly learned that they needed lawyers who knew the legal system, the laws, and, most importantly, the language of this new country. In 1853, heads of four district associations appeared before the Committee on Mines and Mining Interests of the California legislature to promote a positive image of the Chinese community and to complain about the increasing violence against Chinese in the mines and the court's unwillingness to receive Chinese testimony. This effort led to the committee's rejection of the proposals for radical changes in the licensing laws (McClain 1994). Understanding the importance of political lobbying, in 1860 the CCBA hired, with the assistance of a Protestant missionary, a lawyer-lobbyist to represent the Chinese community on an ongoing basis in Sacramento. Pushed by Senator William Stewart of Nevada, the Chinese leaders were successful in persuading the U.S. Congress to incorporate protections for the Chinese in Section 16 of the Civil Rights Act of 1870 (McClain 1994).

Between 1880 and 1900, Chinese litigants were involved in about twenty cases heard by the U.S. Supreme Court over issues of merchandise to be imported for cooking, healing, and decorating needs and over the taxation of imported goods (McClain 1994). In 1873, in the wake of widespread urban unemployment and fierce hostility toward the Chinese, San Francisco began arresting Chinese for violation of the "cubic air" law, which was passed in 1870 and required that every house or room occupied as a lodging should contain at least 500 cubic feet of air space for each adult resident. Another ordinance required laundry shops in wooden buildings to be licensed or closed for business. Between 1873 and 1884, fourteen ordinances were passed by the Board of Supervisors to restrict the approximately 300 Chinese laundries in the city (Lyman 1974). The Chinese responded by refusing to pay bail or fines and by filling jailhouses (Daniels 1988). Five Chinese in San Francisco, incensed by the proposed discriminatory ordinances, asked a Methodist minister to read to the Board of Supervisors a translation of a lengthy statement of protest. Chinese laundrymen formed a powerful protective trade association in the 1870s called the Tung Hing Tong. This laundrymen's guild advocated noncompliance (to ignore the law and continue operating) and developed a legal fund to pay attorneys' fees and court costs in a class action suit[22] against the city of San Francisco and triumphed (McClain 1994). Half a century later, in New York, Chinese laundrymen formed the CHLA (Chinese Hand Laundry Alliance) to fight a discriminatory city ordinance. They hired two lawyers and were successful in bargaining for lower business fees. They also fought against the CCBA in court concerning a fingerprinting requirement and, with the assistance of the Chinese left, fought a slander suit against the editor of a conservative newspaper, *Chinese Journal* (Kwong 1979).

During the bubonic plague quarantine of 1900, Chinese resisted with indignation the idea of inoculating a community based on a few cases of outbreak. They gathered at the offices of the Six Companies and in front of the residence of the Chinese Consulate to demand forceful actions to prevent compulsory inoculation. They shut down businesses to signify opposition to the infringement on personal liberties and the lack of protection and services from city health officials to Chinese living within the district. They also opposed a racist embargo line drawn so that not a single Caucasian business was affected. They then took the San Francisco Board of Health to court in the cases of Wong Wai[23] and Jew Ho[24] and triumphed (McClain 1994).

One area of economic issues that specifically affected the livelihood of Japanese immigrants was the Alien Land Law. The California Alien Land Law of 1913 was the first legislation to deprive the Japanese of any substantial property rights based on federal naturalization statues— even though in 1912 Japanese owned less than 0.12 percent of the agricultural lands in the state.[25] Although this law generated many law suits, most of the cases were Superior Court cases that were not appealed and were not recorded in official court reports. The one exception was *Suwa v. Johnson*.[26] To plug loopholes in the 1913 act, voters approved the 1920 Alien Land Initiative by a margin of three to one, prohibiting any leases of land to aliens, instituting a criminal provision for violations, and greatly expanding the state's ability to confiscate the land. Eleven landmark cases, nine in California and two in Washington, were reported during the next five years. The intent of the law was clearly to drive the Japanese farmers out of their main economic activities. A review of escheat proceedings instituted by the California Attorney General's Office under the Alien Land Laws showed that, from 1912 to 1946, seventy-three of the seventy-six persons charged were Japanese, two were Chinese, and one was Asian Indian (Chuman 1976).

In the beginning, the Japanese immigrants of northern and southern California each responded by forming a land litigation committee under the separate leadership of the JAA and Central Japanese Association of Southern California. As the battle unfolded, the two central bodies joined forces and shared the cost of all legal expenses (Ichioka 1988). They brought four types of test cases into the Supreme Court. The first round of legal battles engendered optimism because of the victory in the Yano case.[27] In this case the California Supreme Court held that the parents of a young American-born girl of Japanese descent, to whose name they had transferred some acres of land, were able to serve as her guardians. But it resulted in more stringent proposals to amend the 1920 Alien Land Law Act. More stunning to the Japanese was that the Supreme Court upheld the prohibition against the leasing of agricultural land, the purchasing of stock in land companies, and the awarding of cropping contracts. As a result, Japanese lost 30 percent of their owned or leased landholding acreage between 1920 and 1925, owing to their inability to make outstanding payments. The Japanese Americans' right to farm was not protected until 1948 when Oyama successfully attacked the 1920 act on grounds of unconstitutionality and violation of his Fourteenth Amendment rights.[28]

Acquiring equal access to education was another theme of participation in the lives of the early immigrants. From 1871 to 1884, Chinese children in San Francisco were excluded from public education and parents engaged themselves in a fourteen-year struggle petitioning the reopening of an evening school for the Chinese (Low 1982). At first, thirty-nine Chinese businessmen petitioned the Board of Education and the Committee on Evening Schools to no avail. In 1878, the Chinese community gathered 13,000 signatures to petition the state legislature for access to the public school system and faced another defeat. After 1882, Chinese parents began to focus on the question of equal rights for their American-born children and they changed the tactic to litigating for equal access to public education. In *Tape v. Hurley*,[29] Joseph Tape, a Chinese immigrant married to a white woman, challenged the San Francisco School Board's decision to deny admission of his 8-year-old daughter, Mamie, to a local public school based on her racial origin. He received support from the Chinese Consul who sent a letter of protest to the Superintendent condemning the denial as being inconsistent with the treaties, the Constitution, and U.S. laws. Although the judge ruled favorably for Mamie Tape to be admitted to an all-white school, her opportunity to go to an integrated school was delayed by bureaucratic tangles and closed off by the creation of a separate primary school for Chinese children in Chinatown (McClain 1994). Thus, the ultimate effect of the Tape case was decades of segregation for Chinese American youth.

Nisei parents staunchly opposed segregation of their children from whites. They boycotted the San Francisco Board of Education's decision to consign some fifty Nisei to the Oriental School after the 1906 earthquake. The Japanese American community leaders appealed strategically to the people and government of Japan for support (Wollenberg 1995). Private classes were held to tutor the students until President Theodore Roosevelt intervened and had the school board rescind the decision and exclude Japanese Americans from segregation requirements. Nevertheless, Japanese Americans paid a high price for this victory because of the resulting Gentlemen's Agreement to limit Japanese immigration (Hata 1978; Daniels 1962).

Outside of Chinatown, Chinese parents also lacked the freedom to send their children to the nearest public school. Dr. Wong Him's claim for equal protection for his daughter Katie was denied by a federal court in 1902 (Low 1982).[30] After the decision, the Six Companies issued thousands of circulars protesting the city's Board of Education policies and hired a former Baptist missionary to lobby the legislature for a change in the law. Years later, a similar attempt was defeated in Mississippi in the case of *Gong Lum v. Rice*.[31] A wealthy and respected Chinese merchant and father of Martha Lum, a 9-year-old girl born in Mississippi, challenged the "separate but equal" doctrine by refusing to send his daughter to a segregated school for nonwhite children. To strike a middle ground, several local communities eventually established separate schools for the Chinese (Loewen 1971).

Although de jure segregation in primary education for Chinese and other nonwhites in California did not end until the repeal of segregation provisions in 1947, Chinese American secondary school students were able to gain admission to white schools because of parental resistance. A segregation attempt in 1900 was met with a threat from Chinese parents to withdraw all their children from the Chinese Primary School. By the late 1920s, when another segregation proposal was on the table, the Chinese American community was able to avert the school board's plan with a coalition of support from both Chinese and non-Chinese organizations and individuals (Hendrick 1977).

Seeking Redress for Mob Violence

In case after case, Asians were not passive recipients of discrimination. They skillfully used whatever resources were within the diasporic community and the legal and political structure to improve their status. This section reveals another fascinating story of the Chinese attempts to seek legal redress for and political protection from racial violence. According to McClain (1994) and others, Chinese responded to anti-Chinese violence either by suing or threatening to sue the perpetrators or the municipalities for compensation of their losses. They often did so after engaging their homeland government in attempts to resolve the conflicts with the local and federal governments through diplomatic channels.

As specified in Article III of a bilateral treaty of 1880, the American government had ultimate responsibility for the safety of the Chinese in the United States—including the initiation of legal action against the wrongdoers and the provision of monetary compensation to the victims. Representatives of the Chinese government were frustrated when the federal government refused to interfere with the jurisdiction of state authorities. After the massacre in Rock Springs, Wyoming, in 1885, which involved the killing of at least twenty-eight Chinese workers by a white mob irritated by the former's refusal to join a proposed strike, a major diplomatic confrontation occurred between the State Department and the Chinese legation in Washington, D.C. (Tsai 1986). Heeding in part the pleas from the Chinese government, President Cleveland dispatched an army escort to Rock Springs to protect Chinese residents and investigators in the wake of the riot. Later that year, responding to a series of anti-Chinese incidents in the Seattle area, he sent in a part of the Fourteenth Infantry Division (Chan 1991a). Nevertheless, he was unwilling to admit federal responsibility for the criminal acts.

Troubled by the rising level of anti-Chinese violence, Chinese diplomats and the CCBA tried to take prompt action and send protests and pleas for help on behalf of the Chinese victims on the heels of major incidents. For instance, on the very day of an incident in 1886 that involved the raiding and forced deportation of some forty-six workers from the Chinese quarter, the consul general in San Francisco and legal consul

Frank Bee pleaded with the governor of California to take immediate action for this and other anti-Chinese riots nearby (McClain 1994). When a copycat act was reported four days later in Oregon City, Oregon, the Chinese diplomats decided to force federal intervention through a constitutional litigation. Although the resulting Supreme Court case denied the Chinese the right to equal protection, it was considered symbolic of the Chinese reaction to racial violence. The decision also removed all constitutional obstacles for Congress to enact legislation punishing those guilty of violating the treaty rights of the Chinese. When *Baldwin*[32] was in process, a group of Chinese merchants in Eureka, California, pressed action against the city government in the circuit court for damages due to negligence (189). Earlier, in the 1875 Watsonville incident, the Chinese filed three lawsuits demanding a total of $205,000 in damages from the perpetrators. The U.S. Congress, without admitting any liability, eventually appropriated a total of some $425,000 for the compensation of the survivors of the Rock Springs riot and of other anti-Chinese disturbances, distributed under the supervision of the San Francisco Consulate (McClain 1994).

INVOLVEMENT IN HOMELAND POLITICS

Although the immediate concern of most immigrants is to find a foothold in American society, many groups of Asian immigrants were known to have involved themselves extensively in improving conditions of their homelands in Asia. A major reason for this was because immigrants perceived a symbiotic relationship between the international status of the homeland and their fortunes in the adopted land. Many Chinese immigrants attributed their mistreatment in America not to some generalized antipathy among the American public toward racial minorities but to their homeland government's ineptitude and weakness in the international arena (Kwong 1979). Many Issei understood that their greater ability over other early Asian communities to form families was due to the military and diplomatic strength of their homeland government. Their exclusion from the American body politic further strengthened their identification with Japan. Between 1937 and 1941, after the outbreak of the Sino-Japanese War, Issei demonstrated their intense patriotism by lending moral, financial, and material support to Japan's war effort (Ichioka 1990). Their participation in collecting war funds and relief supplies and propagating pro-Japanese opinion paled, however, when compared to what was accomplished by their Chinese counterparts.

For early immigrants from Korean and India, their political priority was to help liberate a nonfree homeland, and they endorsed radical means to achieve the goal of independence. For those Chinese who attributed their deprived status in America to a weak homeland government, their first reaction to problems in China was to strengthen rather than overturn the existing regime; many did so by making financial contributions. They remitted money to China to fund Ch'ing government modernization, famine relief, and defense efforts and to purchase Ch'ing titles (Tsai 1986). Later, frustrated and angered by the hapless Ch'ing officials' inability to fight internal corruption and to resist Western imperialism, Chinese Americans would contribute generously, first to the reformist (Protect the Emperor Society) and then to the revolutionist (Revive China Society) parties, to help rebuild China. Profits generated from the various commercial enterprises set up with the donated money were used to underwrite such programs as military training, education, and newspaper advertising. However, money raised by the Subscription Bureau of the Zhigontang, which functioned as the financial arm of the revolutionary union, led to the ultimate downfall of the Manchu Dynasty.

To improve their own fortunes in the United States, many Chinese continued to send money after 1911 to help the new republic construct roads, public buildings, schools, and hospitals, especially in the Province of Guangdong (Tsai 1986). Following the Japanese invasion of China in the 1930s, and particularly between 1937 and 1945, some 25 million U.S. dollars were sent to the Chinese government from San Francisco, New York, Chicago, Los Angeles, and other American cities in the hope of alleviating the suffering of wartime refugees and for the purchase of uniforms, tanks, and airplanes. During the Sino-Japanese conflicts in the 1930s and 1940s, thrifty Chinese would donate whatever money and time they could spare to save a troubled homeland. To these economically exploited, socially segregated, and politically disenfranchised Asians, support for the building of a strong homeland was equivalent to accessing greater protection and political stature in the United States.

The extraordinary willingness and ability of the overseas community to provide financial support and other assistance to the people and gov-

ernment of the homeland had brought more than a reputation of generosity to the immigrant community. In fact, competition from rival
political factions of the homeland for the moral and material support of
their overseas brethren often contributed to the polarization of the ethnic community along ideological and class lines (Lai 1976; Armentrout
Ma 1990). For the Japanese, their intense patriotism during the Sino-
Japanese War in the 1930s formed a "crucial, but theretofore neglected,
background to the wartime internment of Japanese Americans"
(Ichioka 1990, 274). Within the artificially tiny Korean immigrant community in Hawaii and the United States,[33] effectiveness of the united
effort to free the homeland was undermined by the contention among
nationalist leaders over ideology and strategy. Among Asian Indians,
the deep-seated splits in class, religion, and politics were temporarily
withheld in the pursuit of homeland independence, but the radicalism
of the Ghadar Party probably heightened the level of interrogation of
Indian activists in America and delayed the political integration of
Asian Indians into the American mainstream (Melendy 1977).

Nevertheless, many Chinese Americans benefitted from the participation in these homeland-related activities by being able to construct a
new ethnic identity in America. During the Sino-Japanese conflicts in
the 1930s and 1940s, the patriotism of the New York Chinese was so pervasive that it cut across family, clan, village, and party divisions, despite
discouragement and repression from the nationalist government after
its adoption of nonresistance and appeasement policies (Kwong 1979).
A coalition of anti-Japanese groups called the Chinese Citizens' Patriotic League of New York was formed in response to the massacre of
nearly 4,000 Chinese civilians by the Japanese army in Tsinan in 1928.
A demonstration organized by the Patriotic League attracted over
10,000 Chinese representing 148 organizations and groups. They sent
cables to President Coolidge urging him to take a stand against the
Japanese aggression as a threat to world peace. The League also raised
funds, collecting $70,000 from the community in five months. When
organized protest was not the official policy, individuals and small
groups persisted in their patriotic activities, raising funds to send to the
troops and refugees. Women (whose roles are featured in a later chapter) played a vital part in these wartime relief activities.

Chinese Americans also instituted "people's diplomacy," reaching
out aggressively to the U.S. public for their monetary and political sup-

port (Kwong 1979). They began with an information campaign educating the public about what was going on in China and explaining the reasons for the war against Japan. They called for a boycott of Japanese goods. An "Aid China" rally sponsored by a U.S. Congressional Committee attracted 15,000 people, of whom only 2,000 participants were Chinese. The boycott earned endorsement from many leftist groups including the CIO chapters. A march in New York asking American women not to buy Japanese silk stockings was supported by 2,000 women, including many movie stars. However, the most aggressive effort by the Chinese Americans was to stop U.S. companies from selling scrap iron to Japan. With support from the mainstream labor movement, Chinese set up pickets at piers in both New York and San Francisco from which cargo ships were known to take scrap iron. When the United States joined the war on the same side as China in 1941, the American public attitude toward Chinese Americans changed from contempt to admiration. There was active lobbying in Congress on behalf of the Chinese to repeal the Chinese Exclusion Act (Riggs 1950). With President Roosevelt's executive order calling for an end to racial discrimination in the defense industry, the Chinese, formerly denied access to the industrial labor force as well as to most white-collar jobs, were suddenly released from the low-paying service "ghetto" to which they had been restricted.

An organization that was able to successfully achieve the dual goal of improving the fortunes of the Chinese in China and those in America was the CHLA (Chinese Hand Laundry Alliance), founded in 1933 by a group of Chinese laundrymen frustrated by the failure of traditional community organizations to protect their economic interests (Yu 1992; 1998). Inspired by the democratic principles in America and a growing sense of nationalism in China, members of the grassroots organization donated and raised funds to advocate military sanctions against the Japanese invasion of China and to publish the *China Daily News* informing readers of China's domestic situation and Chinese Americans' opinions on U.S. politics. The CHLA pioneered a mandatory monthly contribution system among its members before the contribution system was adopted by the entire community. Some of its young members set up a flying school in the hope of going to China as volunteers in the Chinese Air Force (Kwong 1979). The CHLA's ability to challenge the authoritarian community power structure while asserting its dual political identity as concerned citizens of both China and America contributed to the gradual transformation of the Chinese in America into Chinese Americans.

WARTIME PATRIOTISM AND DISSENT

Although Asian Americans may be highly involved in homeland affairs, this does not mean that they are not willing to die for the host country. In fact, in spite of official policies of exclusion, discrimination, and oppression, tens of thousands of Asian Americans demonstrated their patriotism by volunteering for wartime services in the U.S. armed and civilian forces. They also did so in the hope of gaining an ascension in social and political status through the granting of citizenship, veterans' benefits, and professional employment opportunities. Nevertheless, as shown in the section on naturalization, WWI veterans of Filipino, Japanese, Chinese, and Korean origin had to fight the legal and political system for the promised citizenship. The military exploits of Japanese, Filipino, and Chinese American soldiers during WWII not only accelerated U.S. victories in Europe and the Pacific, they also helped reduce white prejudice against Asian Americans and rescind discriminatory laws prohibiting the immigration and naturalization of Filipino and Japanese immigrants.

The earliest record of Chinese American involvement in U.S. warfare is of the fifty-one soldiers and seamen who fought from 1861 to 1865 for both the Confederate and Union forces in the Civil War (Lowry and Milligan 1999). When the United States was preparing to go to war with Spain, the New York branch of the CERL disclosed a proposal to form a Chinese American militia company (Zhang 1998). Although this service was not needed, more than eighty Chinese served in the U.S. Navy's Asiatic Squadron and won a decisive victory in the Battle of Manila Bay in 1898. These veterans were denied participation in the postwar victory celebration and they were not permitted to receive U.S. citizenship. During WWI, many American-born Chinese were drafted and served honorably. The New York Chinese also responded enthusiastically to raising war funds; the Chinese Merchants Association in New York pledged $50,000 to the Liberty Loans (Bonner 1997). Between 1940 and 1946, almost 16,000 Chinese Americans served in both integrated and segregated units in the Army, the Navy, and the Air Force

(Tsai 1986; Daniels 1988; Lim and Lim 1993; Phan 1993). This figure represented well over 20 percent of all Chinese adult males in the United States. In New York, about 40 percent of eligible Chinese males were drafted, the highest of all ethnic groupings (Kwong 1979). Many welcomed military service as an opportunity to learn special skills that would be useful in civilian life and to earn veterans' benefits. Many Chinese GIs did so out of a strong sense of both Chinese nationalism and American patriotism (Yung 1995).

During both WWI and WWII, the U.S. Navy actively recruited Filipinos to serve specifically as mess stewards with no prospect for promotion (Melendy 1977; Espiritu 1995). Under a 1918 amendment, these Filipino veterans were allowed to petition for citizenship if they served for at least three years and received an honorable discharge. Upon the outbreak of WWII, many Filipinos in the United States attempted to volunteer for military service but were unable to until a change in the draft law in 1942 permitted the enlistment of nationals (Melendy 1977). Over 7,000 Filipinos (many who gained their citizenship through mass naturalization ceremonies held prior to their induction into the armed forces), served in the segregated First and Second Filipino Infantry Regiment (Espiritu 1995). They conducted pre-invasion intelligence work in the Pacific but received little recognition for their contribution in expediting the recapture of the Philippines in 1945 (Melendy 1977). For those Filipino veterans incorporated into the U.S. Armed Forces in the Far East, their citizenship rights were rescinded in 1946 and not restored until 1990 (Espiritu 1995). The fight for the restoration of full veterans' benefits to them had not been completely resolved by the late 1990s despite decades of aggressive lobbying (Marquez 1999).

Japanese Americans' reactions to government mistreatment during WWII highlight the hybrid and paradoxical nature of Asian American wartime participation. Because the Issei leaders were interned very early on and since the Nisei leaders of the JACL urged maximum cooperation, there was virtually no resistance to the evacuation order except by a few individuals (Irons 1983; Chan 1991b). Yasui, Hirabayashi, and Korematsu challenged the constitutionality of the curfew and exclusion order but failed.[34] Endo, a Nisei woman, was successful in challenging the constitutionality of the detention, which eventually won the release of herself and other internees.[35] Out of pragmatic concerns, the JACL leaders charted the strategy of "constructive cooperation" to demonstrate their good citizenship and to preserve their privileged "middle-class" position in the pre-internment era (Takahashi 1997). Out of a different set of concerns, the Nisei progressives and radicals also adopted a cooperative stance in order to triumph over what they saw as fascism and militarism. This convergence of the right and the left within the Japanese American community was a curious phenomenon made possible only by the internment.

To further prove their loyalty as Americans, some 23,000 Nisei— about half from Hawaii and the other half from the mainland—served with high distinction in segregated combat units in the European theater and in military intelligence in the Pacific (Daniels 1988). They fought for a government that put a total of 120,313 Japanese Americans under the custody of War Relocation Authority centers. Regardless of this irony, the largest Japanese American unit in the army, the 442nd Regimental Combat Team, fought heroically and became the most decorated unit of its size during the war. Some Nisei soldiers did express bitterness about the discriminatory practices and ambiguity about their role in the military (Daniels 1988). For the politically left Nikkeis (overseas Japanese) serving in the Office of Strategic Services (OSS), the concepts of loyalty and disloyalty were politically constructed terms. Their resistance to the racist and "Black propaganda" strategies of white OSS officers was based on a concept of loyalty that emphasized the saving of the Japanese people and culture from destruction as well as the creation of a democratic postwar world (Schonberger 1990).

Those internees who protested, albeit small in number, did so through work stoppages, mass demonstrations, hunger strikes, renunciation of U.S. citizenship, refusal to answer positively to the loyalty question, and draft resistance (Daniels 1988; Chan 1991b). As in the case of compliance, their reasons for resistance ranged from the ideological right, or the anti-American/pro-Japan stance, to the ideological left, or the pro-American/anti-discrimination stance (Daniels 1988). Supporters of the "right opposition" were usually Issei but the leaders were often Kibei (born in the United States, reared in Japan). An example of this opposition was the Manzanar riot of 1942, which began when several Kibei were arrested for attacking a JACL leader. Another example happened in 1942 when camp residents at Poston, Arizona, protested the beating of several Kibei leaders who were suspected of organizing a petition drive protesting the use of barbed wire around the camp (Bailey 1971). The incident of draft resistance at Heart Mountain, Wyoming, provided an excellent example of the "left opposition," when refusal to obey the JACL instructions was considered a defense of the American democratic tradition (Daniels 1988). The coexistence of the left and right opposition or the bipolar resistance among Japanese Americans defied the assertion of a unidimensional and conformist community response due to traditional Japanese cultural values and philosophy of life. Both the resistance in Poston and in Manzanar could be perceived as continuous manifestations of a preexisting, underlying layer of resistance potential against white racism among Japanese Americans (Okihiro 1973). Paradoxically, the apparent accommodation could be de facto resistance in disguise because of the articulation of anti-administrative sentiments through the retention of traditional matrices of Japanese institutions, values, and relationships by camp residents.

CONCLUSION

From farmfields to battlefields and from labor camps to court rooms, Asian Americans staged a multiplicity of campaigns for inclusion and equal treatment prior to the modern era of civil rights and electoral politics. The sheer size and diversity of their participation profiled in this chapter speak loudly against any characterization of Asians as uniformly passive and inconsequential in the American political system. Transcending the image of victims in a racist and exploitative political and economic order, early Asian immigrants were able to respond, and sometimes received surprisingly large rewards. When political action was deemed necessary, the initial response of the Chinese and Japanese communities was to form umbrella organizations and seek recourse in the American systems through judicial, diplomatic, legislative, and administrative means. They were skillful in identifying and using their own resources and extracting support from both the homelands in Asia and the adopted land. The Filipino, Korean, and Asian Indian communities responded in more proactive styles, primarily due to limitations in community resources and the besieged and colonized status of the homelands in Asia.

The preeminent political orientation of the early Asian American community may appear to be a conservative one, in part because of the dominance of the Chinese and Japanese immigrant leaders who had the resources, knowledge, and skills to work the system, but also because of the perceived necessity to promote and preserve their social and economic standing in their new home, America. Their struggles for inclusion set many precedents in the civil rights, immigration, and naturalization litigation of the United States and, in turn, changed the social structure and identity of the ethnic community. Far from being docile and obedient, numerous others were sympathetic to the leftist and socialist ideals and participated courageously in the diversification of the American labor unions and the democratization of homeland governments. Through both activism and resistance, Asians in America were able to construct a new identity, not as ethnics, but as ethnic Americans, and to share it with the community as a whole. Because of political participation, the shift in identity from being ethnic to ethnic American (for the foreign-born) and from being American to ethnic American (for the U.S.-born) was inaugurated. This, in turn, might have finally permitted the transformation, however slowly or provisionally, of their group image from perpetual foreigners to one of equal and worthy Americans in the post –WWII era. But, as told in the next chapter, the making of Asian America involves another level of identification called panethnicity, which, because of its indefinite, unfixed, and situational character—made more so by the significant restructuring in community population and external social, economic, and political conditions—will not be an easy concept for many in the community to absorb. Conceivably, for those immigrants arriving after 1965 (who did not participate in nor were informed about the struggles that led to ethnic change and acceptance), the transformation of their identification from ethnic to panethnic Asian American may be even more difficult to chart. Nonetheless, during this era, the convergence of shifting community structure and the presence of persistent and new forces in the social, political, legal, and global economic order of the American society and elsewhere also produced numerous participation opportunities to help forge a more coherent community than predicted by demographics alone.

2 Constructing a Community That (Almost) Cannot Be

Contemporary Movements Toward Liberation and Empowerment—After 1965

"The scope and depth of the issues raised require a full hearing and report to educate this nation about the inaccurate assumptions and stereotypes perpetuated about Asian Pacific Americans and legal permanent residents; the impact upon and injury to Asian Pacific American and immigrant communities both politically and socially from this conduct; and the need to hold institutions and public officials accountable for their irresponsible actions."
—from *Petition to U.S. Commission on Civil Rights* (Chen and Minami 1998, 77)

THE STORIES of individual activism and group struggles described in the first chapter suggest that, prior to the mid-1960s, peoples of Asian descent sought to negotiate a repressive system for their best possible space in American society and polity. They used a variety of political strategies from active resistance to accommodation, of tactics from protest to litigation, and of styles encompassing both the left and the right ends of the political spectrum. Their explicit forms of political expression reflected the confluence of a complex dynamic between internal community structure and external legal, social, political, and international context. Their participation earned them not only a rightful place to survive and thrive in America but helped transform the identity of the immigrant community from alien to ethnic American. A similar shift in identity also took place in the native-born population, only the movement was from an assimilationist identity to a pluralistic one that accepted and appreciated dual cultural roots. The result of the convergence of these identity movements prior to the mid-1960s was the emergence of a new phase of ethnic identity for Chinese, Japanese, and Filipinos in America. These three groups were the only populations of Asian ancestry enumerated in the 1960 Census.[1] It would take a strand of coalition-building movements to forge a new group identity that transcends ethnic-specific boundaries. This chapter depicts the birth and growth of the Asian American community and panethnic identity after 1965.

CONTINUITY AND CHANGE IN COMMUNITY STRUCTURE: COMPARING 1960 TO 1990

At the onset of the 1960s, the combined Asian population in America was no more than 0.5 percent of the U.S. population (see table 2.1). Although tiny in size, the population was far from homogeneous in geographic distribution and demographic makeup. The population center of the Chinese was in San Francisco, that of the Japanese, Filipinos, and Koreans was in Honolulu, and that of the Asian Indians was in New York City. About four out of ten Chinese in the United States called California their home state; less than two out of ten Asian Indians could make that claim in 1960. In terms of population size, the ethnic community was dominated by the Japanese, whose population was mostly native-born and had a relatively balanced gender ratio. The Chinese population was less than half of the size of the Japanese; it was mostly foreign-born and male, but to a lesser degree than that of the Filipino population. During this period, about as many Filipinos were born in the United States as in the Philippines.

Three decades later, the population structure of the Asian American community appears to have undergone a fundamental and multidimensional transformation. The bottom half of table 2.1 presents the basic demographic characteristics of the six major Asian American groups in 1990. Compared to similar statistics for 1960, a number of observations can be made. First, the total size of the population has grown eight fold, whereas the general U.S. population has increased only by 39 percent. Second, the number of ethnic groups has dramatically expanded. In 1960, only three of the five early Asian American groups were large enough to be enumerated. In 1990, over thirty Asian ethnicities were identified; though only one new ethnicity, Vietnamese, was included in the top six category. The additional ethnicities originated mainly from Southeast and South Asia as well as from the Pacific Islands.[2] Third, the order of population subgroups by size has changed. The Japanese majority was replaced by the Chinese and Filipino plurality and followed almost in equal numbers by the Japanese, Korean, and Asian Indian population. Fourth, the geographic center of the pop-

TABLE 2.1   Demographic Characteristics of Major Asian American Groups, 1960 and 1990

	Chinese	Japanese	Filipino	Korean	Indian	Vietnamese	U.S. population (total)
1960							
N (×1,000)	236	473	182	14.2[a]	8.7[a]	N.A.	179,326
Asian population (% among)	26	52	20	1.5	1	N.A.	
California (%)	40	34	37	26	18	N.A.	
Hawaii (%)	16	44	39	29	0	N.A.	
Top City	San Francisco	Honolulu	Honolulu	Honolulu	New York		
Foreign-born (%)	40	22	49	N.A.	N.A.	N.A.	5
Female (%)	43	52	37	N.A.	N.A.	N.A.	51
1990							
N (×1000)	1,645	848	1,407	799	815	615	248,710
Asian population (% among)	23	12	20	11	11	8	
California (%)	43	37	52	32	20	46	
Hawaii (%)	4	29	12	3	<0.001	<0.01	
Top City	New York	Honolulu	Los Angeles	Los Angeles	New York	San Jose	
Foreign-born (%)	69	32	64	73	75	80	8
Female (%)	50	54	54	56	46	47	51

Source: U.S. Bureau of the Census (1963, Tables 7, 8, 11–13, 16–18, 34–36; 1964, Table 100; 1993a, Tables 253, 277; 1993b, Table 123–129; 1993c, Tables 1, 3–5).

Notes: Figures for Chinese, Japanese, and Filipinos in 1960 were based on the 25 percent sample data. The 1960 Census included, for the first time, figures from Alaska and Hawaii. It was also the first in which most respondents had a chance to classify themselves with respect to race. Geographic distribution figures for 1960 were adapted from the appendix of Melendy (1977; 1984). N.A. = "not available."

[a]Figures are for nonwhite, foreign-born only, taken from U.S. Bureau of the Census (1964, Table 366). The Indian population in 1960 included the combined foreign-stock from India and Pakistan.

ulation has shifted. Each group increased its presence in California while experiencing a decrease of population share in Hawaii over the last thirty years. Although the largest city of residence for both Japanese and Asian Indians remained the same, large Chinese communities could be found on both the East and the West Coasts in 1990, while at least one third of the population for each ethnicity except Asian Indians settled in California. Fifth, the census showed a concentration of birthplace in Asia. Each group had a foreign-born majority in 1990 except for the Japanese, even though the latter also saw an increase in the percentage of foreign-born from 1960. Sixth, the census revealed a more balanced gender ratio. In 1960, only the Japanese had near parity in gender ratio. Thirty years later, each group is more or less equal in terms of the number of men and women in the population.

In a sense, except for the birthplace of the population, which tends to be located in Asia, the trends of population expansion, ethnic diversification, feminization, and California-centered migration observed between 1960 and 1990 are more an acceleration of than a departure from the trends developed within the first two decades after WWII. Nevertheless, significant changes did occur in the community size, ethnic and gender composition, place of birth, and geographic distribution of the population, coinciding with changes made in the domestic legal, political, social, economic, and international structures over the last thirty years. These external forces help explain the creation and maintenance of the population trends observed above. They also provide opportunities and create barriers in the making of a panethnic community known as Asian America—a term foreign to the ears of those who participated in the census of 1960 and that may continue to sound strange to many Asians residing in America today.

FACTORS ACCOUNTING FOR THE DEMOGRAPHIC CHANGE

The most important reason for the dramatic increase of the Asian American population after 1960 is the 1965 Immigration Act. This Act removes the discriminatory national origin quota system put in place since 1924 and limits each nation in the eastern hemisphere to a maximum of 20,000, or a total of 170,000 per year. Three types of immigrants are preferred under this act: those who possess occupational skills needed in the U.S. labor market; those who are directly related to U.S.

citizens or permanent residents; and those who are vulnerable to political and religious persecution in their native country. In addition, the parents, spouses, fiancees, and unmarried children under the age of 21 of U.S. citizens could be admitted as special immigrants exempt from the quota limitation. Whereas many surmised that it was not the intention of the drafters of the act to change significantly the historical dominance of the European immigration (e.g., Daniels 1990; Briggs 1992; Reimers 1992; Yang 1995), Asian immigrants steadily increased their representation among all immigrants to the United States after 1965 and reached a peak of 52.7 percent in 1982 (U.S. Immigration and Naturalization Service 1992). Most of the post-1965 immigrants from Asia came from a middle-class, educated, and urban background and entered under the provisions of family reunion (Hing 1993). The act initially drew in higher proportions of highly skilled occupational immigrants. The economic recession of the early 1970s forced the federal government to restrict the immigration of Asian professionals, particularly medical professionals. This policy was somewhat reversed in 1990 with the hope of recruiting more Asian workers to meet the U.S. demand for skilled workers in a competitive global economy.

Clearly, the astronomical rise of the post-1965 Asian immigration cannot be separated from the phenomenon of post-WWII global economic restructuring. One dimension in global restructuring involves the gradual shifting of industrial manufacturing to less developed nations where production costs are cheaper. In the case of the United States, accompanying the phenomenon of plant closures and massive layoffs for unionized domestic workers is an increasing need to import highly skilled foreign labor. Asia was positioned to become a major source of American high-tech labor because the Asian middle-class and professionals had been predisposed to U.S. culture, values, and practices through the establishment of educational systems highly similar to that of the United States in their emphasis on the capitalist ideology, individualistic goals, democracy, and modernization (Liu and Cheng 1994). In addition, during the post-WWII era, the United States was heavily involved in setting up export-oriented economies that require "constant infusions of foreign capital, technology, and highly educated persons" in East Asia (Liu and Cheng 1994, 88). The massive U.S. postwar economic investment in this world region helped the dramatic economic revival of Japan and rapid economic development in Taiwan and South Korea, but it also created a mismatch between the supply and demand of labor in the Philippines, Taiwan, and South Korea.

This became a "push factor" for the U.S. immigration of highly educated labor from these origins. A similar case happened to the former British colonies of Hong Kong and India where the U.S. linkage was tied more by economic than by political or military needs.

Not all post-1965 Asian immigrants are middle-class professionals, however. About 2 out of 10 immigrants from Asia between 1965 and 1989 were semiskilled or unskilled workers (Liu and Cheng 1994). Their emigration to the United States was influenced by some of the same factors that encouraged middle-class Asians to leave Asia. These included U.S. ideological indoctrination, cultural assimilation, and family reunification provisions on the "pull side," and regional wars, domestic political instability, and economic hardship on the "push side." The war in Vietnam and the subsequent military conflicts in Cambodia (Kampuchea) and Laos created the push factor for three major waves of Southeast Asian refugees to America. In April 1975, as Saigon fell, about 132,000 refugees from South Vietnam resettled in all fifty states of the United States. Between 1979 and 1982, about 270,000 "boat people" arrived. In each subsequent year up to 1992, an average of 24,000 Vietnamese entered, mostly as refugees; more entered as non-refugee immigrants after 1990. Unlike those who entered in 1975, the post-1975 refugees and immigrants came mostly from rural backgrounds, with little education, knowledge of English, or transferable occupational skills, but with experiences of prolonged stays in refugee camps, often after surviving traumatic experiences at sea or over land involving deaths of relatives, rapes, beatings, and robberies (Routledge 1992; Rumbaut 1996). As political refugees, they often faced a triply disadvantaged situation of adaptation by having a tumultuous war experience in their country of origin, the rupture of cultural and social relations in transit, and lack of preparation and—particularly for the first wave of refugees—preexisting community structures in the host country (Haines 1996). Although they were able to receive federal government assistance in food, housing, jobs, and medical care for various lengths of time, they were not able to resettle as a group in one locality. Further, the peak year of their arrival (1980) coincided with both the influx of Cuban and Haitian refugees in South Florida and the most severe economic recession since the Great Depression in the United States (Rumbaut 1996). This, coupled with the image of a failed war in Southeast Asia, contributed to rising hostility in the public mind and reduced benefits for the new arrivals. As a result, Southeast Asians registered lower in socioeconomic achievement among Asians in the 1990 census, and the policy of forced dispersal failed to prevent the secondary migration of the Vietnamese and other Southeast Asian groups from all over the mainland to California.

International events such as these help account for the Asia dominance in birthplace and the diversification of class and ethnic origins of the Asian American population. The intensive U.S. military involvement in East Asia also helps to balance the gender ratio of Asian Americans with the immigration of war brides or women married to U.S. servicemen stationed in Asia. From the passage of the amendments to the War Brides Act in late 1940s, which put wives and children of U.S. citizens on a nonquota basis, to the end of the Vietnam War in 1975, almost 166,000 Asian women entered because of their marriages to G.I.s (Reimers 1992). These women's sponsorship of their working-class family members to the United States further diversifies the class structure of the Asian American population. Unresolved political differences relating to divided homelands in Asia—such as among mainland China, Hong Kong, and Taiwan; between South Korea and North Korea; and between former South and North Vietnam—provide major sources of fragmentation in the construction of a community of Asian descent in America. The wartime atrocities the Japanese Imperial Army committed against its Asian neighbors such as Chinese, Koreans, Taiwanese, and Filipinos during WWII is another example. Political conflicts are also fueled by continuous border fights between India and China and between India and Pakistan, and by rising ethnic conflicts within an Asian country or territory such as in Taiwan, Indonesia, Malaysia, and the Philippines. The implication of shifting sociodemographic structures and legal, economic, and international forces on the making of today's Asian American population is that, as the population grows in size, it becomes increasingly more difficult for peoples of Asian descent to consider themselves as all belonging to one pan-Asian community with a common culture and shared concerns.

CONSTRUCTING THE ASIAN AMERICAN COMMUNITY FROM GROUND ZERO: THE NATURE AND DIFFICULTY OF THE PAN-ASIAN CONCEPT

The idea that people of divergent ethnic origins can identify with each other based on certain common characteristics or shared experiences and interests is called panethnicity. It is the organizing principle for building a community among groups with multiple ethnic or tribal origins and involves the shifting in levels of group identification from smaller, national, or tribal based boundaries to larger, supranational, or cross-tribal ones. The development of panethnic consciousness and organizations is, to a large extent, not a voluntary process but determined by the specific political context and social relations within the state. The rise of panethnicity is a process of racialization or the construction of racial identity and meanings that is driven by a dynamic relationship between the specific group being racialized and the governing body (Omi and Winant 1994). The daunting task of constructing and maintaining a politically coherent community within the American context is not unique to Asians (e.g., Nagel 1985; Padilla 1985; Cornell 1988). In fact, it is a challenge faced by all groups, both white and nonwhite, because of the contestable and malleable meanings of race (Omi and Winant 1996; Jacobson 1998).

Panethnic groups are the products of social and political processes (Lopez and Espiritu 1990). The phenomenon of panethnicity calls attention to the coercively imposed and situationally defined nature of racial identity formation through such processes as categorization, or lumping together diverse peoples under a new or reconstituted racial framework (Espiritu 1992). In order to dissolve differences among ethnic groups that are being racialized into one group, panethnicity has to be political in nature (Espiritu 1992). The reason for privileging politics in panethnic organizing is to reconcile oneself with the contemporary reality of race as a "preeminently political phenomenon" (Omi and Winant 1996, 65). The construction of panethnic consciousness not only has to be forged from the political front and led by community organizations that are panethnic in orientation, but it also needs to be embedded within the community's struggles for liberation and empowerment. Panethnic organizing assumes the building of cross-ethnic coalitions so as to function effectively in a competitive and multiracial environment. For historically oppressed and internally diverse groups, panethnic group-based collective action aims to address common political concerns of inequality, exploitation, and subordination. With the legitimization of racial group rights of nonwhites in the post–Civil Rights Era, multiethnic communities such as American Indians, Latinos, and Asian Americans may become increasingly engaged in panethnic politics.

There are good reasons to argue that Asians in America cannot be considered as all belonging to one community, however it is defined. The demographic trends of rapid expansion and increasing fragmentation and diversification shown in the census statistics indicate one important aspect of the difficulties of the pan-Asian concept. Asians in America do not share the same immigration experiences, lengths of history in America, ethnic and racial origins, English-language proficiency, home languages, religions, and socioeconomic classes. The political and ideological tensions originating in the Asian homelands supply another source of friction in the building of solidarity in the immigrant community. The Asian American history within the U.S. proper also boasts few incidences of interethnic coalition (which is covered in Chapter 5). The oppressive environment created by racial and class subordination and ethnic division, compounded by the military tensions between Japan and other Asian countries in the first half of the twentieth century, provided little incentive for Asians to form cross-ethnic alliances among themselves. Furthermore, when the pan-Asian consciousness was finally formed in the late 1960s, it was limited to a specific constituency whose legitimacy to represent the opinions of the community was almost immediately challenged because of the huge and continual stream of newcomers from Asia beginning at that same time. In a realistic sense, the Asian American panethnicity is an *imaginary* concept used to describe a community that will be difficult to achieve (Anderson 1983). Nevertheless, one of the most remarkable developments in the post-1965 history of Asians in America is the formation and transformation of the panethnic group identity through movements for liberation, justice, and empowerment.

THE RISE AND FALL OF THE INITIAL PHASE OF THE ASIAN AMERICAN MOVEMENT

The first major attempt for political coalition-building across communities of Asian origins occurred in the late 1960s when groups of college-aged, U.S.-born, middle-class male and female activists mostly of Chinese and Japanese, but also of Filipino and Korean, origin protested against racist killings in the Vietnam War and mistreatment of the Third World people (Wong 1972; Umemoto 1989; Espiritu 1992; Wei 1993; Omatsu 1994). Their demand for liberation and assertion of racial justice were echoed by "large numbers of community forces, including the elderly, workers, and high school youth" (Omatsu 1994, 21). Campus and community-based organizations such as the Asian American Political Alliance, Inter-collegiate Chinese for Social Action, Asian Americans for Action, East Wind, and "serve the people" organizations formed spontaneously in the late 1960s and early 1970s on the Pacific Coast, the East Coast, and in the Midwest. Their purposes were to raise consciousness, to provide social services to the needy, and to offer mutual support. It was during a meeting in 1968 on the campus of the University of California at Berkeley that the term "Asian America" was coined as an unoffensive and composite label to encompass peoples of all Asian origin (Espiritu 1992; Dirlik 1999).

The initial phase of the Asian American movement resulted from a convergence of sociodemographic changes inside the community and of social and political developments in and outside of the American society and polity since the end of the WWII. It was born in the same era that produced the Black Power, Red Power, Chicano, Young Lords, Antiwar, the New Left, and Women's Liberation movements and was led by a group of primarily English-speaking college students and young social service professionals. These participants came of age in the Civil Rights Era; sensitized to issues of race, inequality, and the colonial exploitation and subordination of people in Asia and other parts of the Third World, they believed in the efficacy of grassroots organizing and social change. Based on an awakened sense of a common destiny, the movement helped transform previously isolated instances of political activism into a nationwide, panethnic political movement for racial equality, social justice, and political empowerment (Wei 1993). Young activists demanded an education more relevant and accessible to their communities so that they could better understand the historical forces shaping the relationships between power and domination and use that knowledge to build a community of common identity and culture. The establishment of the nation's first school of ethnic studies at San Francisco State College (which includes the first Asian American Studies department) was the most obvious accomplishment of the strikes of 1968–69. It set a precedent for later protests that helped establish many Asian American Studies programs across the country and inspired a new generation of activists on campuses across the nation in the 1980s and 1990s. The most important legacy of the movement from this era, however, was the redefinition of the Asian American experience from the power perspective, which presented a knowledge base and an action strategy for activists to make future changes (Omatsu 1994).

Important as it may have been, a basic problem with the movement was its lack of visibility, which could be attributed to the lack of a nationally known leader, an appealing ideology, and a coherent plan of action (Wei 1993). The number of participants was small and geographically dispersed. The call for action was based on the rather obscure and ambiguous racial status of Asian Americans, which was outside of the dominant and dichotomous racial discourse of Blacks and whites. From the eyes of the immigrant generation (who generally took the conservative and legalistic approach to politics as discussed in Chapter 1), the political style of movement activists was too radical to praise or embrace. Women activists were frustrated with male chauvinism even in the most progressive organizations (Espiritu 1992; Wei 1993). In addition to government repression and co-optation, the movement also suffered from rivalries between reformists and revolutionaries, with the former focusing their efforts on working within the political system, and the latter lapsing into sectarianism and the inability to attract many alienated youths after the late 1970s. Furthermore, the ensuing professionalization and institutionalization of what remained of the movement not only distanced community activists from the communities that they served but also exacerbated the division between an emergent professional-managerial class and its working-class constituents (Espiritu 1992; Espiritu and Ong 1994). Yet, according to a leading scholar, the most devastating factor accounting for the demise of the original movement was the broad attack against the poor launched by transnational corporations in the mid-1970s via plant closings, runaway shops, and domestic disinvestments as well as the culmination and institutionalization of the offensive by the neoconservative policies adopted by the Reagan Administration in the early 1980s (Omatsu 1994). As a result, social programs for the poor dwindled, the gap between the rich and the poor sharpened, and the opinion among young, middle-class, professionals of the community shifted toward neoconservative interests that emphasized individual advancement and opposed affirmative action and other "entitlement" programs. Because of these internal and external forces, the progressive movement entered a dormant phase, and the collective identity it promoted failed to register with the communities at large and reach the constant in-flow of new arrivals from Asia.

RECENT TRENDS AGAINST BLACKS AND NONWHITE IMMIGRANTS

The 1965 Immigration Act that transformed the Asian American population was signed into law in the wake of two landmark Civil Rights bills passed by the Eighty-Eighth and Eighty-Ninth Congresses. The barring of employment discrimination and segregation in public facilities and the installation of federal mechanisms to ensure compliance with the Civil Rights Act of 1964 as well as the assurance of fair voting practices in states that lagged behind in ending voting booth discrimination in the Voting Rights Act of 1965 clearly were intended to help Blacks and close the nation's biracial divide. Recent evidence also suggests that Congress passed the Immigration Act with a similar tenor of racial egalitarianism to end the national origin quota system and discrimination against the immigration of Asians as well as that of Southern and Eastern European nationals and African nationals (Chin 1996). The passage of the three acts as well as President Johnson's War on Poverty, the establishment of the Equal Economic Opportunity programs, and the call to move toward a Great Society represented the high-water mark of American racial progressivism. It was as much a catalyst for change for Blacks as for urban Asian Americans (Wei 1993). Nonetheless, the national consensus of racial egalitarianism was undermined almost immediately by the war in Vietnam, difficulties in the domestic economy, the disintegration of the Black civil rights coalition, and the formation of the New Right movement (Levine 1996; Schuman et al. 1997). Disputes over the enforcement and merits of affirmative action and school desegregation surfaced in the 1970s and resulted in significant federal government retrenchment in all areas of civil rights enforcement under the Reagan administration (Sitkoff 1993). Beginning in the late 1980s, the U.S. Supreme Court narrowed the scope of affirmative action policies and applied stringent standards to decide race-related cases, such as ruling that city and state officials may not steer contracts toward minorities except to remedy a clear history of discrimination (*City of Richmond v. Croson 1989*), shifting the burden of proof from employers to employees in workplace discrimination lawsuits *(Wards Cove Packing Company v. Antonio 1989)*, and prohibiting the consideration of race in congressional redistricting after each decennial census *(Shaw v. Reno 1993)*.

The rollback in social programs designated to help Blacks and other minorities came at a time when implicit racial appeals were introduced to the partisan political context (Walton 1997) and evidence of racial discrimination and bias not only persisted but increased. Racial tensions were exacerbated by the 1988 Bush campaign, which used fear tactics to link Blacks to chronic offenders of violent crimes (Jamieson 1992). Reports of racial harassment and violence increased within even liberal colleges and universities (Jaynes and Williams 1989; Wiener 1989). Subtle but significant discrimination was also found among the Black middle class (Feagin 1991), even though their apparent growth, vitality, and success was one of the important gains in Black status in the post–Civil Rights Era. Moreover, concurrent to the ascendance of the Black middle-class was a deterioration or stagnation in the educational, earnings, and residential gaps between Blacks and whites (Jaynes and Williams 1989; Massey and Denton 1993). At the root of the increasing problem of ghetto unemployment and poverty was a basic shift in the nation's economic structure away from manufacturing toward a more high-technology, service-oriented economy (deindustrialization) and the relocation of manufacturing work from inner-city areas to suburban or ex-urban locations (deconcentration) (Wilson 1987). Although the actual amount and effects of these changes remain disputable, these political, social, and economic trends converged with the growing suspicion and distrust among Blacks of the criminal justice system and led to the eruption of race riots in Miami, New York, and Los Angeles in the 1980s and early 1990s.

Importantly, the rise in racial tensions between Blacks and whites in the post–Civil Rights Era has coincided with the growth in anti-immigrant sentiment, which is a direct response to the dramatic transformation of the nation's racial makeup after the 1965 reform in immigration policies and related developments discussed earlier in the chapter. In the three decades since 1965, the influx of new Asian immigration has been accompanied by a significant and steady drop of immigration from Europe and Canada and a sharp rise in the immigration of Latinos from Mexico, Central America, and South America (Passel and Edmonston 1994). As a result, between 1970 and 1990, the Asian and Hispanic American populations grew 400 percent and 133 percent, respectively, whereas the U.S. population as a whole grew by only 22 percent (U.S. Bureau of the Census 1973, 1993a). As of July 1999, Asian Americans and Latinos were estimated to be 4 percent and 12 percent, respectively, of the U.S. population (U.S. Bureau of the Census 1999a). Large numbers of Latino immigrant workers arrived in response to recruitment by U.S. employers, particularly those in the agribusiness and garment manufacturing sectors. In addition, many were driven out of their countries by export-oriented multinational corporations that stripped locals of their land and jobs. Furthermore, many were fleeing political oppression imposed by U.S.-backed dictatorships in Central America (Feagin 1997). Last but not least, restrictions in the 1965 Immigration Act toward western hemispheric immigration and the simultaneous halting of the Bracero program for temporary workers contributed to a sharp rise in illegal Latino immigration (Reimers 1998). The belief that immigrants, especially "illegal" ones from Mexico, are a drain on California taxpayers, compounded by public anxiety about the state's economy and Governor Pete Wilson's endorsement, contributed significantly to the popularity of Proposition 187, a nativist initiative to strip undocumented immigrants and their children of government-sponsored social services, public schools, and nonemergency health care in 1994. Proposition 187 passed the ballot test by 59 percent in the same election year that ended Democratic control of the U.S. Congress. Although the initiative was declared unconstitutional by several federal judges, a number of states such as Florida, New York, Texas, and Arizona followed suit to seek federal reimbursement for costs incurred by state and local governments in providing services to immigrants (Suro 1996). More importantly, the Republican Congress rode on the anti-immigrant tide to propose major immigration reforms.

Soon after the opening of the new Congress in 1995, Representative Lamar Smith (R-TX) and Senator Alan Simpson (R-WY) each proposed, in the names of national interest and financial responsibility, broad and harsh provisions of immigration reform not only to tighten control of illegal immigration, but to curtail legal immigration and limit public benefits to aliens who were not permanent residents nor under humanitarian categories. Particularly troubling to proponents of legal immigration was the proposal to reduce family visas from 480,000 a year to 330,000 and to end visas for siblings and adult children of U.S. citizens. Industries relying on the hiring of skilled temporary foreign workers (H-1B workers) were also upset about the proposed limitations on the hiring and firing of nonimmigrant workers. The high-technology businesses lined up with a broad coalition of immigrants' rights and ethnic and religious groups to separate successfully the legal from the illegal reforms and defeat new restrictions on legal immigration and the employment of H-1B workers (Gimpel and Edwards 1999). They were, however, unable to eliminate the immigration provisions in the welfare reform bill that established restrictions on the eligibility of legal immigrants for means-tested public assistance and broadened the restrictions on public benefits for illegal aliens and nonimmigrants.

In California, the success of Proposition 187 bolstered the state's determination to expedite the reversal of federal policies benefitting racial, gender, and language minorities. In 1996, California voters approved Proposition 209, which attempted to end all racial preferences in state programs and eliminated racial quotas in state university admissions procedures. In 1998, they passed the divisive English-only proposals (Proposition 227), which halted state funding for bilingual education in California public schools. In the same election year, a majority of voters in Washington state supported Initiative 200, which overturned state-sanctioned affirmative action programs. In 1999, Florida governor Jeb Bush ordered the elimination of race and ethnicity factors from university admissions and the prohibition of racial set-asides and quotas in contracting decisions. Other states including Arizona, Colorado, Maine, Michigan, Missouri, Montana, New Jersey, New York, South Carolina, Tennessee, Texas, and Utah have recently debated the adequacy of affirmative action and bilingual programs. Their attempts were echoed by anti–affirmative action and English-only amendments proposed in Congress.[3] To stamp out the troubling trends in race relations, President Clinton launched his Initiative on Race in 1997 and appealed for a renewed national discourse evaluating the state of race relations and equal opportunity in America. Although the precise impact of this initiative is difficult to measure, the Federal Bureau of Investigation's annual Universal Crime Report indicates an increase in hate crime incidents from 1991 to 1998 by 4.4 percent.

The Turning Point: Vincent Chin and the New Asian American Movement

The conservative shift in the social, economic, and political arenas in recent decades has strangled the original Asian American movement, but the deterioration of race relations and the rise of anti-Asian violence has also provided new opportunities to organize an otherwise disparate community. The watershed event in the constructing of a panethnic consciousness regarding the status of Asian Americans as a community was the murder of Vincent Chin in 1982. Vincent Chin was a Chinese American draftsman mistaken as a Japanese by two unemployed[4] Detroit auto workers. They bludgeoned him to death because they believed Japan was responsible for ruining the American auto industry with cheap auto exports. In a controversial plea bargain, each killer was given a sentence of three years' probation and a fine of $3,000. The murder might not have engaged the attention of Asian Americans from all over the nation had it not been for the light sentencing given to the father-stepson team of assailants. In shock and disbelief, the small and fragmented local community formed an organization called American Citizens for Justice (ACJ) to seek prosecution of Chin's killers (Espiritu 1992). At first, only Chinese Americans and their traditional ethnic associations were involved in the case, but the issue quickly drew participation from other ethnic groups and other Asians and non-Asians across the country. The ACJ petitioned the U.S. Justice Department to investigate the possible violations of Chin's civil rights. Although a federal grand jury later indicted the perpetrators on two counts of civil rights violations and convicted one of them, the case was overturned on a technicality by a federal appeals court. Succumbing to the pressure of another round of public campaigning organized by the ACJ, the Justice Department retried the case with a change of venue but failed again to convict the perpetrators.

The Vincent Chin case highlights the Asian American community's vulnerability to anti-Asian violence as well as their feelings of defenselessness in the American legal system. It rekindles the fear in Asian American old-timers and exposes new Asian immigrants to the dark side of the American democracy—the remnants of an unjust and racist system in the post–Civil Rights Era. The tragic case of mistaken identity sensitized Asians of different ethnic origins to the meaning of a common fate and created an opportunity for them to construct a common culture (Nagel 1994). Blaming U.S. economic woes on an Asian American who looked like someone from the Asian country suspected of causing those woes compelled others in the Asian American community to confront once again the inseparable ties between their homelands in

Asia and their experiences in the United States. As a result, the case became a galvanizing issue that created coalescing opportunities for Asians of all ethnic, class, generational, gender, and racial backgrounds to form new panethnic organizations across the nation to monitor, report, and protest anti-Asian activities as well as other issues of concern to the Asian American community. Some of the most prominent Asian American community organizations today had their start in that movement.

The Chin case also provides a blueprint of action for both the community and the government on how to react to similar incidents. It sets an important precedent, giving activists and advocacy groups a reason to press on even after state and local justice has been miscarried. It establishes a remarkable record of participation for others to emulate. For example, between 500 and 1,000 Detroit Asians attended an ACJ rally in May 1983, making it the largest local event ever in support of an Asian American cause. During the 21-month period beginning in March 1983, the ACJ raised close to $83,000 nationwide. The letter-writing campaign to government officials and the press generated more than 15,000 letters to the Justice Department alone and forced the indictment of Chin's killers. It also appealed to electoral politics. In response to the request of the ACJ, Norman Mineta, a Japanese American congressman, wrote the U.S. Attorney General to act on the Chin case. In response to constituency pressure, the Los Angeles City Council joined other governmental bodies in petitioning the Justice Department to investigate Chin's murder. Chin's mother and ACJ representatives also addressed the founding meeting of the Democratic Party's Asian Pacific American Caucus. Last but not least, the Vincent Chin case facilitated the passage of bills in state and federal governments to better address the issue of hate crimes. In Michigan, state laws were changed so that second-degree murder charges could no longer be reduced to manslaughter. In 1990, Congress passed the Hate Crime Statistics Act to develop and implement a uniform system of collecting more accurate data at the federal level on crimes motivated by prejudice against race, ethnicity, national origin, religion, and sexual orientation.

The national campaign to seek justice for Vincent Chin ushered in the second phase of the Asian American movement. Although, as an ongoing project of political construction whose formation is shaped by forces from both inside and outside of the community, it is difficult to characterize with any precision the current shape of the movement; participation patterns in and after the Chin case suggest both continuity and change from the previous phase. As in the first phase, participants were mobilized by issues of subordination, injustice, and disenfranchisement that they perceived as affecting all Asian Americans. They inherited the tradition of grassroots organizing in structuring the multiethnic community into a more politically cohesive and vocal one. They formed panethnic and multiracial coalitions with other ethnic and racial groups to strengthen their positions. They also shared the original movement's deficiencies in the absence of prominent national leaders, a comprehensive pan-Asian agenda, and an umbrella organization to implement such an agenda. Still, much of the landscape of Asian American political activism has been energized in the post–Vincent Chin era because of the growing anti-immigrant and anti-minority sentiments on the local and national political scenes.

More than the Imaginary: Possibilities in Panethnic Community Building

In reaction to the retrenchment in immigrant and minority rights and because of the expansion and transformation of the demographic base of the community, the second phase of the Asian American movement has been reinvigorated by the participation of a much broader range of constituency in ethnicity, class, ideology, and nativity. The major ethnicity of activists expanded from Chinese and Japanese to include people of Filipino, Korean, Asian Indian, Vietnamese, and other South and Southeast Asian origins. Together, they are resisting attempts to roll back affirmative action, ethnic studies, family immigration, bilingual education, and social welfare for legal permanent residents. Rather than being on the periphery, these are major issue areas that link activists' concerns to the core of American mainstream politics. Organizing along the traditional lines of young, liberal-minded, college-educated students and social service professionals against limitations on family immigration and social welfare, for instance, are the politically conservative new immigrants and a growing number of active senior citizens. Equally important, they have channeled their actions through a vibrant network of new panethnic organizations or ethnic-specific organizations with panethnic concerns that increasingly view issues affecting all

Asian Americans from a policy framework and attempt to find solutions through legal and political recourse. With this new perspective, the movement has been transformed to election-centered politics, and community organizations have behaved more and more like interest groups.[5] New political organizations specializing in voter education, voter registration and turnout drives, leadership training, and other aspects of an election campaign were created to raise political consciousness and mobilize mass-based political participation. To function more efficiently and effectively in the national environment, the Asian American organizational network also realized the necessity of establishing a permanent multifunctional political coalition to supplement the single-issue, ad-hoc coalitions. This idea took shape in 1997 when, spurred by relentless news coverage and political battling over the fund-raising practices of Asian Americans, the first national pan-Asian civil rights coalition, the National Council of Asian Pacific Americans (NCAPA) was born.

Yet, fundamentally, the most critical issue facing Asian Americans after the Vincent Chin incident remains the construction of a common group identity, which, as informed by the panethnicity literature, is most viable through the formation of panethnic political coalitions (Espiritu 1992). The rationale of panethnic community building is strikingly similar to that of ethnic community building discussed in the previous chapter. To survive and thrive in a new environment, umbrella organizations that facilitated political participation and empowerment were formed within each of the larger early Asian American communities. One of them, JACL, has been able to distinguish itself as the most established and visible Asian American organization on the national political scene. However, its leadership may be lessening because of a changing demographic structure and the plethora of new organizations formed in recent years. In the post-1965 era, repetitive and often contentious attempts to create credible intra-ethnic umbrella organizations have occurred within the Chinese, Filipino, Korean, Asian Indian, Vietnamese American, and other Asian American communities that have experienced significant new immigration and increased diversification. Some examples of these include the Organization of Chinese Americans (OCA), Korean American Coalition (KAC), National Association of Korean Americans (NAKA), National Federation of Filipino American Associations (NFFAA), National Federation of Indian-American Associations in North America (NFIA), India Abroad Center for Political Awareness (IACPA), National Alliance of Vietnamese American Service Agencies (NAVASA), and Southeast Asian Refugee Action Center (SEARAC). Major functions of these ethnic organizations are to foster unity, encourage cooperation, and promote participation at local, state, and national levels.

Meanwhile, the persistence of racial hegemony and hierarchy as well as the increasing intolerance of racial and cultural diversity have compelled the formation of panethnic organizations among Asian Americans to address more fully fundamental issues of equality, rights, and power that affect them all. The first major pan-Asian political organization was the 1986 founding of the Asian American Voters Coalition, which included national and local organizations representing Chinese, Japanese, Filipino, Korean, Asian Indian, Vietnamese, and Thai Americans (Feagin and Feagin 1999). Some recent examples of national panethnic organizing include the Asian American Institute of Congressional Studies (AAICS), Asian Pacific American Labor Alliance (APALA), Asian Pacific Islander American Health Forum (APIAHF), National Association of Asian American Professionals (NAAAP), National Asian Pacific American Bar Association (NAPABA), National Asian Pacific American Legal Consortium (NAPALC), and the U.S. Pan–Asian American Chamber of Commerce (USPAACC). There are also many other panethnic organizations located in major cities such as New York, Los Angeles, San Francisco, Chicago, Philadelphia, Boston, Detroit, Atlanta, Dallas, and Houston.

Organized either at the ethnic-specific or panethnic level, these organizations generally share the same mission of advocacy, education, information, and networking. Nearly all of the national organizations named above have a national office in Washington, D.C., to facilitate advocacy and coalition building, which has primarily been on liberal issues.[6] Forces that compel the formation of panethnic organizations also demand ethnic-specific organizations to address issues that are increasingly pan-Asian in scope. Through the identification of common ground and the experience of working with each other on one or more policy areas, the idea of a pan-Asian American community and identity begins to take shape among active participants in these organizations. Importantly, the rise of panethnicity has apparently not taken place at the expense of ethnic-specific interests. To the contrary, as a study on ethnic enumeration politics for the 1980 and 1990 censuses clearly shows (Espiritu 1992), ethnic-specific concerns have received greater attention because of efforts made by panethnic organizations to promote an awareness of different cultures and needs. Espiritu and Wei brilliantly document such activities and other examples of panethnic community building between the late 1960s and early 1990s. The following cases illustrate how this movement has evolved in recent years by examining the development of three issues, two of which have transfixed the previous generation of movement participants. These cases show that, although changes in the community structure may complicate the concept of community for Asian Americans, concurrent changes in the social and political context that threaten the primary interests of the community may also present organizing momentum for a more coherent community than predicted by demography. In the end, this is a story about a community that almost cannot be—if not for an inordinate amount of resistance, perseverance, coordination, and determination from within the community to make it be; and not without the pervasive and negative forces external to the community which, through racial categorization and racist attacks, help make it be.

REACTING TO ANTI-ASIAN VIOLENCE

Seven years after Vincent Chin's murder, an American-born Chinese, Jim Ming Hai Loo, was beaten to death by two brothers who claimed that their brothers "went over to Vietnam and never came back." Again, an Asian American was blamed for the alleged misdeeds of Asians abroad; again, the actual ethnicity of the Asian in question did not seem to matter—whether Chinese, Japanese, or Vietnamese, "chink," "Jap," and "gook" were all synonymous. The cases of both Chin and Loo illustrate a central organizing principle in combating anti-Asian violence: All Asian Americans are in the same line of fire. In the eyes of the attacker, the Asian victim is never an individual human, but rather a symbol of foreign threat. This makes the issue of anti-Asian violence a handy one for panethnic coalition building and empowerment (Sehgal and Yang 1992).[7]

By 1989, however, Asian Americans were much better equipped to react to the crime and to act on behalf of the victim's family. It not only took the local Chinese and other Asians less than a month to form the Jim Loo American Justice Coalition to ensure the prosecution of the assailants, but representatives from Asian American civil rights organizations elsewhere such as the D.C.-based national OCA, the San Francisco-based Asian Law Caucus (ALC), the New York-based Asian American Legal Defense and Education Fund (AALDEF), and the Detroit-based ACJ promptly offered their support (Espiritu 1992). In addition, the legal system was more responsive at both the local and federal levels and resulted in, "the first successful federal prosecution of a civil rights violation case in which the victim was an Asian American" (Espiritu 1992, 159). More importantly, based on the experience of working together on the Jim Loo case, a number of antiviolence groups from across the nation formed a National Network Against Anti-Asian Violence (NNAAV) in 1990 (Sehgal and Yang 1992). The coalition offered courtroom monitoring, meetings with prosecutors and law enforcement, and support for the victim's family in the Loo case; it also had an agenda of education, change, and prevention for future cases. The NNAAV coalition included the ACJ, AALDEF, ALC, the California Attorney General's Asian Pacific Advisory Committee, OCA, and JACL as well as the Committee Against Anti-Asian Violence (CAAAV) and the Break the Silence Coalition (BTS).

In New York, the CAAAV has served since 1986 as a focal point for action not only against racial bias violence but also against police brutality, discriminatory labor practices, and stereotypical portrayal of Asians in the media (Wei 1993; Geron 1996). Some of CAAAV's founding members included activists from the AALDEF, JACL, OCA, the Organization of Asian Women, Korean American Women for Action, and Khmer Association in the United States. Over the years, it has grown from a loosely organized coalition to a funded nonprofit with a paid staff and forty active volunteers. Arguing that officers in the New York Police Department were the largest perpetrators of violence against Asians, CAAAV adopted proactive and coalitional strategies to address the issue of hate violence from a systemic angle. For example, it joined the National Congress for Puerto Rican Rights (NCPRR) to organize a citywide civil disobedience in 1995 by blocking the Manhattan Bridge in protest of racial violence and police brutality. It led a nationwide campaign of over forty civil rights organizations to demand the reconvening of a grand jury that had refused to indict the white offi-

cer who allegedly shot from behind Yong Xin Huang, a 16-year-old student playing in his friend's driveway. By providing direct assistance to
victims of anti-Asian violence, lobbying local and state governments,
pulling together multigroup and often multiracial protest coalitions,
and engaging in other means of direct action, CAAAV has earned the
reputation of being one of the most highly visible and most confrontational Asian Pacific American (APA) groups.

On the West Coast, the Break the Silence Coalition (BTS) has performed a similar function. Formed in the wake of the first Bay Area
Anti-Asian Violence Conference in 1985, BTS provides direct assistance
to victims and communities affected by violence while promoting
awareness of multiculturalism through outreach and training. The
grassroots nature of the organization allows it to take advocacy positions and serve as a liaison between victims, police, and government
representatives. When Chinese and Korean store owners were harassed
and beaten by a gang of ten white youths in the Bay Area, BTS served
as the bridge between the victims and the Alameda City Human Relations Department, providing translators and assisting in the police
investigation (Sehgal and Yang 1992).

Grassroots organizations like CAAAV and BTS often work very
closely with local legal advocacy groups such as the AALDEF in New
York, the ALC in San Francisco, and the Asian Pacific American Legal
Center (APALC) of Southern California. These three legal organizations formed the National Asian Pacific American Legal Consortium
(NAPALC) in 1993 to provide better access and networking as well as
more effective litigation, advocacy, public education, and public policy
development at the national level. Headquartered in Washington D.C.,
the priorities of this leading APA civil rights coalition have expanded
from anti-Asian violence, voting rights, and immigration into affirmative action, welfare reform, language rights, and Census 2000 over the
last several years. Its work on anti-Asian violence has featured the
annual release of the "Audit of Violence Against Asian Pacific Americans." In addition to monitoring and documenting hate violence and
pushing for stronger hate crimes legislation, it also provides legal representation for hate crimes victims and participates as amicus curiae in
support of hate crimes statutes being constitutionally challenged in
various states. This strategy of collaboration between community-
based support, outreach, and street activism, and legislative and liti-

gation expertise at the nation's capital is a new development in the second phase of the Asian American movement (Sehgal and Yang 1992). It has proven remarkably effective not only in helping victims win justice, but also in directing the attention of national political leaders to initiate programs addressing specific problems. Partly because of NAPALC's efforts, the White House hosted the first national Conference on Hate Crimes in November 1997 to highlight key proposals exploring better hate crime identification, legal enforcement, and education strategies.

It is no exaggeration to suggest that groups that have developed around the issue of anti-Asian violence are among the strongest and most dynamic in the second wave of the Asian American movement. Unfortunately, they find themselves in too much demand. Contrary to the national trend of declining crime rates, hate crimes against Asians have risen in each year since the collection of such statistics began.[8] The rapid entry of Asian Americans into formerly homogenous communities may be one reason for the increase. The rising popularity of hate groups, the scapegoating of immigrants for local and national problems, and the perpetuation of Asian Americans as foreign objects by the mainstream press and politicians are other possible reasons. Several heinous crimes reported in 1999 suggest that this rising tide of anti-Asian sentiment is part of the national antagonism against peoples of difference. Nevertheless, the reactions of the community also show that Asians Americans may be increasingly more able to think beyond ethnic, nativity, and geographic lines and act together as a group while collaborating with non-Asian groups, politicians, and the U.S. government to find solutions to this issue.

In July 1999, Woo-Joon Yoon, an Indiana University student from Korea, was gunned down outside of a Korean Methodist church by a white supremacist in an Independence Day shooting spree that also killed a Black man and left six Orthodox Jews, two other Black men, and a Taiwanese student wounded. A memorial service sponsored by Bloomington United, an organization formed to respond to racist literature distributed by the assailant, was held eight days later and attended by 3,000 people (Park 1999). Speakers included U.S. Attorney General Janet Reno, Benjamin Johnson, director of President Clinton's One America, the mayor of Bloomington, the chancellor of the University, and other community and religious leaders. Several Asian American student leaders led a panel discussion on hate crimes prevention and college Democrats sponsored a university-wide town hall meeting to discuss the issue. Nationwide, Asian American organizations such as the National Korean American Service and Education Consortium (NAKASEC), Filipino Civil Rights Advocates (FilCRA), IACPA, NAPALC, and OCA were galvanized to push for passage of the 1999 Hate Crimes Prevention Act, which would add sexual orientation, gender, and disability as categories covered under federal hate crime laws (Dang 1999). The bill (S.622), introduced by Senator Edward Kennedy (D-MA), and passed by a voice vote in the same month Yoon was killed, would also permit a federal investigation regardless of whether the victim was exercising a federally protected right and would empower federal prosecutors to act if the states were unable or unwilling to do so.[9] Since 1991, the FBI has reported more than 50,000 hate crimes, but the Department of Justice has brought in only thirty-seven cases under the current Hate Crimes Act.

The fate of Asians, Jews, and Blacks were linked in two other incidents. In August 1999, a white supremacist killed Filipino American postal worker Joseph Ileto and wounded five others at a Jewish Community Center near Los Angeles. Eight months later, a white male in Pittsburgh shot to death a Jewish woman, three Asian men of Indian, Chinese, and Vietnamese descent, and a Black man; he also paralyzed another Asian Indian. In both incidents, a number of pan-Asian organizations (e.g., NAPALC, NCAPA, and NAPABA) and umbrella ethnic organizations (e.g., NFFAA, FilCRA, IACPA, and OCA) promptly joined the local Asian American civil rights groups to hold rallies, raise memorial funds, and demand justice. They also called for the immediate confirmation, after years of undue delay, of Bill Lann Lee as the Assistant Attorney General for Civil Rights at the Justice Department, demanded the swift passage of strong hate crimes legislation at the local and federal levels, and insisted upon vigorous enforcement of the laws. In addition, they participated in the National Day of Remembrance, which was organized by the nation's multiracial civil rights community to mourn the death of Ileto and other hate crime victims. Instead of Asians fighting hate crimes by themselves, these hate-motivated shooting rampages became galvanizing events that united Americans of all colors to demand legal and political changes to address related issues.

RENEWING DEMAND FOR ASIAN AMERICAN STUDIES

The college campus traditionally has been the bastion of political activism. In the late 1960s, student protests led to the establishment of the nation's first ethnic studies degree programs at San Francisco State University and the University of California at Berkeley. At that time, there were comparatively few Asian American college students. Most of them were U.S.-born, from the West Coast, and of either Chinese or Japanese origin. By the late 1990s, Asian Americans represented 6 percent of the nation's college population and have reached critical mass on many of the best college campuses (where much of the scholarship that defines American identity is produced) (Hong 1998). At Harvard, Yale, Cornell, Stanford, and Northwestern, about 1 out of 5 undergraduate students is Asian.[10] That ratio is twice as large at the Universities of California at Berkeley and Los Angeles, and higher at Irvine. Even in institutions such as the University of Maryland at College Park and the University of Texas at Austin, where their location had isolated them from the first phase of the Asian American movement, Asians comprised about 14 percent of the undergraduate student bodies in 1998. These campuses were some of the sites within the last decade where Asian American students demanded, in political styles reminiscent of campus activism of the 1960s, an equal right to study about themselves.

The first wave of a widespread push for Asian American Studies (AAS) ended in 1973, when the national economy declined and support for AAS programs dwindled (Wei 1993). By the end of 1980s, when fewer than half of ethnic studies programs survived the period of contraction and consolidation (Wei 1993), the stage was set for a resurgence in student activism. There are at least six reasons to account for the renaissance. One is the continuing failure of mainstream academia to recognize and integrate the experiences of Asian Americans into mainstream curriculum (Maehara 1995). Another is the outright resistance of universities and colleges to the concept of AAS or the to idea of an educational reform whose concerns about institutional racism, class exploitation, sexual subordination, and cultural hegemony strive to make American schools "more equitable, inclusive, and open to alternative perspectives" (Hune 1996). A third reason is the continuing need to address the recruitment, retention, and promotion issues affecting Asian American faculty, whose overall tenure rate has been below the national average (Wei 1993). The renewed interest in Asian American studies also was triggered by the controversies over Asian American admissions that facilitated a transformation in the political discourse from support for racial remedial programs and minority group rights to opposition to liberal education, affirmative action, and ethnic studies in the late 1980s (Takagi 1992). Also, decades of new Asian immigration and high birth rates among certain subgroups have led to a dramatic increase in the number of college-aged Asians. The surging of Asian Americans on to many campuses has further pushed issues of group identity, representation, and empowerment to the academic front and pointed out the deficiencies in the extant structure of academia to address such concerns. Last but not least, the success of student activism in the late 1960s and the East Coast students' organizing efforts in the late 1970s and early 1980s permitted efficacy in political action and created an organizational basis for a new generation of disillusioned students (Wei 1993). The convergence of all these factors has linked grievances to action and explains the revival of student participation in AAS politics (Euchner 1996).

Socially conscious students often resort to direct action tactics after they have been frustrated by the administration's lack of response to their repetitive pleas made through conventional channels within the system for a particular program. Such was the case with Asian American students at Northwestern University where, after three years of futile effort, students held a twenty-six day hunger strike and three rallies in 1995 to demand AAS course offerings and a permanent faculty member to serve as temporary program director. In April 1996, about 100 Northwestern students, disappointed at the administration's progress, showed up at a vigil to commemorate the one-year anniversary of the hunger strike. A similar commemoration was held at Princeton, where, in 1995, seventeen students occupied the president's office for thirty-five hours to protest the administration's lack of commitment to Asian American and Latino studies while supporters held four rallies outside. The sit-in and rallies were broadcast on NBC's New York affiliate. The events at Northwestern and Princeton took place within the context of a national movement for race and ethnic studies when the month of April 1996 was the designated national month of action. The idea of the national action was born a year before at the 1995 East of California Association for Asian American Studies Conference. The conference sought to create a sustained effort to end isolated struggles on individual campuses and to bring to the attention of the national media attempts by students and faculty to engage university administrations in a more substantive dialogue on the creation and maintenance of ethnic studies.[11]

A broad coalition of more than 1,000 Asian American students from 11 campuses, mainly in the Northeast, participated in the unprecedented push for AAS (Yip 1996). They were supported by Asian American students and faculty in at least thirty other schools and community organizations nationwide. On many occasions, other students of color also lent their support. Various forms of protest action were exercised during and around the month-long movement. At Columbia University, four students launched a fifteen-day hunger strike on April 1. They were supported by more than 100 students who participated in a five-day sit-in at the president's office demanding an ethnic studies department with Latino and Asian American programs; twenty-two of them were arrested by city police. Months earlier, twenty-five Asian, Hispanic, and African American students occupied the office of the Columbia College Dean for three hours and taped the sit-in to broadcast on a local NBC news affiliate; 200 students held a candlelight vigil that evening in which students and local community activists gave speeches. Students also petitioned concerned individuals and organizations across the nation to e-mail letters of support to Columbia's administrators. Cross-campus alliances were further solidified by vigils held at Cornell in support of Columbia students and by support actions staged by students at Harvard, Yale, Northwestern, and campuses of the City College of New York, who organized a citywide rally to protest cutbacks of their programs. Students at Yale, Amherst, and Harvard also sponsored conferences to educate themselves and others about the importance of ethnic studies. Finally, students at Smith and Harvard met with administrators to discuss their need for ethnic studies programs.

Compared to the Asian American student movement in the late 1960s, participants in the 1990s shared the general goals and participation styles of their predecessors but differed in ideology, focus, and resources, and in class, ethnic, and geographic representation. As before, students pursued the goals of "strengthening identity and pride, promoting history and culture, and ending individual and institutional racism" (Wei 1993, 151) through mass rallies, protest marches, sit-ins, teach-ins, and hunger strikes. However, unlike before, students focused their energies on reforming the educational system rather than trying to overturn it. They also did not feel the need to provide community services, which had been mostly served by professional social service organizations. Participants were much higher in number, more diverse in ethnic origins, and came mostly from either immigrant families with upper-middle-class backgrounds or refugee families. They were also much less sympathetic to Marxist-Leninist and Maoist ideologies (Wei 1993). The epicenter shifted to schools in the Northeast, but schools in California and the Midwest remained in the limelight and were joined by schools in the mid-Atlantic and the South. The movement itself was less bloody and much more sophisticated in operation—thanks in large part to Internet technology, which permitted the creation of an instant cyber-community with a few keyboard strokes and an extensive network of outside support and pressure to the administration. Students ensured that their actions received major media coverage by frequently feeding major local media outlets with video footage and press releases updating the situation. The contemporary movement also enjoyed much greater organizational support and intercampus coalition-building opportunities. The Association for Asian American Studies was established in 1979, and the East of California Network was founded in 1991 on the campus of Cornell University and consisted of twenty-three institutions of higher education. The East Coast Asian Student Union (ECASU), the West Coast's Asian Pacific Student Union (APSU), and the Midwest Asian Student Union (MASU) are regional networks uniting student organizations of many campuses, holding annual conferences that move from college to college to foster communication and address issues (Wei 1993; Jer 1994).

This new phase of student movement is the culmination of recent attempts by students and faculty at other campuses such as Stanford and the Universities of California at Irvine, Los Angeles, and Berkeley. The result of the 1993 struggle at UC Irvine was particularly noteworthy: The thirty-five-day rotating hunger strike and a sit-in of an ethnically diverse group of 100 students at the chancellor's office produced an unprecedented statement of mutual understanding between students and the administration (Tsang 1993). The settlement came days after ULCA hunger strikers won a promise to improve the Chicano Studies Program. Some UCLA protesters showed up to express their solidarity with the UC Irvine students. The 1996 movement was followed by more protests and demands elsewhere. Student protesters at the University of Maryland, College Park, stormed into the president's office in 1997 to demand the immediate implementation of the AAS Program for which they had been asking for more than two years. At the University of Texas at Austin, frustrated students staged a 1999 sit-in to protest the interim dean's decision to deny the appointment of their favorite candidate to the directorship of the new AAS Program that they had demanded for six years. Ten were arrested and charged with misdemeanor criminal trespassing. Weeks earlier, students at UC Berkeley who were frustrated by continuing cutbacks in ethnic studies staged takeovers, hunger strikes, and mass rallies over a three-week period. They were supported by students of all colors and ethnicities from other departments on campus and from other schools including Stanford and San Francisco State. Over 130 were arrested by campus police during early morning raids. This ended when a tentative agreement was reached between the Chancellor and the Ethnic Studies Department to fill three vacant faculty positions and to hire two new professors each year for the following two years.

Because of these struggles, some schools were able to establish their AAS programs with relative ease, due to the administration's preemptive strike to prevent conflicts and the offering of AAS courses on many campuses nationwide. Such was the case with programs at UCLA, Cornell University, University of Southern California, and University of Pennsylvania. These changes added pressure to existing programs and led to such improvements as the addition of an AAS major at UCLA in 1994. Finally, an ethnic studies program was established at Columbia in May 1998, and Northwestern hired its first AAS professor in 1999. Thus, despite the antiestablishment orientation of AAS and its struggle against a national retreat from racial concerns, the number of AAS programs has actually grown. In 1999, according to the Association for Asian American Studies' Directory of AAS Programs, the number of AAS programs offered either as independent or affiliated academic units stood at close to fifty nationwide. At least twelve additional schools offered courses on Asian Americans, although only eleven out of 50 programs permitted students to declare a major in AAS.

Most importantly, for participants and observers, such collective political action across campuses may be a direct stimulus to forge a larger sense of community and identity; for some, it helps deepen the belief in the collective fate of Asian Americans as a vocal, participating part of nonwhite America. The experience of participation may also provide critical training grounds for new generations of Asian American leaders who are most likely to take their dedication with them after they leave college. This ensures the development of an active, informed community. Nevertheless, the construction of a common Asian American identity faces challenges from the continuing balkanization of ethnic diversity, which may present a serious obstacle to political organizing because of the different levels of political consciousness of students from various ethnic communities (Wei 1995). Class inequality may complicate the situation in that students of Filipino and Southeast Asian origins have complained about the dominance of student organizations by those of Chinese, Korean, and Asian Indian backgrounds (Lee 1998).

STRUCTURING THE VOICE AND THE VOTE: PANETHNIC POLITICAL ORGANIZING AND BEYOND

According to Espiritu, the most significant political development in recent Asian American history may be "the emergence of the pan-Asian entity" (1992, 163). The previous cases are just two of the many recent incidents of panethnic organizing in the continuing evolution of the Asian American movement. In truth, given the antagonism against immigrants and minorities, a survey of recent political actions taken by community organizations at the national level strongly suggests that ethnic politics have become panethnic politics. Each call for action is a call to look beyond primordial boundaries and to work with mainstream institutions on mainstream issues. Nevertheless, because the new Asian immigration in the post-1965 era coincided with the crucial transformation of the Pacific Rim into new centers of global economic power, the sharp growth in the levels of trans-Pacific transfer in capital, personnel, and commodity have necessitated a reconceptualization of the very boundaries of Asian America in diasporic or transnational terms (Dirlik 1999). Increasingly, the community has been asked to address transnational rather than panethnic politics. The following prominent examples of political organizing in the late 1990s illustrate this trend toward panethnic and transnational politics.

Voter Registration

In 1996, citing continuous assaults from Congress on the immigrant community, a coalition of nineteen Asian American national organizations, led by the OCA, formed the first National Asian Pacific American Voter Registration Campaign. More than 100 APA groups and agencies across the country participated in the unprecedented and multiethnic effort that eventually registered 75,000 new voters. The campaign produced an award-winning public service announcement featuring twenty-one Hollywood Asian American celebrities. It also set up a multilingual toll-free number to allow Asians to receive information on how to get registered as well as information on upcoming voter education and get-out-the-vote activities. Because of the success of these efforts, similar projects were planned for the 2000 election in which OCA, along with IACPA, NFFAA, and NAPALC, was on the board of a multiracial, national coalition called Youth Vote 2000. This was expected to be the nation's largest, most diverse non-partisan coalition ever established to encourage civic participation of those aged 18 to 30. At least 18 APA organizations participated in a coalition that included representation from all major ethnic groups.

In addition to the national campaign, numerous local panethnic-oriented organizations such as Vision21, Chinese Americans United for Self Empowerment (CAUSE), Asian American Voter Coalition, APALC, and AALDEF have conducted voter education, citizenship classes, leadership training, and voter registration and Get-Out-The-Vote (GOTV) drives on a regular basis.

Reactions to Campaign Finance Controversy

In 1996, with the national voter registration drive in full gear, accompanied by an unprecedented number of strong APA candidates running for all levels of office, and the positioning of APAs in prominent fund-raising roles,[12] the election year was poised to be a watershed one for Asian Americans in politics. Instead, the fund-raising scandal, which broke into the newswire weeks before the general election, not only rocked the community's dream for meaningful participation, but left behind feelings of stigmatization and alienation for the politically involved (Wu 1997a, 1997b). In November 1996, following allegations of improper political contributions solicited by three individuals (John Huang, Charles Trie, and Johnny Chung) at an April 1996 event at the

Hsi Lai Buddhist Temple in California, the Democratic Party, through its governing arm, the Democratic National Committee (DNC), directed an audit of approximately 1,200 contributions made from 1994 to 1996 by Asians. Donors with Asian surnames were investigated and interrogated by anonymous callers about their citizenship, source of the donation, and personal finances, and they were asked to authorize release of a credit report to the DNC. Some were told that if they refused to provide the requested information, their names would be released to the press (Chen and Minami 1998). For many Asian Americans, what transpired in the 1996 presidential elections and afterwards constituted the most severe infringement on civil rights in the group's recent political history. The national media and prominent politicians perpetuated biased assumptions and stereotypes about the Asian American community.

Organized protest, however, did not emerge until the appearance of Chinese stereotypes on the cover of the March 24, 1997, issue of the biweekly magazine *National Review*. Major Asian American community and advocacy groups initiated a media education campaign to teach the difference between Asian Americans and Asian foreigners (Wu 1997c). According to various media reports, community individuals and campus groups also protested vehemently against remarks made by John O'Sullivan, editor of the conservative magazine, who openly debated with the executive director of OCA, Daphne Kwok, about the editorial decision to use the racially offensive images.

The scandal also provided an incentive for political organizing. Some community elites were convinced that money raised by John Huang and about a dozen other figures of Asian descent represented the class interest tied to transnational Asian capital and multinational corporations, which tends to undermine the American democratic process (Wang 1998). They formed a historic grassroots organization, Asian Americans for Campaign Finance Reform (AAFCFR) to change practices in mainstream politics. It called for a vigorous investigation of the wrongdoings of all persons involved and advocated major campaign reforms to eliminate or reduce the influence of money in the electoral process. However, other elites, especially those linked to established community civil rights organizations, considered this demand to overhaul the system and prosecute the misdeeds of fellow Asian Americans to be too disruptive and harmful to the claim of equal protection and rights for all Asian Americans. Perhaps a more significant development (from the perspective of panethnic community building) was the 1997 formation of the NCAPA from over twenty community organizations. Headed by Daphne Kwok, the Council aspires to provide a much-needed and long-awaited national leadership that is sophisticated in the American system, can respond in a swift, unified, and forceful fashion, and can communicate with and command the respect of the political establishment (Kang 1997). Since its inception, the Council has intervened on issues such as hate crimes, media misrepresentation and underrepresentation, and the appointment of Bill Lann Lee.

Finally, in protest of the perverse patterns of racial stereotyping, scapegoating, and discrimination directed at the APA community by the nation's most important and powerful institutions, such as Congress, major political parties, public officials, and the news media, fourteen national organizations and four individuals formed a coalition to petition for a hearing to the U.S. Commission on Civil Rights. Petitioners include the NAPALC, OCA, JACL, CACA, KAC, NAKASEC, IACPA, APALA, APALC, NAPABA, APIAHF, AAFCFR, the Philippine American Foundation, and the Committee of 100. They charged that members of the nation's most influential institutions had acted irresponsibly and carelessly to the allegations of wrongdoing by scapegoating and stereotyping Asian Pacific Americans and immigrants.[13] They said that the xenophobia infecting the campaign finance reform debate had made its way into legislative proposals. Both Democratic and Republican members of the House and Senate introduced nine different bills that would prohibit campaign contributions by legal permanent residents, some of which would bar independent expenditures by legal permanent residents as well. Whereas the petitioners supported a full investigation into any and all substantial allegations of misconduct, they demanded that "the investigations, statements and policy choices of Congress, political parties, and public officials, and reportage by the news media be fair, informed, accurate, and free of racial and anti-immigrant bias" (Chen and Minami 1998, 358).

Appointment of Bill Lann Lee

As a result of the campaign money scandal, some observe that the community experienced a paradigm shift in its political participation (Sterngold, 1999). Instead of relying on donations as the primary means to influence, APAs turned their attention to lobbying for political appointments such as the aggressive campaign for the appointment of Bill Lann Lee. Lee was nominated in July 1997 to be Assistant Attorney General for Civil Rights at the Justice Department. A distinguished civil rights lawyer with impeccable credentials, Lee had headed the Los Angeles office of the Legal Defense and Educational Fund of the National Association for the Advancement of Colored People (NAACP), the nation's foremost civil rights group. His confirmation was expected to be quick, but conservatives on the U.S. Senate Judiciary Committee objected to Lee's views on affirmative action and prevented a Senate vote. Over the Senate Committee's objections, President Clinton appointed Lee acting chief of the Department of Justice Civil Rights Division. In order for Lee to be confirmed as the nation's top enforcer of civil rights and become the highest ranking APA in the Clinton Administration, ten national organizations signed an open letter to Senator Orrin Hatch (R-UT), chairman of the Committee, urging his support for an expeditious full Senate floor vote. The NCAPA organized a signature-gathering campaign and called for a national action day with press conferences and support rallies held in Washington, D.C., Los Angeles, San Francisco, New York, Philadelphia, and Salt Lake City. This was the highlight of a series of calls for action in the preceding two years; using the Internet, activists urged local communities to participate in letter-writing and phone campaigns and in-person contacts with senators on the Committee to influence their votes.[14]

80-20 Initiative

Another indication of the paradigm shift in APA political participation was the launching of a first-ever national nonpartisan Asian American political action committee (PAC) for the 2000 elections. In addition to gaining political appointments and vigorous prosecution of hate crimes, the PAC focused intently on lifting the glass ceiling. To achieve the stated goals, APAs were asked to withhold financial and other forms of support to any presidential candidates in the primary election who failed to pledge commitment to the PAC's request for equal justice in the workplace. In the general election, supporters were asked to form a bloc vote (ideally at an eight to two ratio) and cast their votes for the candidate favored by the PAC. Organizers argued that Asian Americans are strategically located in key presidential election states with some of the largest electoral college votes. For instance, 54 electoral college votes are in California, where APAs are 12 percent of the population and about 6.5 percent of voters. A total of forty-eight electoral votes are in New York (thirty-three) and New Jersey (fifteen), where APAs are 5 percent of the population in each state. They planned to pour organizational energy into these key states to structure a swing vote. Until mid-Febrary 2000, only a Democratic candidate, Bill Bradley, responded in kind to the pledge. In return for his support, the PAC helped publicize and sell tickets for Bradley's fundraising events (Lee 1999). Vice President Al Gore rushed in his written statement of support hours before the deadline to avoid being boycotted by the organization in the primary election, a decision arguably not shared by his Republican opponents. On August 27, 2000, twenty-six of the thirty-three delegates to the 80–20 convention voted to endorse Gore, thus turning the PAC into a partisan operation.

In addition to the challenge of competing for attention from heavyweights among the presidential candidates of major parties, a more fundamental issue for the initiative is the delivering of the promised bloc votes. Leaders envisioned a two-stage strategy to accomplish this: first, to unite the Chinese American community; and second, to organize other Asian American communities in the formation of a Pan Asian American Committee (PAAC). What the PAC needs to address, at the time of this writing, are means to overcome other barriers such as differences in political ideology, foreign policy concerns, class, gender, geographic location, and nativity within and across Asian American communities. Besides structuring the direction of the vote, it also needs to mobilize participation and turnout. Although success is uncertain because the initiative is still in search of the best message and strategy to put across, the formation was an important milestone in APA political history, and many lessons can be learned from this unprecedented effort to structure pan-Asian political unity and build political clout.

TRANSFORMING STYLES OF POLITICAL PARTICIPATION: FROM MOVEMENT POLITICS TO ELECTORAL POLITICS

The preceding account of the transformation in political participation styles from movement politics to electoral politics in the post-1965 era should not be seen as a novel development or an irrevocable, uninterrupted, and complete process for Asian Americans. In fact, the history recounted in Chapter 1 shows that some early Asian American organizations attempted to change their fate through lobbying Congress and the administration. As the next chapter shows, Asians in Hawaii ventured into electoral politics as early as the 1920s and have dominated the state's politics since the mid-1950s. Moreover, the recent recurrence of student movements for AAS suggests that at the same time that panethnic organizations were making waves in national politics, the grassroots base of the pan-Asian political community was still fighting for a legitimate space on many college campuses. The unsteady development of panethnicity at the mass level may prove to be an Achilles' heel of these organizations when the community for which they are advocating cannot identify its interests or agree with the interests represented by these elite groups. The rise of transnational issues in community politics may present another challenge to the structuring of political unity (as is discussed later in this book). Nevertheless, the concern over the legitimacy and representation of these advocacy groups may be somewhat mitigated by aggressive outreach efforts to structure and channel the community voice and vote. In addition to direct lobbying, many have allocated resources to and developed expertise on organizing petition campaigns, forging community partnerships, sponsoring internship and leadership training programs, and conducting voter education and mobilization activities.

Perhaps more significant than a shift in the style of participation is the expansion of involvement in electoral politics. In essence, this development in Asian American politics involves the proliferation and entrenchment of panethnic organizations in mainstream election-centered politics. The rise of Asian American panethnic organizing and consciousness (as described earlier in the chapter) can be attributed to changing community structure and political context since the mid-1960s. Despite their belated and recent entry, the growth and vitality of pan-Asian organizations in electoral politics should also be considered as part of the national phenomenon of interest group proliferation and professionalization during the same era. The system has been transformed in both the number and the types of representation. Between 1977 and 1991, the number of interest group representatives located in Washington, D.C. grew from 4,000 to over 14,500 (Petracca 1992). The city has become a headquarters for not only lawyers and law firms, nonprofit associations, and business corporations, but also citizen groups, state and local governmental entities, and foreign interests. Rather than conceiving policymaking in "iron triangles,"[15] recent scholars have identified the process as captured in loosely formed "issue networks" (Heclo 1978; Salisbury et al. 1992). In addition to lobbying Congress and the White House and participating in Supreme Court litigation, interest groups are now actively involved in electoral politics and are armed with direct-marketing techniques for mobilizing voters, selecting candidates and issues, raising campaign funds, and maneuvering initiative and referendum campaigns in local and state politics (Rozell and Wilcox 1999). These changes in the interest group system have taken place amidst other changes in the American political system that include but are not limited to: the decline of major political parties, the rise of social movements, the proliferation of new communication technologies, the expansion of federal bureaucracy, the emergence of interest group patrons, and the dispersion of power resulting from structural changes in Congress[16] during the 1970s (Petracca 1992). As a result of post-Watergate reforms in campaign finance,[17] the number of political action committees (PACs) exploded, particularly those affiliated with corporations and ideological groups, and the amounts of money involved in political campaigns skyrocketed.[18] Changes in Democratic Party rules after 1972 also gave interest groups greater influence on party nominations. Finally, the high-level involvement of interest groups in American politics stems from the decentralized form of American government, weak political parties, and unique characteristics of U.S. elections such as frequent elections, candidate-centered campaigns, low levels of voter turnout, and the winner-take-all contests in single-member districts (Rozell and Wilcox 1999).

Because of the transformation in the American interest group system, Asian American advocacy groups have greater opportunities to take a more active role in lawmaking. Although most of the Asian American groups are of the 501(c)(3) status, which bans congressional lobbying activity or taking part in partisan electoral activity but permits issue advocacy, their rise and conduct are shaped by the same forces accounting for the advocacy explosion after 1965. As interest groups, their rise in the last two decades can be understood, in part, using Truman's (1951) disturbance theory, which postulates that major disturbances within the political environment motivate people who perceive their interests as adversely affected to band together to improve their lot.

Inherent in group politics, however, are a number of problems that affect the assessment of its prospect and influence. First, not all community members have the same will and capability to organize themselves. Given the extreme heterogeneity of the multiethnic population, this is certainly a problem that no one can afford to ignore. Second, the interests of the "haves" may be overrepresented. As observed by Schattschneider (1960), the beneficiaries of group politics are people in higher socioeconomic brackets, those with more money and better organizations. For an immigrant community such as Asian Americans, the "haves" may be better defined as those who possess greater English communication skills and social networks. The native-born minority among Asian Americans, in this regard, may have a larger say in mainstream political matters than the foreign-born majority. Third, with increasing entrenchment into the system, groups may be reluctant to challenge the status quo, which they have learned to maneuver. Together, these three factors may cripple the mostly U.S.-born, panethnic group leaders' ability to act on behalf of the community at large, especially on issues arising from the increased levels of capital, material, and personnel transfer across the Pacific.

A case in point was the divergent responses of Washington-based civil rights groups and the academicly centered AAFCFR to charges of campaign finance fraud. Concerned with the problem of foreign money, the AAFCR condemned the misbehavior of the accused individuals and argued that fundamental changes in the American campaign finance system were needed to uproot corruption that hurt the democracy and its people, especially the extraterritorially connected Asian Americans. However, the Beltway groups, refusing to tinker with a system that had accounted for their ascendence in national politics, opted to express concern only about the vulnerability of Asian Americans to guilt by association. To be sure, the latter's emphasis on the need for equal protection and justice to all was vital and rightful. Because of the blurring of the line between Asia and America by the restructuring of the Pacific Rim economy, having real or perceived political ties with the Asian homeland could render any Asian American suspect as American (Dirlik 1998). However, their aversion to criticism of a government and a system that had a long history of exploitation and abuse of the people these groups had existed to serve in the first place was a concept rather unsettling to supporters of the AAFCFR and to others who were concerned about the civil rights future of the community. This division in political response to the multidimensional transnational politics underlines the limitation of panethnicity and liberal ideology as organizing principles in the future of Asian American politics. The rift it created among panethnic elites presages a very serious challenge to the structuring of political unity among Asian Americans at the dawn of the new century.

Conclusion

In response to internal community and external political forces, panethnic-oriented organizations have emerged to play a vital role in transforming Asian American political identity and participation in contemporary U.S. politics. Like umbrella ethnic-specific organizations, panethnic organizations were formed as political coalitions to protect and promote community interests. For a racialized group like Asians that is historically marginalized and demographically small and heterogeneous, panethnic organizations are vital for cultural construction and identity formation. Their indispensable role in community building and empowerment is consistent with the stories of other multiethnic nonwhite groups (Padilla 1985; Vigil 1987; Cornell 1988; Lopez and Espiritu 1990; Nagel 1996). Yet, in part because of these organizations' prominence in structuring the identity and voice of an emergent political community, some have observed Asian Americans to rely in an unusual degree on the "politics of other means" (Erie and Brackman 1993, 47). Rather than pursuing power through conventional mass political means such as voting and demonstration, Asians have depended heavily on elite-based tactics such as litigation, campaign donations, and lobbying to influence politics and policy. In hindsight, the reliance on political contributions from big donors in Asia as a means of participation has certainly backfired in formidable ways for the aspiring political community in recent years (Wang 1998). More importantly, inherent in group politics is the classic "free rider" problem when potential beneficiaries or the majority members of the community opt not to contribute time or money, leaving the burden of participation to volunteer or professional political activists whose political stand may be ideologically more extreme than the community at large. As a result, a study focusing on the political activism of social and political elites and their organizations is likely to overestimate the degree of panethnic community unity and political integration while underestimating the weight of ethnicity, class, ideology, and other cleavages as barriers to political participation facing the mass of Asian Americans.

To provide a broader understanding of Asian Americans and political participation, the next chapter presents an overview of their involvement in formal means of political participation as individual elites and rank-and-file members. The evolution of Asian American participation in direct electoral politics as candidates, public officials, and voters is investigated at both national and subnational levels. The chapter pays special attention to the differences between Hawaiian and mainland Asians, to the contributions of Asian Americans in Congress, to the construction of the pan-Asian community, and to the degree Asians have been able to participate as equals to other racial groups in elections and in government.

3   Participation in Electoral Politics
Evolving Patterns in Hawaii and Mainland States

"Nothing is impossible."
> —Wing Ong, Arizona state legislator, 1946–50, 1966–68

THE PRECEDING accounts of political participation by Asian Americans, both before and after 1965, provide ample evidence to undermine the notion that Asian Americans, by default, are apathetic to American politics. To the contrary, each Asian American group has a segment of the population that has been highly active in pursuing the goals of equality, integration, and independence through legal, bureaucratic, administrative, legislative, and mass democratic means. Notwithstanding, prior to 1965, their participation was mostly outside the radar of mainstream American politics. Even in the post-1965 era, when changes in legal, political, economic, and racial orders made mass-based electoral politics a possibility for the majority members of the growing community, their participation has remained most visible at the organized elite level. Individual-level participation of Asian Americans in electoral politics as candidates, voters, donors, campaign volunteers, and participants in other election-related activities has been more an exception than a norm, despite recent hypes over the campaign finance controversy (Lien 1997a). The apparent deficit of direct participation in electoral politics has generated a long list of journalistic accounts and scholarly depictions that project a triangulated group image of cultural docility, socioeconomic success, and political complacency (e.g., Petersen 1966; Kitano 1969; Sowell 1983, 1994; Jo 1984; Bell 1985; Jo and Mast 1993). This chapter attempts to alter this image by focusing on the evolving patterns of participation of Asians as candidates, elected officials, and voters in the American electoral processes—both in Hawaii and on the mainland. An obvious but often forgotten fact is that in Hawaii, Asian American participation in electoral politics began early, and the nonwhite population has been in control of the island state's politics since the mid-1950s. How have Hawaiian Asians risen to political dominance? What impact have the congressional delegates from Hawaii and other Pacific states had on the construction of the Asian American community and identity? How do mainland Asians compare to their Hawaiian counterparts in terms of the trajectories of electoral success at national and subnational levels? I stress, among other arguments, that the situation in Hawaii provides not only another forceful testimony to the fallacy of the cultural deficiency theory in predicting Asian American political behavior, but that it points to the necessity of incorporating history, geography, sociopolitical and economic contexts, in addition to individual-level factors, in explaining the multifaceted relationship between Asian Americans and U.S. politics. I also argue that a major reason for the lack of participation of mainland Asians lies in our electoral structure, which suppresses the participation potential of small, nonwhite, language minorities. An analysis of Asians in Hawaii and major mainland states shows that having more representatives in government may help mitigate underparticipation by mobilizing voting participation in the mass.

THE RISE OF ASIANS IN ELECTORAL POLITICS: THE CASE OF HAWAII

Although Chinese began to arrive as contract laborers three decades earlier than the first major wave of Japanese immigration to Hawaii in the mid-1880s, Japanese soon became the largest ethnic group on the islands. In 1900, Japanese were 40 percent of the territory's civilian and military population, followed by Hawaiians at 24 percent, whites at 19 percent, and Chinese at 17 percent (Haas 1992, table 1.1). This reversed the ethnic distribution of the Hawaiian population from barely 15 years earlier when Hawaiians were the largest group at 55 percent, followed by Chinese at 23 percent, and whites at 21 percent (Haas 1992, table 1.1). Part of the reason for the ethnic change had to do with immigration regulations. Hawaii passed a Chinese Exclusion Act in 1886 and adopted the U.S. Chinese Exclusion Act after 1900, when federal laws prevailed over Hawaii except in cases where there was a clear argument for exemption because of unique local conditions (Haas 1992). Between 1894 and 1908, over 140,000 Japanese plantation workers arrived. They were recruited to serve as a counterweight to the relatively large and increasingly "unruly" Chinese workers (Daniels 1988). Although many disgruntled Japanese workers left for California after contractual failures, the sheer size of the remaining population at the turn of the twentieth century suggested that they were poised to become one of the first Asian American groups to enter Hawaiian politics. However, the potential to become a leading group was not realized without resistence from the white oligarchy. The 1790 Naturalization Act, which prohibited nonwhite immigrants from acquiring citizenship, was applied to Hawaii from 1900 on; the majority of the immigrant population was prevented from becoming citizens and voters until after WWII. Although Asians born in Hawaii were given the franchise by the Treaty of Reciprocity of 1887, white elites, fearing the potential voting strength of Asians, sought to strip citizenship from Chinese and Japanese who were citizens prior to annexation. Their attempts were successfully challenged in the U.S. District Court of Hawaii, which decided in 1901 that citizens of Hawaii automatically became U.S. citizens under the Organic Act (Haas 1992).[1] Filipino nationals, however, were unable to become citizens before 1946 because of the colonized status of the Philippines.

Filipino workers were recruited to replace striking Japanese workers in the early 1900s. They were preferred over other foreign workers for their illiteracy, their ineligibility for citizenship, and the lack of a diplomatic presence from the homeland government in Hawaii. Nevertheless, the Filipino workers soon found that they were underpaid and would follow the path of other immigrant groups and strike for equal pay. Because most foreign workers were unable to speak each others' languages and because the plantation owners, operating on a strategy of divide and rule, intentionally kept workers segregated and racially stratified, interethnic union was rare. During WWII, the mainland-based International Longshoremen's and Warehousemen's Union (ILWU) gained momentum by combining Filipino and Japanese workers into a powerful bloc of workers, building cross-ethnic solidarity through such activities as baseball games and bowling leagues (Haas 1992). In preparation for postwar strikes, the ILWU encouraged Filipino and Japanese members to show solidarity by voting for Democratic candidates (Daws 1968). The ILWU was successful in organizing a cross-ethnic strike in 1946 and another one in 1949, which effectively brought Hawaii into a recession. Its success also drew the persecution of ILWU leaders by white Republican elites through House Un-American Activities Committee investigations. This neutralization of the leftist faction within the Democratic Party, coupled with the refusal of the Republican Party to coopt upward mobile Japanese into prominent positions, opened up opportunities for leaders such as Nisei war heroes to quickly ascend in local Democratic Party ranks (Haas 1992). After Japanese immigrants were permitted to seek naturalization in 1952, they constituted the largest voting bloc of Hawaiian voters and were able to deliver a landslide victory for the Democratic Party in 1954.

Success for Japanese Americans in Hawaiian politics did not come easily or occur instantly. Nisei involvement in electoral politics can be traced back to 1917 when the Republican Party began to recruit Japanese for membership (Hosakawa 1969). At the time, 179 Nisei were registered to vote. Japanese voters made up 3.5 percent of the electorate in 1922, when the first Nisei ran for office. Several Nisei ran as Republicans for seats in the territorial legislature during this decade, although none were successful. By contrast, because of the relatively larger voting power of the second generation, Chinese Americans were able to be elected to a number of territorial and county positions before 1930 (Fuchs 1961). Chinese voters constituted 4.3 percent of the registered voters when William Heen was elected as the city and county attorney in Honolulu in 1919. This came two years after Heen's appointment to a position that was previously held only by whites and native Hawaiians. The first Chinese entered the Honolulu Board of Supervisors and the territorial House of Representatives in 1927. Growth of Chinese interests and power in American politics in the 1930s produced legendary figures like Hiram Fong, who was later to be elected to the U.S. Senate. The majority of appointed and elected positions at that time, however, were held by Hawaiians.

When Noboru Miyake delivered the first Japanese electoral success in 1930 by becoming a county supervisor, Japanese were 13.5 percent of the electorate. That percentage rose to 31 percent in 1940 when 15.6 percent of the legislators elected were Nisei (Haas 1992, tables 2.10 and 2.11). If Japanese had voted as a bloc, they could have acquired greater political representation. But, according to Hosakawa, they did not (and would never have) because their partisanship as either Republican or Democrat was a greater factor than their ethnicity. Besides, bloc voting was discouraged by community leaders for fear of being considered un-American. The JACL's adoption of nonpartisanship in electoral politics was in response to the liberal criticism that ethnic bloc voting was unpatriotic and anti-American (Takahashi 1997).

Despite the strategy of accommodation, Hawaiian Japanese suffered discrimination of various sorts because of the oligarchical rule that tried to contain both the Hawaiian and the local Japanese influence (Fuchs 1961). Concern over the Japanese vote deepened when the military actions taken by the Japanese imperial regime were considered a potential threat to U.S. interests in the Pacific (Haas 1992). Prospective Nisei voters often found that they had to go to greater lengths to prove their citizenship and eligibility to register, such as getting sworn statements from midwives or other knowledgeable persons (Fuchs 1961). Before 1940, U.S.-born Japanese (and other Asian) workers on the plantations were introduced only to Republican candidates and instructed to vote only for the approved slate of G.O.P. candidates (Fuchs 1961). The escalation in the number of Japanese voters among plantation workers and the entry of union leaders as political bosses lessened the dominance of the white sugar-planter-merchant-missionary oligarchy. Between 1931 and 1944, the percentage of eligible voters among Japanese male and female workers rose from 19 percent to over 50 percent (Akamine 1993).

Their sheer size and contributions to the economy became major reasons for the island Japanese to be put under martial law immediately after the attack on Pearl Harbor (Anthony 1955). For all practical purposes, Japanese Hawaiians were not interned behind barbed wires except for the 930 Japanese Hawaiians who were interned in mainland camps and the 540 who were kept in small camps on Oahu. Instead, residents lived under a military government whose absolute powers exceeded those enforced against the southern states after the Civil War (Haas 1992). For instance, all residents were fingerprinted; their mail was subject to censure; the writ of habeas corpus was suspended; and a large portion of the population lost their prewar jobs in areas considered vital to the security of the island. During the war, not a single Nisei sat in the territorial legislature, but Nisei captured 13.3 percent of the legislature in the first postwar election (Haas 1992, table 2.11). The growing power of Nisei in Hawaiian politics, facilitated by the rapid rise of the voting-age sector of the ethnic population and the continuing strong grasp of Japanese on the island economy, became a cause for concern whenever the issue of statehood was raised in the national Congress. Southern Democrats in particular feared that representatives from a multiethnic state like Hawaii would doubtlessly support the integration of Blacks (Bell 1984).[2]

The Asian presence in Hawaiian politics increased significantly in the late 1940s and early 1950s. This was due mainly to the entry of heroic Japanese American WWII veterans of the famed 100th Battalion and 442nd Regimental Combat Team into the political arena. After the "Democratic Revolution of 1954," the stewardship of island politics was stripped from the hands of the white oligarchy, and ethnicity became a more salient factor than partisanship in the politics of this multiethnic state (Boylan 1992). Between the mid-1950s and mid-1980s, Asian Americans occupied more than half of the leadership positions in the state legislature as president of the Senate, Speaker of the House, and chairs of key committees (Cooper and Daws 1985). In 1990, Japanese were 22 percent of the state's population, 35 percent of the registered voters, 37 percent of legislators, and 55 percent of the civil service administrators (Haas 1992). Chinese also occupied a relatively advantaged position, with a share of 6 percent of the population, 8 percent of the registered voters, 9 percent of legislators, and 9 percent of the civil service administrators. Conversely, whites were 33 percent of the population, 28 percent of registered voters, 24 percent of the legislators, and 20 percent of the civil service administrators. Filipinos were 15 percent of the population, but only 10 percent of registered voters, 7 percent of legislators, and 2.2 percent of the civil service administrators. The Filipinos, who were regarded as junior partners in the liberal coalition, did not receive their fair share for their solidarity with the Japanese in the union movement. They suffered from institutional racism inherited by Japanese American leaders from their white predecessors (Haas 1992). Nevertheless, with the 1994 and 1998 election of Ben Cayetano into governorship, prospects for Filipino ascendence in Hawaiian politics has been greater than ever.

Although the grip of Japanese Americans in Hawaiian politics may be diminished by the rise of Filipinos and Hawaiian natives in state politics, these statistics still provide a clear illustration of the persistent and central position of Japanese Americans in contemporary Hawaiian politics. The case of Hawaiian Japanese presents a powerful antithesis to the popular assertion that Asian Americans are culturally apathetic and politically inexperienced, and therefore inept in electoral politics. However, the case of Hawaiian Filipinos shows that not all Asian American groups are equal in terms of access and power, even though different Asian ethnic groups may share similar experiences of discrimination and exploitation in the development of their history in America. Furthermore, the present-day dominance of Asians over whites in Hawaiian politics demonstrates that it is racial position, not race per se, that may be the source of stratification and conflict. The Hawaiian case illustrates that historical and contextual factors dealing with ethnic group formation and local political economy are important variables to consider when assessing the political participation status of Asian Americans. Finally, the Hawaiian story is vital to the understanding of Asian American politics because of the national impact and implications of the Asian American legislators from the Aloha state.

CONGRESSIONAL REPRESENTATION BY ASIANS FROM HAWAII, THE PACIFIC ISLANDS, AND MAINLAND STATES

The influence of Asian Americans in Hawaiian politics extends far beyond the islands, owing in part to the disproportional American representation system, the two-party system, the campaign finance system, and the single-member district and majority rule characteristics of U.S. elections. The combined features of the American political system not only favor majorities and incumbents in any jurisdiction but also magnify the influence of representatives from sparsely populated states in the upper chamber of the national Congress. Although Asian Americans nationwide comprise a tiny percentage of the U.S. population, their demographic dominance and high partisan cohesiveness in a single state, Hawaii, have helped provide a rather secure access to seats in Congress. When Hawaii received its statehood in 1959, the nation saw for the first time congressional delegates of Asian descent elected by a largely Asian American constituency.[3] Whereas their presence was highly significant to the lifting of Asian American "self-image and confidence" in political participation (Daniels 1988, 311), the more important contribution of the men and women sent to Congress from Hawaii and the Pacific Islands has been their abilities both to represent the interests of their local constituents and to contribute to the constructing of a more viable political community for Asian Americans nationwide. A summary of these and other Asian American members of Congress is listed in table 3.1.[4]

A total of seventeen individuals, including five from American Samoa and Guam,[5] served in the U.S. Congress between 1957 and 2000. Although not all belonged to the Democratic Party or were of Japanese origin, these congressional members from Hawaii or the U.S. territories

TABLE 3.1   Asian Pacific Americans Who Have Served in the U.S. Congress

Name	Ethnic Origin	State	Party	Service Years
Senate				
Hiram Fong	Chinese	Hawaii	Republican	1959–77
Daniel Inouye	Japanese	Hawaii	Democratic	1963–
Spark Matsunaga	Japanese	Hawaii	Democratic	1977–90
S.I. Hayakawa	Japanese	California	Republican	1977–83
Daniel Akaka	Hawaiian-Chinese	Hawaii	Democratic	1990–
House of Representatives				
Dalip Singh Saund	East Indian	California	Democratic	1957–63
Daniel Inouye	Japanese	Hawaii	Democratic	1959–63
Spark Matsunaga	Japanese	Hawaii	Democratic	1963–77
Patsy Mink	Japanese	Hawaii	Democratic	1965–77, 1990–
Norman Mineta	Japanese	California	Democratic	1975–96
Daniel Akaka	Hawaiian-Chinese	Hawaii	Democratic	1977–91
Robert Matsui	Japanese	California	Democratic	1979–
Patricia Saiki	Japanese	Hawaii	Republican	1987–91
Jay Kim	Korean	California	Republican	1993–99
David Wu	Chinese	Oregon	Democratic	1999–
Mike Honda	Japanese	California	Democratic	2001–
Nonvoting Delegates in the House				
Antonio Won Pat	Chamorro	Guam	Democratic	1973–85
Fofo Sunia	Samoan	American Samoa	Democratic	1981–89
Vicente Blaz	Chamorro	Guam	Republican	1985–93
Eni Faleomavaega	Samoan	American Samoa	Democratic	1989–
Robert Underwood	Chamorro	Guam	Democratic	1993–

Sources: American Enterprise Institute for Public Policy Research, 1980 to present, *Vital Statistics on Congress*, Washington, D.C.: Author. Congressional Quarterly, Inc., 1965 to present, *Politics in America*, Washington, D.C.: Congressional Quarterly Press. Congressional Quarterly, Inc., 1965, *Politics in America, 1945–1964*, Washington, D.C.: Congressional Quarterly Press. National Journal, 1972 to present, *The Almanac of American Politics*, Washington, D.C.: Author.

in the Pacific are similar in their career paths and representative roles. All were born American and most of those from Hawaii were reared in immigrant families; many had to work their way into and through college. Five of the eight members had a degree in law from prestigious mainland institutions such as Harvard (Hiram Fong and Spark Matsunaga), George Washington (Daniel Inouye), Chicago (Patsy Mink), and the University of California at Berkeley (Eni Faleomavaega). The other three received degrees in education from the University of Hawaii (Daniel Akaka and Patricia Saiki) and the University of Southern California (Robert Underwood). Before entering national politics, all but one had served in distinctive positions in state politics and were involved as local party activists. Each may claim to have been a champion of women's or minority rights or both, in part because many had encountered personal discrimination based on race or gender or both in their career paths. Both Fong and Inouye, for example voted in favor of the Civil Rights Act of 1964 and the Voting Rights Act of 1965. Fong was one of the key architects of the sweeping immigration reforms passed in 1965. His contributions included the redrafting of the immigration bill to remove the discriminatory provisions against people from the Pacific and Asia (Zia and Gall 1995). Mink, having entered into politics before the civil rights and women's movements, faced many stereotypes and discrimination based on her race, ethnicity, and gender. Both her campaigns for the territorial Senate and the U.S. House were underfunded and not favored by the Democratic Party. However, she managed to triumph as an advocate for the underdog by introducing and supporting legislation to improve women's pay, early childhood education, and women's access to education. The most significant was the enactment of the Title IX of the Higher Education Act Amendment of 1972 (Arinaga and Ojiri 1992; Davison 1994; Zia and Gall 1995). A more recent example was Akaka's speech on the Senate floor during Senate campaign finance hearings in 1997. He lashed out at major media outlets for "giving inappropriate and misguided attention" to the ethnic heritage of those involved in the controversy as well as for their failure to differentiate between Americans of Asian background and foreign Asians. He also appealed to the public and his colleagues to refrain from assigning guilt by ethnic association. As a result, Akaka received a barrage of racist phone calls and death threats.

Although not personally interned, those in service during the time when the Japanese American redress issue was debated in Congress demonstrated through their supportive actions that their conception of representation was more than a reflection of constituency opinions; they were elected also to fulfill their roles as advocates of justice and rights. Inouye took the lead early on in the redress movement that resulted in the improbable passage of the Civil Liberties Act of 1988 (the redress bill), which offered a formal apology and $20,000 in reparations to each surviving Japanese American interned during WWII. For reasons explained later, the success would be improbable without the proper alignment of societal, individual, and institutional factors (Maki, Kitano, and Berthold 1999). Instead of asking the U.S. government to issue monetary compensation from the start, he advised and pushed for establishing a less controversial congressional study commission that would hold public hearings and report findings of facts and factors behind the evacuation and internment. The report by the Commission on Wartime Relocation and Internment of Civilians (CWRIC) turned out to be pivotal in changing public opinion about the redress movement both inside and outside of Congress. Although he did not actively lobby individual senators as the other Nikkei senator did, his leadership position as the second-ranking Democrat in the Senate Appropriations (Sub)committees was crucial in securing redress as an entitlement program and obtaining a larger sum of money to cover the budget shortage after passage of the 1988 bill (Hatamiya 1993; Maki, Kitano, and Berthold 1999).[6] "Spark" Matsunaga, reputed to be one of the hardest working and most personable senators around, was the main Senate leader who personally lobbied all ninety-nine other senators at least once and solicited seventy-five cosponsors—an unheard-of number for major civil rights legislation—thus making the redress bill filibuster-proof (Hatamiya 1993; Zia and Gall 1995). Two other members also expressed support: Akaka provided much needed assistance in the funding stage of the 1988 bill, and Saiki served as a witness in the House Judiciary Subcommittee hearing held in 1987 (Hatamiya 1993).[7]

Mink eloquently explained this perceived role of an advocate when she proclaimed, "It is easy enough to vote right and be consistently with the majority . . . but it is more often more important to be ahead of the majority and this means being willing to cut the first furrow in the ground and stand alone for awhile if necessary" (Arinaga and Ojiri 1992, 251). Not shy of displaying their ethnic background and island roots, Hawaiian delegates had a disproportionately large influence on appointments, judgeships, and the hiring of Hawaiian natives and Pacific Islanders in staff positions (Nash 1998a). As Americans of various ethnic origins, they have demonstrated an ability to serve not only their ethnic community interests but the interests of the pan-Asian community and the greater American community. This profile bears similarity to some of the Asian American congresspersons elected from the mainland, but departs significantly from that of others.

Compared to their colleagues from Hawaii and the Pacific Islands, the career paths of the congresspersons from the mainland make them almost seem like a different breed. Four of the six members were born outside of the United States; the two U.S.-born members were both of Japanese origin and from northern California. Three were elected to the House from municipal positions; two had no prior experience of public office-holding; and none had served in state legislatures. Before entering public service, their occupations included farming (Dalip Singh Saund), education (Samuel I. Hayakawa), business (Morman Mineta and Jay Kim), and the law (Robert Matsui and David Wu). Ideologically, two were Republicans and extremely conservative; others were Democrats, but none could be labeled as extremely liberal. Importantly, no person was elected from a district that was more than 10 percent Asian; instead, all came to represent a majority white constituency. The lack of an ethnic mandate from the majority of their constituents may have limited each person's willingness and ability to represent ethnic-specific and panethnic interests. As a strategy to survive and thrive, some also went to the extreme to downplay their Asian ancestry. This was particularly true with the two Republican members whose partisanship appeared to supercede ethnicity in their legislative decisions.[8]

Yet, other Asian Americans elected from the mainland have managed, in one way or another, to join their counterparts elected from Asian majority districts in the Pacific region and serve a representative role that is not bound by geographic or ethnic lines. For instance, as a Nisei who spent three years growing up in Camp Heart Mountain during WWII, Norman Mineta was determined to use his office to right the wrongs caused by the internment. He successfully pushed for passage of a bill in 1978 granting previously denied retirement benefits to interned Japanese American civil servants. His commitment to the redress efforts was not solidified, however, until after the CWRIC report. From 1983 on, his office became the operational headquarters on the Hill. His staff played a key role in formulating the legislation, cooperating with other congressional offices and committee staffs, and coordinating with the lobbying and letter-writing efforts of community groups. He personally approached every colleague who might lend support, attended every House hearing on redress, gave testimony in various committees, and gave a floor speech in front of the full chamber on the issue. Robert Matsui, who was interned as an infant until four with his American-born parents, played a similar role. Together, they were responsible for getting the redress bill out of committees (Hatamiya 1993; Zia and Gall 1995). In 1988, Norman Mineta signed the redress and reparations bill on behalf of the House.

The passage of the 1988 Civil Liberties Act was considered an improbable legislative success because it was achieved by a numerically negligible, geographically concentrated, relatively affluent, politically fragile, and historically "silent" minority population. Furthermore, it took place under the negative context of massive federal budget deficits and elevated anti-Japanese sentiment because of wide U.S.-Japan trade imbalance. The success was also considered unlikely because of the unprecedented attempt to demand not only an apology and an education fund, but also monetary compensation from the federal government for an injustice done more than forty years earlier under the aegis of national security and other concerns (Hatamiya 1993; Maki, Kitano, and Berthold 1999). When the redress bill was debated in the 100th Congress (1987–89), there were six Asian American congresspersons; all but one was of Japanese origin, but only two out of the group were interned during WWII. Although the mass relocation and incarceration of a group of Americans (two thirds of them were citizens and almost all resided on the West Coast), was unquestionably one of the most serious violations of civil liberties and rights in the U.S. history, this fact was not widely known to the national legislators, let alone their constituents. Yet, facilitated by the relentless efforts of the Japanese American community—which included a class-action suit, a reopening of wartime court cases, the holding of fact-finding community hearings, the seeking of a broad coalition of support, a Smithsonian Institute exhibition, and aggressive grassroots letter-writing and phone-calling campaigns—Asian Americans in Congress, led by Senators Inouye and Matsunaga and Representatives Mineta and Matsui, were able to convince their non-Asian colleagues to look beyond narrow electoral interest and vote for a moral and constitutional cause. In the end, the success of the redress movement was a triumph of a community effort that contained many elements but would not have been possible without the clout and commitment of these congresspersons.

There are other examples of the expansive conception of representation held by Asian Americans in Congress. For instance, to demand a more accurate and speedy count of the Asian and Pacific Islander (API) population, both Mineta and Matsui played instrumental roles in having the API population counted on a 100 percent basis on both the short and long forms of the 1990 census and through a nine-category check-off rather than a write-in system (Espiritu 1992). Earlier, they collaborated with Asian American members from Hawaii and community advocacy groups to prod the formation of an Asian Pacific American Advisory Committee for the 1980 census for a more complete count of the population. Each also introduced amendment bills to fix the omission of Asians from the list of designated minorities eligible for small business contracts and higher education funding. In a similar vein, both Robert Underwood and Eni Faleomavaega have played watchdog roles to ensure that peoples of Guam and Samoa, other Pacific Islanders, and other indigenous peoples were eligible for coverage under relevant federal legislation and programs.

The fact that not all congresspersons with Asian faces can be expected to support policy proposals promoting the panethnic community underlines the idea that "pan-Asian identity is not a natural, inevitable coalition" but a politically constructed one in the pursuit of social justice (Matsuda 1996, 171–79). Nevertheless, the preceding account of the ability of Asian Pacific American members in Congress to advocate the rights and justice for and beyond their geographic constituency does not imply that they can always be expected to speak up on civil rights issues affecting the panethnic community, especially those dealing with transnational concerns.[9] The effusive representative roles beyond fixed boundaries performed by the majority of Asian Americans in Congress highlight the dialectical relationship among ethnicity, panethnicity, and "extraterritoriality"(Wang 1998) within the community and help explain the disproportional amount of campaign funds each often received from outside districts. With important exceptions, and regardless of prior preparations, Asian Americans in Congress usually learn the ropes well, and their quality of representation is reflected in the high reelection rates of many. Unfortunately, and doubtlessly, their political fortunes can also be tarnished by the negligent behavior of other Asians, American or not. Because of campaign finance problems such as those with Jay Kim,[10] each has to take extra caution to weed out any possible source of questionable funding. This issue, as part of the campaign finance scandals involving Asian money in American campaigns, also ill-influenced the fortunes of those who aspired to enter Congress in 1998. Matt Fong, a Republican candidate for the U.S. Senate in 1998, was forced to return within 24 hours a $100,000 campaign donation from a controversial Chinese American, despite his grave need for funds to challenge successfully the incumbent Democratic Senator from California. He lost the election, in part because of the shortage in campaign funds.

Development of Participation as State and Local Officials

Although there are obvious exceptions throughout the electoral history of Asian Americans, holding elective offices at state and local levels is usually a prerequisite to winning national offices. The optimal number of Asian American elected officials in Congress depends on the extent of Asian American participation in office-holding at state and local levels. An examination of the evolution of Asian American participation at local and state levels is therefore in order. Except for a few pioneers, mainland Asians did not begin to run for public office with some frequency and success until the 1970s. The difficult start could be directly attributed to a historically hostile racial environment and racist policies preventing immigration, public employment, equal education, citizenship, and voting.[11] These were the same tactics used in Hawaii in the 1920s and 1930s to postpone as long as possible the emergence of the Japanese vote. However, Hawaiian Japanese were able to benefit from the lifting of legal and political barriers and prevail in politics since the mid-1950s, primarily because of their sociodemographic dominance, the entry of Nisei war heroes into politics, and the persecution of white, leftist, Democratic Party leaders around the 1950s. This was a unique set of conditions not likely to be matched in any other locality or time.

On the U.S. mainland, early accounts of Asian Americans running for public office were scarce and sketchy. The first Asian Americans to run for public office were often leftists and of Japanese or Chinese origin. The earliest record was in 1906 when Benjamin Chow ran as a Socialist candidate in Massachusetts' 1st district and received less than 4 percent of the vote (Cho 1999a). In 1934, Karl Hama (Yoneda) ran on the Communist Party ticket for the 22nd State Assembly seat in San Francisco. Despite an intense anti-Japanese sentiment, he received 1,017 votes from a district with Blacks, whites, and other Asians but less than 100 registered voters of Japanese ancestry (Yoneda 1983). That same year, a Japanese labor attorney ran unsuccessfully as the Republican candidate for Seattle's thirty-seventh Assembly seat. Before 1950, the only recorded history of electoral success on the mainland was Wing F. Ong of Phoenix, Arizona. At age 14, he was detained on Angel Island for three months upon arrival as an immigrant born to a U.S.-born Chinese. He got his first exposure to American electoral politics while working as a houseboy for Arizona's governor. In 1940, he lost his first campaign for the Arizona state legislature by seventeen votes. After the defeat, he went on to earn a law degree and campaigned for the same office in 1946, becoming the first Asian on the mainland to be elected to a state House. Between 1940 and 1968, he ran in eight campaigns and lost five, but was able to gain a seat in the state Senate in the last two years of his public service (Nagasawa 1986). Ong set an example of winning high electoral offices with an immigrant background and without a large number of ethnic votes. As a Democrat, he advocated for teachers' benefits, opposed tax hikes, and scorned Communism. Although his motto was, "Nothing is impossible," he was unable to obtain appointment as an ambassador to China despite Senator Goldwater's support (Nagasawa 1986).

The first mainland Asian woman to win an elective office, March Fong Eu, was a third-generation Chinese American from California. She had a doctoral degree in education from Stanford University and was elected in 1956 to the Alameda County Board of Education. She became the first Asian woman ever elected to the California State Assembly in 1966 and as Secretary of State in 1974, an office that she held for the next twenty years (Zia and Gall 1995). The first Asian to be elected to the California Assembly, however, was Alfred Song, a third-generation Korean American born in Hawaii. An attorney by trade, he won the open seat election with a loan of $3,500 and many non-Asian volunteers from the Democratic Party. Prior to his election in 1962, he served as a city councilman in Monterey Park, California, and held key party positions. He moved up to the state Senate in 1966 and stayed there until 1978 (Song 1980). Tom Hom, a Republican, served briefly in the California Assembly from 1969 to 1970 and had been a city councilman in

San Diego for several terms in the 1960s. Other Chinese Americans who made electoral history in the 1960s included Wing Wu of Providence, Rhode Island, who ran as a Republican for the House of Representatives in 1960 but lost his bid in a Democratic sweep, and Wing Luke, who was elected to the City Council of Seattle in 1962 and became the first person of Chinese descent to win a public office in the Pacific Northwest (Sung 1974). In Tucson, Arizona, Soleng Tom was elected to the school board in 1964. By the late 1960s, both Oakland and Berkeley also saw their first Chinese American city council member (Lai 1992).

The first Nisei to be elected to a mainland state legislature was Seiji Horiuchi of Brighton, Colorado (Hosakawa 1969). He was an agricultural consultant who ran as a Republican in a Democratic district in 1961 and won comfortably. In Washington state, Carl Ooka was the first Nisei elected to be a county commissioner in Kittitas County. In Gardena, California, Bruce Kaji was elected city treasurer in 1959, and Ken Nakaoka, a real estate broker, was elected city councilman in 1966 and mayor in 1972. Three other Japanese Americans served on Gardena's city council in the 1970s (Kubota 1980). Frank Ogawa, a wholesale nurseryman, served in Oakland's city council. Several other Nisei were elected mayors of rural communities in California and Idaho in the 1960s (Hosakawa 1969).

In 1973, Democrat George Chinn became the first Chinese American appointed to the San Francisco Board of Supervisors. Four years later, Gordon Lau became the first Chinese American elected to the Board. The first Korean American to be elected to the school board was Gene Roh of Berkeley, California, in 1973. Roh advocated bilingual education for minorities in general and for Asian immigrants' children in particular (Choy 1979). A Japanese American city councilman from Gardena, Paul Bannai, became the first of his ethnicity to serve in the California State Assembly in 1973. He was joined by another Japanese American, Floyd Mori, in 1975. The following year saw the election of Mae Yih to the Oregon Legislative Assembly, a body where she still maintained a seat in 2001. In nearby Seattle, Ruby Chow became the first Chinese American city council member. In New York, the first Chinese American woman was elected to a school board in 1974 (Lai 1992). In the South, Chinese Americans were elected mayor or sheriff in states like Arkansas, Mississippi, and Louisiana (Lai 1992). Evidence of the emergence of the Asian American participation in electoral politics outside

of Hawaii and California could also be found in a political roster prepared by Nakanishi in 1978 (1980) where Japanese Americans were
shown to be elected to local or state positions in Nebraska (Omaha),
Oregon (Ontario), Colorado (Denver, Pueblo, and Ft. Lupton), Utah
(Salt Lake City and Draper), Idaho (Idaho Falls), Maryland, and Pennsylvania. Most of the roster, however, was comprised of seventy-six
Asian Americans holding federal, state, or local offices in California and
sixty-one federal or state officials of Asian ancestry in Hawaii. Nearly
all were of Japanese or Chinese descent.

Twenty years later, the national political roster directed by Nakanishi and Lai (1998) listed over 1,200 elected and appointed officials of
Asian or Pacific Islander origin.[12] Close to 400 held key elective positions in the federal, state, and municipal governments as U.S. senators
and House representatives, state governors, state senators and representatives, mayors and city council members, and judges. This reflects
about a 10 percent increase from data collected in 1996. Of these key
positions, 147 (or about 38 percent) were from Hawaii, 129 (or 33 percent) were from California, and 31 (or 8 percent) were from Washington. These statistics unveil not only a phenomenal rise in the size of elite
participation and continued dominance of Hawaiian and Californian
Asians, but also an increased participation of mainland Asians residing
in states east and north of California. In the late 1970s, a number of
Asians were elected to state assemblies, city governments, and school
boards in states in the Pacific Northwest, Mountain West, South, and
the East. In 1998, Asians were found to hold key state and municipal
government positions in thirty-three states, including many places
where there was no Asian representation two decades ago. These states
include, but may not be limited to, Alaska, Illinois, Kansas, Massachusetts, Michigan, Minnesota, Missouri, New Jersey, New Hampshire,
Ohio, Oklahoma, Tennessee, Texas, West Virginia, and Wyoming.[13]

Another change that has occurred during the last twenty years is the
increased frequency of Asians occupying higher or more prominent
offices. This may reflect not only the growing sophistication and savvy
of Asian Americans running political campaigns and the emergence of
highly qualified candidates, but also the increased acceptance by the
mainstream electorate of officials with Asian faces. For instance, in 1984,
S. B. Woo, a Shanghai-born physics professor, became the first Asian to
win a lieutenant governorship in Delaware, a state without a large

Asian American population. He did so with a Chinese name and accent and without prior experience of holding a public office (Zia and Gall 1995). His stunning success was replicated by Cheryl Lau, a third-generation Chinese American Republican woman born in Hawaii. A music professor turned deputy attorney general, Lau was elected Nevada's Secretary of State in 1992 as a political newcomer and in a year when Democrats won the majority of the races (Zia and Gall 1995). In 1996, another third-generation Chinese American made history by becoming the first mainland Asian American to be elected a state governor. Gary Locke became the third governor and Democrat of Asian origin in the United States, after George Ariyoshi (1974–1986) and Ben Cayetano (1994–) of Hawaii. Prior to the 1996 Washington-state election, he served as the Chief Executive of King County, the nation's thirteenth largest, where he gained national praise for his work on Seattle's growth management plan. He was elected to this position in 1993 after serving for eleven years in the Washington state legislature. His election to the governorship was considered a milestone for the national Asian American community, not only because he was elected from a state whose electorate was only 4 percent Asian, but because Locke had worked for Asian American causes throughout his career and pledged to continue doing so to help Asian Americans raise their voices in the national political arena (Zia and Gall 1995; Locke 1998).

A third change in recent years is greater ethnic representation among elected officials beyond Japanese or Chinese descent. One ethnic group that has entered the electoral arena in steady progression is Filipino Americans. Although a disadvantaged minority compared to Japanese and Chinese in Hawaii, Filipinos have attained a significant degree of political representation in the island state (Okamura 1997). The first Filipino American legislator, mayor, state cabinet member, and state supreme court justice all were elected or appointed there. Outside of Hawaii, Filipinos are best represented at the local level as town mayors (Delano and Vallejo, California), in city councils (Kodiak, Arkansas; Carson and Daly City, California), and local boards of education. Filipinos also served as state legislators in Maryland, Washington, and West Virginia, but not in California. David Valderrama, a Democratic Party activist who lived in the Philippines for the first twenty-seven years of his life, became, in 1990, the first Filipino American to be elected to a mainland legislature. His Maryland district was 2 percent Asian among the registered voters. Among other accomplishments, he was a central figure in Maryland's fight against the English-only initiative (Lim 1994; Zia and Gall 1995). Two years later, Velma Veloria, another immigrant and longtime community activist, was elected the first Filipina and Asian American woman to the Washington state legislature (Picache 1992). Other Filipino Americans who made electoral history in the 1990s include Pete Fajardo of Carson, California, who became the first Filipino to be elected to a city council on the mainland, and John Amores, who was the first Asian to be elected a state representative in West Virginia.

Another group that has expanded its participation in electoral politics outside of California is Korean Americans. Paul Shin, who was adopted by an American dentist and moved to the United States at age 18, became the first Korean American to be elected to the Washington state legislature in 1992. He ran unsuccessfully as a Democrat for Congress in 1994 and for lieutenant governor in 1996. John Lim, another immigrant born and raised in South Korea, was elected to the Oregon State Senate in 1992 and 1996. He ran for the Republican nomination for governor in 1990 and finished a strong second; he ran unsuccessfully for Congress in 1998 and received over 151,000 votes.

Three Asian Indians made their way to state legislatures in the 1990s. Kumar Barve, a third generation Asian Indian American, was elected to the Maryland House of Delegates in 1990 and became the first of his ethnicity ever to be elected to a state legislature. Nirmala McGonigley, also of Asian Indian descent, served from 1992 to 1996 as a Wyoming state representative and ran unsuccessfully in 1996 to fill Senator Alan Simpson's seat. Second generation Asian Indian American Satveer Chaudhary was elected Minnesota's first Asian state representative in 1996. He won the bid to the state senate in 2000. These individuals became active long after the departure of Congressman Dalip Singh Saund in the early 1960s.

In addition to Korean Americans and Asian Indians, Southeast Asian refugees also debuted in American political life in the 1990s. Tony Lam was elected to the city council of Westminster, California, and became the first Vietnamese-born American to hold an elected office in 1992. He was elected from the nation's largest Vietnamese enclave "Little Saigon," and this fact distinguished him from many Asians in office. The second Vietnamese refugee to win an elective office in America was

Van Thai Tran. On November 7, 2000, he placed first in a field of eight competitors for two open seats on the city council of Garden Grove, California. Both are Republicans from the conservative Orange County. Choua Lee, who came from Laos in 1976, was elected to the St. Paul school district in 1991. She was the first Hmong person in the nation to be elected to public office.

A fourth and less cogent development in recent years is the establishment of more equitable political representation of Asians in localities with high concentration of Asians. Although, in theory, having a greater share of the population may increase Asians' likelihood of receiving political representation (Alozie 1992), in reality, this seldom happens outside of Hawaii, where Asians are two-thirds of the electorate. Excluding Hawaii, the electoral history sketched previously suggests that Asian candidates tend to score greater electoral successes in jurisdictions with a very small percentage of Asians in the population. This curious phenomenon may reflect as much the willingness of non-Asians to vote for a qualified Asian in jurisdictions sparsely populated by Asians as the resistance of non-Asians to the rapid ascendence of Asians to positions of power in areas of Asian concentration. Unless Asians in the electorate reach a critical and cohesive mass, the rapid expansion of the nonwhite population may engender a sense of threat to the status quo among non-Asians and thus become a liability, rather than an asset, to Asians running for offices (Lien forthcoming). This may explain the absence of or delayed electoral empowerment of Asians in major population hubs on the mainland.

In Los Angeles County, the county with the nation's highest Asian American population (they comprised over 13 percent of the population in 1998), there was no Asian representation on the city council or county board of supervisors after the departure of Michael Woo. The former top legislative aide to a powerful state senator was elected upon his second attempt to the city council from a district with a 5 percent Asian population in 1985. He quit the post to run a strong but unsuccessful campaign for mayor in 1993. In San Francisco, a city with a strong and prolonged presence of Asians, who represented 30 percent of the population in 1990, the first Asian did not get elected to the city governing board until the late 1970s. Between 1996 and 2000, with three Asians serving on the eleven-member board of supervisors (Mabel Teng, Leland Yee, and Michael Yaki), Asians were given a taste of equal representation. That taste turned bitter when the number of Asians was stripped down to one during the December 2000 run-offs conducted under the city's first district-based election in over twenty years. However, a positive development occurred in the school board race when a third Asian (Eric Mar, who joined Edward Chin and Frank Chong) was elected to the seven member board in November 2000. In Monterey Park, California, which boasted the highest concentration of Asians in any mainland city (57 percent in 1990), only two Asians (Judy Chu, 1988–, and Sam Kiang, 1990–1994) were elected to the city council in the 1990s. A similar frustration may be found across the coast in New York City. Despite its being the largest Asian American city in 1990, where Asians comprised nearly half of the population in Flushing, no Asian was ever elected to the city council, state assembly, state senate, or the U.S. Congress.[14] With less than 20 percent of Asians in Flushing eligible to vote in the Democratic primaries where elections are decided, the lack of political unity, more than the lack of numbers, may be the culprit for the lack of representation for New York Asians (Dao 1999).

A fifth and related trend over the years is the persistent gap between running and winning. Compared to the rise in the number of elected officials, growth in the number of unsuccessful candidates may be equally dramatic (Nakanishi 1996). Especially illuminating is the amount of failed attempts made by well-qualified Asian American elected officials on the mainland to ascend to higher offices. Michael Woo's campaign to become mayor of Los Angeles was one of the more well-financed, serious campaigns. So was Monterey Park Council-woman Judy Chu's recent attempt for a state assembly seat. More recent examples were former California State Treasurer Matt Fong's and Oregon State Senator John Lim's campaigns for the U.S. Senate in 1998. Other Asians who had made remarkable but unsuccessful runs for the U.S. Congress in the last two decades include: Dan Wong (R, CA-34, 1982), Tom Shimizu (D, UT-2, 1986), S.B. Woo (D, DE Senate, 1988 and DE at large, 1992), Lily Lee Chen (D, CA-30, 1988), Sang Korman (R, CA-21, 1988 and 1992), Albert Lum (D, CA-30, 1992), Mark Takano (D, CA-43, 1992 and 1994), Esther Yao (R, TX-25, 1992), Peter Mathews (D, CA-38, 1994 and 1998), Binh Ly (R, FL-19, 1994), Paul Shin (D, WA-2, 1994), Ram Uppuluri (D, TN-3, 1994), Yash Aggarwal (DL, NY-20, 1996), and Cheryl Lau (R, NV-2, 1996).[15] A positive trend in recent elections may be the emergence of strong candidates (Nash 1998b). Though he was defeated, John Lim raised more than $300,000 in campaign funds and received over 35 percent of the votes in Oregon, a state with a 3 percent Asian population in 1998. More impressive was the record of Matt Fong, who raised over $8 million in campaign money and garnered 3.1 million (or 44 percent) of the votes.

The above discussion on political representation at national and subnational levels indicates that Asian Americans have been elected from backgrounds diverse in nativity, immigration generation, gender, class, ethnicity, and prior experience of public service. Asian-born immigrants could win, but more victories were won by U.S.-born generations. Women could win, but more offices were won by men. Whereas second-generation Japanese Americans made many electoral histories, more were made by the first and third generations of other ethnicities. Reflecting the chain migration history of Asian immigration and settlement patterns, most of the mainland Asian Americans were elected from the West Coast and were of Japanese or Chinese origin, but a growing number of elected officials of Filipino, Korean, Asian Indian, and Southeast Asian ancestry have been elected from California and elsewhere. Most of them served in local offices as school board officials, fewer in city councils, and only a few in state assemblies. As an indication of Asians' greater ability to overcome minority status and white prejudice, there has been a phenomenal growth rate in recent years of Asians appointed to judicial benches at state levels. Nevertheless, at the dawn of the new millennium, history is still waiting to be made at many levels of public offices, by many ethnic groups, and in many places in the nation. One political frontier, the President's cabinet, welcomed its first Asian member in July 2000. Norman Mineta, who resigned from his House seat in 1995 to accept a private position with a leading company in the defense industry, was sworn in to serve as Secretary of Commerce in the final six months of the Clinton Administration. Although significant, this was a dream that had been deferred since 1996 when Chang-lin Tien, a world-renowned scientist in the field of energy and then Chancellor of the University of California at Berkeley, was rumored to be a frontrunner for the Secretary of Energy post. The bubble burst after news revealed that Tien had forwarded a letter of recommendation to the University of California Regents for the son of James Riady, a central figure in the fund-raising scandal from Indonesia.

ASSESSING THE EXTENT OF ELITE PARTICIPATION IN GOVERNING

Despite great electoral gains over recent decades, the Asian American community outside of Hawaii continues to suffer from a lack of representation in political bodies at federal, state, and local levels of government. Their lack of equal participation in governing can also be assessed by comparing the group's share in the population to the group's share of governing elites in the legislative, executive, and judicial branches of government. Applying the logic of proportional representation, Asians should have participated in the governing of the American democracy at the rate of 3.1 percent in 1992 and 3.7 percent in 1998 (see table 3.2). Yet, a cursory review of the group's participation in the operations of U.S. government reveals a huge gap between ideal and reality. In the 106th Congress (1999–2001), there are no more than seven congresspersons, including two nonvoting House members, in both chambers who are of Asian or Pacific Islander ancestry. The 1.3 percent percentage of representation is the lowest of all racial groups. Although, thanks to the two senators from Hawaii, Asians have a greater ratio of representation in the upper chamber than other nonwhite groups, that ratio is still below the national population share.

Besides underrepresentation, another potential issue for the community is asymmetrical representation. As of 1999, of the six congresspersons ever elected from the U.S. mainland, only one was not from California (Wu, D-OR, 1998–). In the 106th Congress, only one of the five voting members was elected from California (Matsui), three came from Hawaii, and all were moderate to liberal Democrats. Given that in 1998, the API population in California was 37 percent of the national total while the population in Hawaii was only 7 percent of the national total, the case of geographical asymmetry may seem obvious. A similar situation is the asymmetry in ethnic and gender representation. Japanese Americans comprised only 12 percent of the national API population in 1990, but three of the five voting members in the 106th Congress are Japanese and one is also the only woman legislator in the Asian delegation. Their ability to speak for the multiethnic community may be limited by the skewed geographical, ethnic, partisan, and ideological distribution of the Capitol Hill team. Yet, their records of service suggest that this concern may be mitigated by the panethnic nature of their representation.

TABLE 3.2   Political Participation in Governing by Asian Pacific Americans and Other Racial Groups

Population (% of)[a]	Asian	Black	Latino	American Indian	White	Total N
1992	3.1	11.9	9.5	0.7	74.4	254,995,000
1998	3.7	12.1	11.2	0.7	72.3	270,299,000
Members in the 106th Congress, 1999–2001 (% of)						
House	1	9	4	0	86	435
Senate	20	0	0	1	97	100
Local Elected Officials in 1992 (% of)						
Total	0.1	2.7	1.4	0.4	95.4	493,830
County	0.1	3.1	1.6	0.3	94.9	58,818
Municipal	0.1	3.7	1.4	0.6	94.1	135,531
School District	0.2	5.2	3.0	0.7	90.9	88,434
Special District	0.2	1.0	0.9	0.6	97.5	84,089
Federal Executive Branch and U.S. Civilian Labor Workforce, 1998 (% of)						
U.S. Civilian	3.7	11.0	10.8	0.8	73.6	N.A.[b]
Federal	4.1	17.1	6.4	1.9	70.6	N.A.
White-Collar Employees in Executive Branch Agencies						
Total	4.4	16.3	6.2	2.0	71.1	1,563,644
Professional	7.5	8.2	4.2	1.3	78.6	345,566
Administrative	2.9	13.6	6.0	1.4	75.5	400,234
Senior Executive	1.8	7.8	2.4	0.8	87.1	N.A.
Federal Judicial Appointees to U.S. District Courts (% of)						
1985–88 (Reagan)	0.6	3.1	4.3	0.0	91.9	161
1989–92 (Bush)	0.0	6.8	4.0	0.0	89.2	148
1993–96 (Clinton)	1.2	19.5	6.5	0.6	72.2	169
Federal Judicial Appointees to U.S. Courts of Appeals (% of)						
1985–88 (Reagan)	0.0	0.0	0.0	N.A.	100	47
1989–92 (Bush)	0.0	5.4	5.4	N.A.	89.2	37
1993–96 (Clinton)	3.4	13.8	10.3	N.A.	72.4	29

Sources: Population information taken from resident population estimates of July 1, 1992, and July 1, 1998, in U.S. Bureau of the Census (1999a). Members of the 106th Congress taken from *Vital Statistics on Congress 106th Congress*. Local elected officials in 1992 taken from U.S. Bureau of the Census (1995, Tables 18–9, 21–4). Information on the 1998 Federal Executive Branch and civilian labor workforce taken from U.S. Office of Personnel Management (1999). Information on Federal Judicial Appointees taken from Goldman and Slotnick (1997).
[a] Entries are percentages of distribution across each row.   [b] N.A. = "not available."

Compared to elite participation at the national level, the community's share of political representation was worse at the local level where only .2 percent of the nation's school and special district offices and 0.1 percent of the nation's county and municipal offices were estimated to be held by Asians in the most recent government survey (see table 3.2). Asians again scored the lowest among all racial groups. Absence of office-holding in these lower positions is an indication of the community's inability to overcome the lack of a political infrastructure for empowerment. Outside of Hawaii, there is a severe case of Asian American underrepresentation in the political system, even in areas with a substantial Asian population. In California, a state where over 12 percent of the population was Asian, only one out of the fifty-four-member congressional delegation and two out of the 120 state legislators in 2000 were of Asian descent (Assemblymen George Nagano and Mike Honda, both Democrats). The situation improved after November 2000 with the elections of Mike Honda to the U.S. House of Representatives and of two Asian American women, Wilma Chan and Carol Liu, to the state assembly. Some places, however, may be making better progress. For instance, in Washington, where less than 6 percent of the population was Asian, the state's chief executive and two of the state's legislators were Asian. In 1998, the state also had thirteen city council members, seven school board members, and eighteen judges who were Asian, according to the *Almanac*, compiled by Nakanishi and Lai (1998). Apparently, although the figures are low overall, the extent of Asian incorporation may vary greatly from one locality to another and it does not necessarily correspond to its population share or size.

The evidence of Asian underrepresentation in other branches of the federal government is somewhat mixed. As shown in table 3.2, Asians were represented in the federal executive branch workforce at a rate slightly above their share in the population or civilian labor force in 1998. Among nonwhites, both Blacks and American Indians, but not Latinos, also participated beyond their share in the population. Yet, the "overrepresentation" of Asians and other minorities in the federal workforce is a result of their concentration in certain occupational categories. For Asians, they were overrepresented in the professional but underrepresented in the administrative categories. Among the topranking employees of the federal civil service, the senior executive service, Asians only accounted for 1.8 percent of the group. In the federal judicial branch, no Asians have ever been appointed to the Supreme Court. Figures reported in table 3.2 show that few Asians were appointed to the U.S. district courts or U.S. Court of Appeals under the Reagan and Bush Administrations. The situation improved under the Clinton Administration. Although the percentage of Asians appointed to the district courts was still below its population share, that of Asians appointed to the Courts of Appeals was almost equal to its population share during Clinton's first term of office. With rare exceptions, this brief survey of the participation status of Asians in the levels and branches of government paints a rather bleak picture pertaining to their ability to participate as equals in democratic governing and jurisprudence. Hopefully, the historic appointment of two Asians to President George W. Bush's cabinet (Norman Mineta to the head of the Department of Transportation and Elaine Chao to the Secretary of Labor) in 2001 is the beginning of an end to the observed trend.

EMERGENCE OF PARTICIPATION AS VOTERS AND VOTING RIGHTS ISSUES

An important reason for the difficult translation of population growth to increased participation in governing for Asians on the mainland is the lack of voter participation. As an immigrant community that continued to expand at an astronomical rate in the 1990s, the likelihood for individuals of Asian descent to cast a ballot in an American election may be hindered by as fundamental a factor as the failure to meet the eligibility requirements or the lack of information in ethnic enclaves. To cast a vote, one needs to register, which, in addition to age limitation, requires U.S. citizenship.[16] Historically, the deprivation of U.S. citizenship of Asian immigrants has been used as a means to exclude Asians from participating in the American political mainstream. Without citizenship, Asian immigrants were rendered powerless by not being able to vote, to serve in public office, or to receive tangible and intangible political dividends because of their participation. Unlike immigrants from Eastern and Southern Europe, mainland Asians were seldom the target of mobilization by machine politics, nor could they gain a foothold in local political power bases. However, not having citizenship was only part of the excuse for the exclusion of Asians. In the latter part of the nineteenth century, many European immigrants were recruited to vote despite their noncitizenship, and laws were changed to make them eligible in the absence of U.S. citizenship.[17] For Asians, the story was different. Their sustained disenfranchisement can only be understood by taking into account both race and alienage factors.

Prior to the repeal of discriminatory naturalization laws in the 1940s and 1950s, only the U.S.-born generation, the majority of whom were under the voting age, and a very small number of citizens naturalized primarily before the exclusion acts were eligible to vote. Although there is no systematic account to document the history of voting participation of these early Asian Americans on the mainland, after WWI, many American-born Chinese became increasingly aware that their vote was their primary protection against discrimination (Tsai 1986). In New York, the Chinese American Voting League, put together by the Democratic Party as part of a coalition uniting minorities and labor, conducted highly successful campaigns to turn out the ethnic vote for Franklin D. Roosevelt in 1932 and 1936 (Chen 1941). Believing that the way to change injustice was through the ballot box, the JACL encouraged every eligible member to vote; certain local chapters would even apply sanctions against those who failed to vote (Hosakawa 1982). However, some faced unexpected obstacles when attempting to register to vote. For instance, the voter registration office in San Francisco had no listing for Japanese. When a Nisei went to register to vote and was asked of his race, the clerk could find only "White, Black, or Mongolian" listed. A Japanese category needed to be created to permit the Nisei to register (Hosakawa 1982). During the internment years, in an attempt by the WRA to socialize Japanese immigrants to the American democratic politics, Issei were allowed to vote for the first time in their lives under WRA's concept of promoting "self-government" (Leighton 1945; Takahashi 1997). The foreign-born were relegated to an inferior political status, however, because of the restriction of office-holding to Nisei and in a process that emphasized English as the official language.

With the passage of the 1952 McCarran-Walter Act, which removed any remaining racial restrictions to the naturalization of Asian immigrants, and the enactment of the Voting Rights Act of 1965, which protected Blacks' rights to register and vote in states where discrimination had been most common, prospects for Asians' access to equal participation in the electoral process also improved. Provisions in voting rights that were of particular relevance to Asians were the 1975 and 1992 language amendments. The 1975 amendment to the Voting Rights Act designated Asians as a language minority along with Hispanics, American Indians, and Alaska Natives. Asian American citizens with limited English abilities would be eligible to receive bilingual voting assistance under section 203 if: (1) they reside in a jurisdiction where at least 5 percent of the voting-age citizens belong to the same single-language minority community, and (2) the illiteracy rate of the citizens in the language minority is higher than the national illiteracy rate. Because the 5 percent threshold to qualify for such assistance was too high for any Asian American language community in the U.S. mainland, no one outside of Hawaii could receive coverage under the 1975 law. In 1992, after aggressive lobbying by a broad coalition of community advocacy groups and other civil rights organizations, section 203 was amended to include large Asian American communities that either met the 5 percent test or had at least 10,000 voting-age citizens in a jurisdiction belonging to a single-language minority community with limited English abilities (NAPALC 1997).

Under the 1992 amendment, a total of ten counties in the nation are required to provide voting assistance in five Asian languages.[18] Examples of such assistance include the translation of written materials available to the general electorate, the hiring of bilingual registrars or deputy registrars and trained interpreters to provide oral assistance, and advertisement of the availability of bilingual assistance. A progress report focusing on the 1996 general elections found that section 203 was particularly important to first-time voters; they constituted over 60 percent of those using oral assistance in Southern California and close to 50 percent in the New York area (NAPALC 1997). Although federal monitors greatly enhanced the ability of community-based organizations to encourage effective compliance with section 203, the report indicated that some jurisdictions were not in full compliance with the law. Problems existed in the recruiting, training, and placement of election workers, and numerous poll sites failed to post clearly the availability of language assistance. In addition, severe underestimation of the need for assistance may occur over the decade in high-growth areas because of the use of decennial census data to determine jurisdictional coverage (Ancheta 1998). Given the fact that 40 percent of Asians over the age of five did not speak English "very well" in 1990 (U.S. Bureau of the Census 1993c), the issue of equal access may continue to pose a challenge to the protection of voting rights for a significant sector of the immigrant community.

Another voting rights issue of consequence to Asians is redistricting, which refers to a political process where legislative boundaries are redrawn following the reapportionment of legislative seats to reflect population changes found in each decennial census. Although the purpose of reapportionment is to facilitate the equal opportunity of every American to influence the outcome of elections, political boundaries often have been drawn to impair the opportunities of racial minorities to elect candidates of their choice (Davidson 1994). Asian Americans have complained that their political power might have been diluted by redistricting plans that split the APA population in an area into several districts. For instance, following the 1981–82 redistricting, Koreatown in Los Angeles was divided into three congressional, four state senatorial, three state assembly, and two city council districts (Ong and Azores 1991). Filipinotown and Chinatown in Los Angeles and in many other areas of APA concentration in the mainland also have experienced similar cases of fragmentation.

To reverse the pattern of fragmentation in California, more than 150 APA organizations formed the Coalition of Asian Pacific Americans for Fair Reapportionment (CAPAFR) during the 1990 round of redistricting (Saito 1998). This was a historic first for the community to band together on this issue. Yet, redistricting as an empowerment strategy is qualitatively different for Asians than for Blacks and Latinos. It is difficult for Asians to satisfy the three-part test of vote dilution established by *Thornburg v. Gingles* (1986), for the population is small in size, geographically dispersed, and politically fragmented (Ancheta 1998). Despite the dramatic rate of population growth, there are only a handful of electoral districts where Asians can or will have the potential to form a majority. Even if Asian-concentrated districts can be created, evidence of pan-Asian bloc voting may not be forthcoming. Boosted by court decisions in *Garza v. County of Los Angeles* (1990), attorneys for Asians argued that the protection of voting rights could apply to a minority population as long as intentional discrimination could be shown. With coordinated efforts from Latinos, the CAPAFR was able to create a number of Asian "influence" state assembly districts by consolidating concentrations of adjacent APA communities (Ancheta 1998). Asians were not the majority in these districts, but, with continued growth, were believed to have the potential to influence future elections. Despite the success, most other Asian populations were divided between districts. Moreover, the new districts still lacked enough voters to change the electoral fate of qualified Asian candidates. Judy Chu, a councilwoman from Monterey Park, lost twice in her bid to an assembly seat in the forty-ninth district.

For the majority of the Asian American adult population who came to the United States as immigrants after 1965, a more direct challenge to their voting rights lies in the need to satisfy the citizenship and voter registration requirements. These two prerequisites to voting have been major barriers to the full franchise of Asians in U.S. electoral systems. Although Asians have been found to compare favorably to immigrants from other world regions in the propensity to seek U.S. citizenship, their citizenship rate in the aggregate has been suppressed by the continuous influx of new immigrants. Between 1975 and 1993, Asians have naturalized two to six years earlier than Europeans and South Americans (Portes and Rumbaut 1996). Their relative speed in adopting U.S. citizenship can be explained by their higher educational levels, greater geographic distance and difficulty in returning to the homeland, and the undesirable political climates in their country of origin. The ability of U.S. citizens to bring in parents, spouses, fiancees, and unmarried children under twenty-one without quota limitation also create a major incentive for their speedy naturalization. After 1994, the threat of losing welfare benefits provided a further push for naturalization. Nevertheless, not all legal permanent residents are eligible for naturalization. Only those who satisfy the minimum legal waiting time requirement may apply. Still, their acquisition of citizenship may be hindered by a combination of factors such as a lack of English-language proficiency, limited knowledge of U.S. history and the Constitution, lack of money and time to go through the arduous citizenship process, distrust in government and its efficacy, and the reluctance to sever emotional ties with the homeland origin. For these immigrants, the journey to the polling booths may never take place or it begins long after their arrival in the United States because of the denied or deferred citizenship. Asians who become U.S. citizens by birth or by naturalization may waste the franchise by not registering.

Prior to 1965, voter registration was used as a device to prevent Blacks and other minorities from voting. A slow but liberalizing trend in registration laws has been evolving at the national level in subsequent decades, evidenced first by the outlawing of poll taxes and literacy tests, then by the abatement of the stringent residency and closing date requirements, and most recently by the passage of the National Motor Voter Act, which attempts to ease the burden of registration for the young, the residentially mobile, and the poor by providing easy access to registration forms in many public places where they would visit (Hington and Wolfinger 1998). Nevertheless, individual U.S. citizens, not the government, still bear the responsibility of registering and re-registering to vote following each move across jurisdictional lines. Flanigan and Zingale (1994) note, "The inconvenience of administrative arrangements for voter registration and the frequent need to re-register have offered greater obstacles to voting than has the imposition of other eligibility standards" (28). The concept of self-registration can be perceived as overtly onerous for Asians who immigrated from systems with government-initiated registration. These citizens may be unlikely to become registered without aggressive voter-registration campaigns. For those with limited English proficiency, their likelihood to register can be hampered if there is inadequate bilingual assistance. Immigration motivation that is political in nature may facilitate the rate of political integration (Portes and Rumbaut 1996). The tendency of recent Asian immigrants to be motivated by economic and family factors rather than by political reasons may not bode well in predicting their participation beyond citizenship. Finally, Asian immigrants may feel that their fragmented districts diminish the power and influence of their votes, thus discouraging them from registering.

The above discussion suggests that the most important obstacles hindering the voting participation of Asians are institutional mechanisms such as English-only ballots, fragmented districts, and citizenship and registration restrictions. Once Asians acquire citizenship and become registered, they are expected to turn out in rates equal to those of other Americans of comparable backgrounds. In addition, the extent of mass participation may correspond to the extent of elite participation (Bobo and Gilliam 1990; Rosenstone and Hansen 1993). According to the elite mobilization hypothesis, Asians residing in localities with greater political infrastructure (such as with more Asian public officials and community groups, political organizations, and the media involved in the recruitment and training of potential candidates as well as in offering citizenship classes and voter education) may be expected to participate in greater rates than Asians residing elsewhere. Thus, Hawaiian Asians may participate in higher rates than Asians in California who, in turn, may register and vote more than eligible Asians in all other American states.

ASSESSING THE EXTENT OF MASS PARTICIPATION IN ELECTIONS OF THE 1990S

The extent to which Asians participated as citizens, registrants, and voters in recent U.S. elections is evaluated empirically using the series of census data collected after each November election as supplemental to the monthly Current Population Survey. For reasons specified in the

Appendix on Methodology, this is the best source to date for estimating the extent of Asian American voting participation. Table 3.3 summarizes the rates of citizenship, voting registration, and election turnout of Asians in the five national elections of the 1990s. The table also provides the rates of Latinos, American Indians, Blacks, and non-Hispanic whites to assess the level of equality in voting participation by Asian Americans as compared to other racial groups.

Citizenship

Under current laws, not all individuals of voting age can register to vote; only U.S.-born or naturalized citizens are eligible to become registered voters. Albeit a nonissue for most Americans, this simple gatekeeping measure has kept close to half of the voting-age Asians in the 1990s from registering to vote. In the first national election of the 1990s, only half of the adult Asians in the survey possessed U.S. citizenship either by birth or by naturalization. This is the lowest rate of all racial groups. In the last national election of the decade, the citizenship rate of Asians remained the lowest. However, because the rate of Asian citizenship grew steadily by 2 percentage points in each succeeding election, the gap in citizenship rates between Asians and the next lowest group (Latinos) was reduced from 8 to 2 percentage points between 1990 and 1998. Whereas every racial group expanded its rate of citizenship over the decade, the percentage change for Asians is the highest of all. Accordingly, Asians possess the fastest growth rate in the share of U.S. citizenry. Table 3.4 reports an estimated 1 percentage point rise in Asians' share of citizenry over the decade. Although this increase in percentage points was smaller than that of Latinos, Asians fared much better than all other groups in terms of the growth rate of individuals holding U.S. citizenship (89 percent) during the eight-year span.

Voting Registration

Since the voting participation rates are generally higher in presidential (or on-year) elections than in midterm (or off-year) elections, separate analyses are conducted for each election series. The chapter also makes distinctions in participation rates between rates that apply to all voting-age respondents and rates calculated only among adult citizens or those who met the eligibility requirements for voting registration. As shown in table 3.3, when registration rates are calculated among voting-age

TABLE 3.3   Percentage Distribution of Voting and Registration in the Elections of 1990–1998 by Race

	Asian	Latino	Indian	Black	White
November 1990 Election					
Citizens (%)	51	59	96	93	96
Registered (%)	28(56)	32(55)	52(55)	59(64)	67(70)
Voted (%)	20(40)	21(36)	35(36)	39(43)	49(51)
among registered	72[a]	65	66	67	74
Reweighted N	2,146	6,492	481	9,469	67,249
Weighted N (×1,000)	4,547	13,756	1,019	20,064	142,492
November 1992 Election					
Citizens (%)	53	58	99	95	98
Registered (%)	31(62)	35(63)	61(63)	64(70)	74(77)
Voted (%)	27(56)	29(54)	51(55)	55(63)	67(72)
among registered	88	83	84	85	91
Reweighted N	2,246	6,506	418	9,204	63,771
Weighted N (×1,000)	5,070	14,688	944	20,777	143,962
November 1994 Election					
Citizens (%)	55	59	99	96	98
Registered (%)	29(52)	31(53)	56(56)	59(61)	68(69)
Voted (%)	22(40)	20(34)	37(37)	37(39)	50(51)
among registered	76[a]	64	66	64	74
Reweighted N	1,958	7,169	392	8,825	59,492
Weighted N (×1,000)	4,772	17,476	954	21,514	145,027
November 1996 Election					
Citizens (%)	57	61	99	96	98
Registered (%)	33(58)	36(59)	61(62)	64(67)	72(73)
Voted (%)	26(46)	27(44)	45(46)	51(53)	60(61)
among registered	79	75	73	80	83
Reweighted N	2,482	6,950	522	8,267	54,819
Weighted N (×1,000)	6,580	18,426	1,385	21,918	145,343
November 1998 Election					
Citizens (%)	59	61	98	96	98
Registered (%)	29(49)	34(55)	57(58)	61(64)	68(69)
Voted (%)	19(32)	20(33)	35(35)	40(42)	47(47)
among registered	66[a]	60	61	66	68
Reweighted N	3,341	9,267	674	10,308	66,810
Weighted N (×1,000)	7,327	20,321	1,476	22,603	146,501

Sources: U.S. Department of Commerce, Bureau of the Census (1992, 1997a, 1997b, 1997c, 1999c). *Current Population Survey: Voter Supplement File*, 1990, 1992, 1994, 1996, 1998 [Computer files]. ICPSR version. Washington, D.C.: U.S. Department of Commerce, Bureau of the Census [producer], 1990, 1992, 1994, 1996, 1998. Ann Arbor, MI: Inter-university Consortium for Political and Social Research [distributor], 1992, 1997, 1999.

Notes: All populations are age 18 and over. Each racial category is mutually exclusive of each other. Entries in parentheses are rates among citizens. All tests of significance are conducted with reweighted data calculated by subtracting the mean adult weight from the final adult weight for each case in order to adjust the size of standard errors.

[a]Chi-square test fails to reject the hypothesis of no racial difference between whites and Asians. All other white-nonwhite differences are statistically significant at the .05 level or better.

TABLE 3.4   Percentage Share of Citizens and Voters by Race in
November Elections, 1990–1998

	Asian	Latino	Indian	Black	White
Share of Citizenry (%)					
1990	1.4	4.8	0.6	11.2	82.0
1992	1.5	4.9	0.5	11.4	81.7
1994	1.5	5.9	0.6	11.5	80.5
1996	2.0	6.4	0.8	11.3	79.6
1998	2.4	6.8	0.8	11.8	78.3
N 1990 (×1,000)	2,298	8,043	975	18,627	136,076
N 1998 (×1,000)	4,344	12,395	1,448	22,603	143,651
Percent Change	+89	+54	+49	+21	+6
Share of the Electorate (%)					
1990	1.1	3.5	0.4	9.7	85.3
1992	1.2	3.7	0.4	9.9	84.7
1994	1.2	4.2	0.4	9.4	84.7
1996	1.7	4.8	0.6	10.5	82.4
1998	1.7	4.9	0.6	10.9	81.9
N 1990 (×1,000)	924	2,894	351	7,912	69,869
N 1998 (×1,000)	1,404	4,068	512	9,044	68,068
Percent Change	+52	+41	+46	+14	−3

Source: See table 3.3.

respondents, they are relatively stable in both election series. When cal-culations are made only among citizens, the rates of Asians have steadily declined in both on-year and off-year elections, even though the sheer size of registrants have generally increased. A similar decline in regis-tration rates for citizens of other races is observed in presidential but not in off-year elections. For Latinos, Blacks, and whites, the rates among cit-izens in 1998 were the same as in 1990, despite a small dip in 1994. Among voting-age respondents, the registration rates of Asians are the lowest of all groups. Racial gaps between Asian and other groups are significantly smaller when citizenship is controlled. Among adult citi-zens, the registration rates of Asians were comparable to those of Lati-nos in every election except 1998, when Asians were 6 percentage points lower. Compared to their white counterparts, citizens of Asian origin are 15 percentage points behind in registration rates during on-years and from 14 to 20 percentage points behind in off-years. These racial gaps in citizens' voting registration in elections of the 1990s cannot be explained away by controlling for differences in socioeconomic status, social connectedness, and residential region (Lien 2000).

Turnout

Among voting-age respondents, the turnout rates of Asians are about the same as those of Latinos in both election series. They also remain relatively stable over time. When only citizen respondents are counted, the Asian rates are generally higher than the Latino rates, except in 1998 when there was an 8 percentage point drop from 1994 among Asians. The rates of other races also dipped in the same period, but not any steeper than the 4 percentage point slide among whites. The greater decline among Asian American citizens in registration and voting rates may be the result of the campaign finance scandals, which painted in a negative light the political participation of Asian Americans. Prior to 1998, the difference between Asian and white rates was about 10 percentage points in off-years and about 15 percentage points in on-years. However, when voting rates are calculated only among those who are registered, Asians turned out at a rate higher than Latinos and were comparable to whites in off-year elections and about 3 to 4 percentage points lower than whites in presidential elections. Being registered makes a big difference for the voting rates of Asians, and this highlights the critical role of registration drives in empowering the community of new Americans. In spite of this bright spot, table 3.4 shows that only 1.7 percent of the electorate in 1998 was estimated to be Asian, a percentage much lower than the community's estimated 3.7 percent share of the U.S. population or the 2.4 percent share of the citizenry. However, Asians again scored the biggest gain in getting more voters to the polls between 1990 and 1998 (a 52 percent increase). In contrast, although whites had a greater share of the electorate than their share of the citizenry, the size of the white electorate was down by 3 percent during the same time period.

State-level Patterns

Although, as a group, the voting and registration rates of Asians may appear low except for the turnout rates among the registered, significant differences may exist from one state to another. Those Asians residing in states with more political elites, organized groups, and other mobilizing agents may be expected to register and vote at higher rates than Asians elsewhere. This hypothesis is examined by studying the voting participation rates of Asians in selected states that have the largest API population. The five largest Asian American states in 1998 were California, New York, Hawaii, Texas, and New Jersey (see table 3.5). They accounted for about two-thirds of the Asian population in the nation. Residents in these states have the potential of influencing up to one-fourth of the electoral college votes in a presidential election. Except for Hawaii, each state has experienced a significant population growth since 1990. Nevertheless, Hawaii is outstanding in terms of the density of Asians in an American state (63.4 percent). California is a distant second at 12.1 percent, followed by New Jersey and New York as a distant third and fourth.

Table 3.6 reports the citizenship, voting registration, and turnout

TABLE 3.5   States with the Largest Asian and Pacific Islander Population in 1998

Rank of State	Estimate Population (×1,000)	% total Asian in nation	% change since 1990	% Asian in Population	% Asian among voters[a]	Number of Electoral Votes [b]
1. California	3,938	36.8	33.6	12.1	6.1	54
2. New York	995	9.3	40.3	5.5	1.5	33
3. Hawaii	757	7.1	8.8	63.4	73.3	4
4. Texas	556	5.2	67.9	2.8	0.4	32
5. New Jersey	453	4.2	63.4	5.6	1.6	15
6. Illinois	403	3.8	37.9	3.3	0.9	22
7. Washington	330	3.1	53.2	5.8	3.1	11
8. Florida	271	2.5	73.4	1.8	0.5	25
9. Virginia	247	2.3	53.4	3.6	1.3	13
10. Massachusetts	223	2.1	52.7	3.6	0.5	12
Nation[c]	10,507	100	40.8	3.7	1.7	538

Source: U.S. Bureau of the Census (1999b).

[a]U.S. Bureau of the Census (1999c). Current Population Survey: Voter Supplement File, 1998.

[b]U.S. Electoral College votes per state for the 1992 election (O'Connor and Sabato 1996, 414, fig. 12-2).

[c]Based on figures for Asian and Pacific Islander population on July 1, 1998, in U.S. Bureau of the Census (1999a).

TABLE 3.6   Voting and Registration of Asians in the Elections of
1990–1998 by Key States

	California	New York	Hawaii	Texas	New Jersey
November 1990 Election					
Citizens (%)	51	36	87	36	43
Registered (%)	29(58)	20(54)	56(67)	21(62)	22(52)
Voted (%)	20(40)	13(37)	51(61)	3(8)	17(37)
among registered	68	68	91	13	74
Reweighted N	864	173	249	71	103
Weighted N (×1,000)	1,831	367	529	149	217
November 1992 Election					
Citizens (%)	45	41	86	42	43
Registered (%)	28(61)	23(58)	56(65)	30(71)	21(47)
Voted (%)	24(53)	21(51)	51(60)	19(45)	17(51)
among registered	86	88	92	63	88
Reweighted N	903	205	232	91	88
Weighted N (×1,000)	2,038	463	523	205	197
November 1994 Election					
Citizens (%)	57	42	84	51	47
Registered (%)	31(55)	19(46)	50(60)	20(40)	26(55)
Voted (%)	25(43)	11(25)	45(54)	14(27)	15(33)
among registered	79	56	90	67	57
Reweighted N	732	177	209	89	86
Weighted N (×1,000)	1,784	431	509	216	209
November 1996 Election					
Citizens (%)	55	50	88	53	42
Registered (%)	32(59)	26(54)	51(57)	35(65)	22(51)
Voted (%)	27(49)	17(35)	42(47)	29(56)	18(42)
among registered	83	65	82	85	82
Reweighted N	992	236	216	136	103
Weighted N (×1,000)	2,629	626	572	361	272
November 1998 Election					
Citizens (%)	61	55	87	44	51
Registered (%)	32(52)	19(35)	52(59)	18(40)	28(55)
Voted (%)	22(35)	12(23)	47(53)	6(13)	15(30)
among registered	69	64	91	31	55
Reweighted N	1,234	315	294	165	105
Weighted N (×1,000)	2,705	692	645	362	230

Source: see table 3.3.

Note: All populations are age 18 and over. Entries in parentheses are those among citizens.

rates of Asians in these states. Among voting-age Asians, the patterns yield overwhelming support for the proposed hypothesis that Asians in Hawaii exceeded Asians in California (who exceeded Asians in the other mainland states) in all three categories of participation. However, the higher registration and voting rates among voting-age Asians in Hawaii and California may reflect the higher citizenship and lower immigration rates of Asians in the states. Between 1990 and 1998, the population of Asians in Hawaii increased by 9 percent and in California by 34 percent; both are lower than the rate of growth in other top Asian states (see table 3.5). Close to nine out of ten Asian respondents in Hawaii were citizens in the study period. The rates in California were much lower, but they were higher than those in the three other mainland states. Although the citizenship rates fluctuated over time in mainland states, each had a significantly higher citizenship rate in 1998 than in 1990. This trend is particularly noteworthy in New York, which had a steady rise in citizenship rates from 36 percent to 55 percent in the eight-year period.

When registration and voting rates are calculated only among citizens, the inter-state gaps shrink significantly and the predicted ranking order of Hawaiian Asians in the lead followed by Asians in California only holds true in one election (1994). In the two presidential elections of 1992 and 1996, Asians in Texas registered and voted at the highest rates. When turnout rates are calculated only among the registered, at least nine out of ten Asians in Hawaii who registered also voted in elections of the 1990s, except in 1996. Although New Jersey could claim to have the second highest turnout rate among the registered in three of the five elections, the turnout rates of Asians in California have been more consistent in both midterm and presidential elections.

Beyond this, it may be difficult and too risky to generalize the pattern of participation at the state level because of the relatively small number of respondents in certain states as well as the likely influence of local political factors. For instance, although presidential elections are considered "high stimulus elections" that tend to increase participation, a competitive gubernatorial campaign in an off-year (as in the case of Hawaii) may have greater stimulating effect on participation. Thus, one notes that among citizens, the ranking order of registration and voting rates across states is not always in the predicted order, especially in presidential election years. However, when an advanced statistical procedure is adopted to control for possible confounding influence on participation such as election type and individual characteristics (income, age, education, gender, length of residence, marital status, employment status, union membership), Asians in Hawaii are found to have a significantly higher likelihood of registration among citizens and voting among the registered than Asians in California who, in turn, have a significantly higher propensity to become registered and turn out than Asians residing either in the three other states or in all forty-eight other states between 1990 and 1998. (Logistic regression results from analyzing merged datasets of the five elections are not shown). Therefore, although the aggregate-level findings suggest that when mainland Asians jump the hurdle of citizenship, they may have the potential to register in as high a rate as their Hawaiian counterparts, both the aggregate- and individual-level results suggest that the turnout potential among the registered would be greater in states that have a larger presence of mobilization agents such as public officials, candidates, ethnic press, and community political organizations. These observations lend strong support to the elite mobilization theory at the state level.

CONCLUSION

How active are Asians in mainstream American politics? Given the diversity of group history and culture, there is more than one answer. This chapter focuses on Asians' roles as candidates, representatives, and voters and contrasts the patterns observed in Hawaii to those found in mainland states. Asians in Hawaii have been able to transfer their sociodemographic advantage into political power because of a unique intersection of history, demography, and politics that has enabled Asians in general and Japanese Americans in particular to participate fully in the electoral process since the mid-1950s. For mainland Asians, their participation in the process has been much more restricted despite significant improvements in political representation and voting rights over recent decades. In fact, there is a severe case of underparticipation in different branches and levels of government, even in communities with a substantial Asian population. This, in turn, may have suppressed the voting registration and turnout rates of the mass. When other conditions are equal, the effect of elite mobilization may account for the greater participation rates of Asians in California than in other mainland states.

Although having representatives of one's race or ethnicity in government is important, there is no guarantee that he or she will be able to represent the community's interest. One barrier interfering with translating symbolic representation into interest representation is the issue of identity. For Asians, this is a particularly thorny one because of the multiple layers and facets of identity formation rooted not only in ethnic origin and skin color, but also in nationality, language, religion, beliefs, cultural norms, nativity, immigration motivation, generation, length of individual stay, and socialization as well as involuntary forces in the larger social and political context. From the evidence shown, Asian American congressional delegates from Hawaii and the majority of their counterparts from mainland states apparently have played a significant role in constructing the pan-Asian community. Despite a sharp contrast in the composition of the constituency, together they helped accomplish the improbable. They helped obtain internment redress for Japanese Americans and political efficacy for Asian Americans. An unanswered question, and one that warrants further investigation, is whether they could have done more for the community. Also, what other contributions have Asian American public officials made in terms of community empowerment?

The lesson from the redress movement is that smallness in size is not an insurmountable obstacle in American politics, but lack of unity and coalition-building viability with other groups is. In the struggles for equality and justice, Asians have shown an ability to form coalitions across ethnicity and race at the organizational and elite levels. How much are Asians able to conduct themselves as individuals in a politically cohesive manner? How much are Asians able to form coalitions with other racial and gender groups at the mass level? These are some of the critical questions to be answered in the following chapters.

4 How Can We All Get Along?

Cross-Racial Coalition-Building Possibilities and Barriers

"Just where exactly did an Asian fit in?"
—Chang-lin Tien (1996, 19)

LIKE OTHER immigrant groups, Asians have been engaged in one struggle after another to become full and equal participants in American democratic politics. Like other nonwhite Americans, their journey to voting booths and city halls has been subverted and deferred by discriminatory legislation and hostile actions. Monumental changes in the social, economic, and political orders on both the domestic and international fronts in the post-1965 era have significantly improved the opportunity structure for Asians to voice their concerns in electoral politics. Still, as noted in the previous chapter, except in Hawaii, Asians are no more than a tiny share of the population and an even smaller share of the electorate at the dawn of the twenty-first century. Given the demographic disadvantage in the national population and the majoritarian bias in the American two-party system, which requires the assembling of large coalitions of diverse interests, it is imperative for Asians to develop political coalitions with other racial and ethnic groups in their pursuit of political power. As shown in previous chapters, Asian elites and organized groups have been able to lead or participate in cross-racial coalitions on issues of social justice, equal rights, and political empowerment. In spite of the belated entry of mainland Asians into electoral politics, they were part of the multiracial coalitions supporting Latino and Black candidates such as Ed Roybal's run for the Los Angeles city council in 1949 (Saito 1998), Jesse Jackson's presidential bids in 1984 and 1988 (Wei 1993), and Lee Brown's campaign for mayor of Houston in 1997 (Saito and Park 2000). They participated as junior partners in Los Angeles mayor Tom Bradley's governing coalition over a twenty-year span (Sonenshein 1993). They were able to negotiate Asian-influence in districts with Latinos in the San Gabriel Valley of Southern California (Saito 1998) and with Puerto Ricans,

Blacks, and whites surrounding New York's Chinatown (Saito and Park 2000). Moreover, as demonstrated in Chapter 3, virtually every successful Asian candidate won because of support from non-Asian voters who are majority white. Granted, there were exceptions in Hawaii and in a very small number of mainland jurisdictions. Still, it is not an exaggeration to suggest that every major political success of the community is a result of cross-racial/ethnic coalition building. Asians have been able to form coalitions with other racial and ethnic groups at the elite level, but how likely is it for Asians to develop parallel relationships at the mass level? Based on the premise that political coalitions cannot last in the absence of public support, this chapter assesses the ability of Asians to forge broad-based, long-term cooperative relationships with other racial groups. It is done by reviewing, first, the structural forces that shaped the racial positions of U.S. Asians. It then examines the historical patterns of interactions between Asians and American Indians, Blacks, Latinos, and non-Hispanic whites. Finally, it addresses mass opinion patterns in the 1990s that were indicative of interracial coalition-building possibilities and barriers among the U.S. public at national, state, and local levels.

CONSTRUCTING INTERRACIAL COALITIONS AND ALLIANCES: AN OVERVIEW OF POSSIBILITIES AND BARRIERS

The concept of political coalition has been construed in different ways. Coalitions may be loosely or tightly organized and cooperation may be tacit or explicit (Eisinger 1976). Coalitions may be based on a shared core when "disparate groups come together because they support a common issue agenda" (Watts 1996, 43). They may also be based on a shared goal that is "instrumental to the realization of more important specific goals that are not shared" (41). In general, political coalitions are short-term working relationships based on the strategic needs of each participant group to maximize its own political power. Because each coalition partner may differ in terms of group solidarity, political clout, resources, and reasons to be incorporated, coalitions are by nature unstable and not designed to last unless some sense of alliance or long-term unity based on common interests, equal partnership, and mutual respect is developed (Rich 1996; Morris 1996). There is also a distinction between governing coalitions formed among political elites out of common strategic concerns and grassroots coalitions formed among voters or the general public based on shared political preferences or causes. A coalition may be a rhetorical construct, that is, negotiated by political elites, with little input from the mass of each group involved. Rather than studying the formation of political coalitions among political elites, which is the main focus of the extant literature, this chapter assesses the viability of building alliances among the masses. Although the preferences of the mass may reflect the influence of elite mobilization, it may also provide a popular basis for elites to maneuver in the coalition-building process. Instead of exploring the possibilities of forming coalitions merely among minority groups, this chapter tries to find the mechanisms that promote interracial peace for all, including alliances formed with sympathetic whites. A racially inclusive focus not only takes into consideration the ever-changing and malleable nature of race, but it may better reflect the contemporary possibilities of cross-racial coalition building in electoral politics involving Asians.

Under what conditions are effective or long-term interracial coalitions most likely to happen? Few theoretical works exist on the creation of biracial, much less multiracial, coalitions beyond the Black and liberal white models (Regalado 1994). Carmichael and Hamilton (1967) proposed four prerequisites for the creation and maintenance of biracial coalitions: identification of self-interest, belief in mutual benefit, recognition of each participant group's independent power base and control over decision making, and agreement on the specific and identifiable goals and issues for each party involved. Although these are useful guidelines, they are limited to temporary political coalitions between Black and white elites; no broad-based or long-term relationship was sought. Some also perceive racial ideology as more fundamental than interest in forging alliances, even though both interest and leadership are also vital elements (Sonenshein 1993). Others argue, however, that the formation and maintenance of stable multiracial coalitions cannot rely solely on common interest and ideology, but are developed "in social interaction where a history of reinforcing behavior breeds trust" (Oliver and Grant 1995, 30). There need to be "*spaces* and *places* in which diverse groups can come together to forge new understandings that recognize distinct group interests . . . through sustained interaction, communication, and the development of trust" (6, emphasis original). Although alliances may be more likely among racial groups of similar social distance or social, economic, and racial status (Meier and Stewart 1991), both status difference and status similarity can contribute to intergroup competition and conflict (McClain and Karnig 1990).

Generally, the formation of long-lasting intergroup coalitions between Asians and others may be assessed at three separate but interconnected levels. The first level of assessment is the between-group level, or factors related to racial interactions. The formation may depend on a list of structural factors revised from Blalock's (1982) theory of inter-minority coalition building: (1) level of contact, especially the presence of bridging personnel or organizations such as intermarried couples, close cross-racial friends, and integrated labor unions or community-based groups; (2) proximity in cultural practices and beliefs; (3) degree of (perceived) economic competition and conflict; and (4) degree of status hierarchicization or relative social and political ranking. Cross-racial coalition is more likely to occur between groups that have high levels of friendly contacts and low incidence or sense of intense economic competition, that are similar in language, religion, beliefs, and values, and that are not too far apart in social and political rankings. These factors affect the degree of interracial trust and efficacy in working together. Groups that perceive themselves as in a "positive-sum" situation in which the gains of one will add to the gains of all are more likely to form coalitions than those in a "zero-sum" competition where the gains of one group are perceived to be made at the expense of another (Blalock 1982).

The second level of assessment is the within-group level, or factors dealing with the formation and maintenance of a multiethnic community. Before a group can be incorporated into the political system, it must have internal unity or be able to coalesce and mobilize as a community (Browning, Marshall, and Tabb 1986). Historically, this possibility for Asians may have been hampered by the serial pattern of labor migration and the practices of segregation (Chan 1991a). In the post–Civil Rights Era, the creation, existence, and sanctity of a panethnic coalition among Asians and members of other racialized groups may also be very much in doubt (Omi and Winant 1994). As explained in Chapter 2, the same forces that facilitated rapid population growth have also contributed to the increased divisiveness within the racialized Asian American community. In addition, the creation and maintenance of a distinct Asian American identity may be challenged by the possibility of total assimilation offered in the American political culture for some ethnic groups, if old ethnic cultural practices are discontinued (Watts 1996). This perception makes it difficult to maintain ethnic ties and formal ethnic solidarity even within the first generation. Furthermore, segments of the Asian population may find it more appealing to organize around class and gender issues than by panethnicity, a concept that may be much more popular among the organizational elites than the mass. The contours of the pan-Asian American community based on public opinion is the subject of the next chapter. Even if a panethnic coalition can be reasonably expected under current situations, the ability of leaders to make bargains may be severely impaired by the lack of a political infrastructure within their respective communities and the difficulty they have in obtaining consensus.

The third level of assessment is the beyond-group level, or factors related not to group characteristics but to the very nature of the U.S. racial system. Because conflict rather than cooperation typifies the interactions between Anglos and nonwhite groups throughout U.S. history (Feagin and Feagin 1999), interracial alliances are often difficult to forge and keep. With whites continuing to dominate racial politics and nonwhites being relegated to subordinate positions, each nonwhite group is enticed to seek a separate accommodation with whites for respective group advancement. The racialization of Asians as a distinctive "model minority" superior to other nonwhite groups may preclude Asians from being considered viable partners in the liberal coalition of nonwhite groups. The perceived advantage of Asians in the socioeconomic sphere may have also convinced many members in the community to accept the "model minority" labeling and fantasize about the group's fictional ability to "make it" by themselves and enjoy an equal political status with whites.

How can we anticipate the construction of long-lasting interracial relationships between Asians and other groups in light of the possibilities and barriers implied by these levels? Which racial group would be the most viable coalition partner of Asians? Where can we identify common grounds for building coalitions? To answer these questions, this chapter begins with an exploration of the erratic nature of U.S. race relations and the distinctive racial positions of Asians. Highlighted is the fact that, despite separate paths, the fates of communities of color are often intertwined and inseparable. Although history has not provided enough examples of the possibilities, a review of historical interactions between Asians and American Indians, Blacks, Latinos, and whites reveals that, in addition to competition and conflict, each group has managed to forge a degree of cooperation with Asians. The viability of Asians to form cross-racial alliances in contemporary times is assessed in terms of their opinion differences with whites, Blacks, and Latinos regarding race relations, support for Asian and non-Asian candidates, general political orientations, and selective issue positions. By studying past interactions and contemporary opinion gaps between Asians and other racial groups, the study strives to identify common grounds and areas of divergence in the pursuit of collective social and political advancement.

U.S. RACE RELATIONS AND RACIAL POSITIONS OF ASIANS

Race relations in the United States are deeply complex and marked by shifting alliances and conflicts between various racial groups. Although few scholars today would question the persistence of white dominance, this is not only the residue of conquest and colonialism, of slavery and segregation, and of termination and exclusion of nonwhite groups; it is also the product of interminority group competition for white approval and conflicts over the rewards of being white (Lipsitz 1998). In order to secure the benefits of whiteness[1] for themselves, communities of color are often forced to make gains at each other's expense. U.S. history is dotted with incidences such as American Indians owning Black slaves, African American soldiers defeating Native and Mexican Americans, and Asian workers being hired to break the unionization effort of Latino and Black workers. During WWII, leaders in the Black community failed to contest the violation of rights of Japanese Americans in the hope that Blacks might profit from the economic dislocation of the Japanese from California agriculture. The NAACP showed its tepid response to the internment of Japanese Americans by presenting a protest resolution that was preceded by twenty-three resolutions on other matters (Kearney 1998). In this process, a nonwhite group can be simultaneously oppressed in one relationship and oppressive in another (Yamamoto 1997). A recent example is the case of *Ho v. San Francisco Unified School District* (1994), in which the historically discriminated against Chinese plaintiffs tried to invalidate the desegregation order meant to provide equal educational opportunities to Black and Latino students. Similarly,

Asian and Hispanic groups filed suit to invalidate Oakland's affirmative action program in city contracting because of the alleged unconstitutional favoritism toward Blacks (Yamamoto 1999).

Yet, because each racial group has been constructed in different ways to sustain the system, it is impossible to fully comprehend the position of any group without understanding the process of racialization for all groups. In truth, "[a]ll racial identities are relational"; communities are *"mutually constitutive* of one another, not just competitive or cooperative" (Lipsitz 1998, 210, emphasis added). To maintain the Anglo supremacy, European immigrants of different colors were mobilized to identify as whites through the collective denial of a lawful and equal presence in the nation's nonwhite population (Saxton 1971). The construction of whiteness was also created by the adoption of a simplified dyad of Blacks and whites in national politics, including progressive projects and coalitions, after the mid-1920s (Jacobson 1998). Meanwhile, the subordinate positions of nonwhite groups were constantly molded by seemingly contradictory actions taken by the U.S. government and the public. Greater freedom of one minority was often followed by the entrapment of another one (Johnson 1998). For instance, the decision to deny citizenship to Chinese immigrants was made in Congress right on the heels of the abolition of Black slavery and the ratification of the Fourteenth and Fifteenth Amendments extending citizenship and suffrage to Blacks. During WWII, the issuance of an executive order establishing a Committee on Fair Employment Practices in June 1941 to permit the integration of Blacks into defense industries was followed by another one sending Japanese Americans into internment camps. Although the hiring of Mexicans as replacement farm workers for the interned Japanese brought a temporary moment of prosperity to the Chicano community (Lipsitz 1998), this was followed by attacks on Mexican American youths wearing zoot suits by mobs of white sailors in 1943 (Lipsitz 1998). In 1948, voters in California who rejected the anti-Asian Alien Land Law Referendum also opposed the Fair Employment Practices measure, which would have prohibited job discrimination against Blacks and Latinos. The *Brown v. Board of Education* (1954) decision was made in the same year Operation Wetback deported en masse Mexican American immigrants and citizens. "Coincidences" like these lend support to the proposition that, when a nonwhite minority was given a break from racial attacks, the animosity was often transferred to another minority, especially one that was perceived as "foreign" and whose subordination would be more socially acceptable and legally defensible (Johnson 1998).

One of the "foreign" minorities is Asian, which has been marked by sociologists as a "middleman minority" because of its relatively small population size, higher general status, and greater income than the subordinate class, but weaker political status than the ruling class (Blalock 1967). Although there has been significant dispute as to the adequacy of treating Japanese Americans and Korean Americans as prototypes of this category from the economic point of view (for a review see Yoon 1997), their political function as a buffer mediating interactions between the dominant and the subordinate groups, tolerated in times of prosperity and peace, and scapegoated in times of stress, seems vindicated by a reading of ethnic history. Depending on the political context, Asians can be simultaneously praised and blamed for their high adaptive capacity and economic success. They are valued as a "model minority" as long as their success is limited to certain economic spheres and does not create a power threat for the dominant class. They are scorned as a "yellow peril" when their cultural values and economic gains are thought to have given them an unfair edge and contributed to the lowering of the economic and social life of other competitive groups. Pivotal to an understanding of the coexistence of ostensibly bipolar and contradictory racial images of Asians is the construction of Asians as perpetual foreigners. Through an ongoing conflation of the domestic and the international, which can be rooted in European colonialism, imperialism, sexism, and racism, Asians have been construed as the "Oriental Others" whose perceived foreignness is a distinct and "deeply ingrained aspect of racial identification of Asian Americans"(Saito 1997, 296) and one that separates the racialization experience of Asians from other immigrant groups. In the end, in their function as a precarious middleman and pawn in the power struggle between the dominant and the subordinate classes, Asians have been used to maintain and justify white supremacy while kept as perpetual outsiders by U.S. society and government.

This focus on the structural position of Asians in U.S. racial politics prescribes a solemn outlook and a serious challenge for interracial coalition building. The historical and contemporary construction of Asians as the "foreigner within" (Lowe 1996) has excluded Asians from becoming a viable alliance or long-term coalition partner in mainstream institutions and politics. As a middleman minority, Asians "may be able to form temporary coalitions with more elite groups when they are needed, but later they are likely to find themselves isolated when the danger of a revolutionary coalition (among lower-ranking minorities) has subsided" (Blalock 1967, 111). The post-WWII social construction of Asians as a superachieving model minority has also generated tensions that form a barrier to coalition building with other oppressed groups. Through the depiction of Asians as one monolithic ethnic group that achieves economic success and social acceptance through education and hard work and without governmental assistance or preferential treatment, Asians are hailed as a poster child used for the denial of racial oppression and discrimination of nonwhites and the disguise of government's failure to help other minorities and poor whites. Furthermore, because organizations have traditionally manipulated position and resource scarcities to divert nonwhites from building coalitions, groups of Asians have found it more feasible to manage their respective political interest in private, low visibility ways (Rich 1996). A few Asians have been made "queue jumpers" by being preferred over other nonwhites in occupational upgrading because of their perceived proximity to whites in socioeconomic status and values. Their token advancement creates the impression of social change but, in reality, does nothing for the collective empowerment of the community. Often their employment takes the pressure off the hiring of other minorities. The interracial competition over scarce jobs, adequate housing, and government services in many urban centers as well as feelings of hostility and mutual distrust and acts of anti-Asian violence have been intensified in recent decades by the neoconservative trend in social, economic, and political policies and other forces discussed in Chapter 2. Asian-owned businesses were targets of harassment, vandalism, and discriminatory city ordinances in California and New Jersey (NAPALC 1997). Asian American political candidates and student activists faced intimidation and threats for their political participation.

HISTORICAL INCIDENCES OF COOPERATION AND CONFLICTS BETWEEN ASIANS AND OTHER GROUPS

Given the precarious middle position of Asians in U.S. race relations, an important first step in exploring ways to get along is to understand the history of group interactions and identify the conditions of cooperation and conflicts between Asians and each of the other major racial groups. With international migration a permanent phenomenon in world history, competition over scarce economic, political, and social resources often followed initial contacts between host peoples and migrating groups (Olzak 1983). Whereas both accommodation and eventual assimilation were observed to have taken place for European immigrant groups (Park 1950), non-European immigrant workers often found themselves trapped in competition in the secondary labor markets with similarly exploited and discriminated local groups over low-paying jobs, limited living spaces, and marginal access to government and social services (Bonacich 1972). Despite a shared history of subordination, oppression, and resistance under European colonization and white supremacy, minority groups often found intergroup cooperation undesirable because of sociopsychological factors such as ignorance, prejudice, ethnocentrism, and mutual mistrust. They also found it nearly impossible because of divisive labor management practices. Interracial coalition-building involving Asians was made more difficult by gaps in religion, language, and other aspects of culture as well as by structural distance in residential patterns and socioeconomic class with other nonwhite minorities. In addition, conflicts between Asians and others could be triggered by tensions in U.S.-Asia relations. Nevertheless, this chapter shows these conditions were insufficient to prevent Asians from forming friendly ties and alliances with Blacks, Latinos, American Indians, and whites out of common interests and needs as well as shared understanding of grievances and aspirations for liberation. The following are highlights of such encounters arranged by race and surrounding issues of class, culture, interracial marriages, and military conflicts between the United States and Asia.

American Indians and Asians

To European explorers, American Indians were Asians. By attempting to "discover" India and its surrounding nations, Columbus encountered the "Indians" (Okihiro 1994). The conquest and colonization of American Indians bear a remarkable degree of resemblance to the European reconstruction and domination of Asians (Okihiro 1994). In general, the relationship evolved along the stages of contact, competition, conflict, and cooperation, and the nature of interactions ranged from mass murder to matrimony (Liestman 1999). When the two groups made their first North American contact in 1788, Indians did not view Asians as interlopers or competitors but skilled coworkers and trading partners. Indians supplied food to early Chinese miners and directed them to rich placer gold beds in southern Idaho. They traded with Chinese workers during construction of the Southern Pacific Railroad. Although both were hired by the Central Pacific Railroad, physical contacts between the two groups of workers were kept to a minimum by segregation rules.

Other early contacts were less propitious. In Washington, two Chinese miners captured by the Colville tribe were killed because the tribal council decided that they were neither white nor Indian (Liestman 1999). Some tribes considered Chinese as socially inferior. In western Nevada, Northern Paiutes threatened to cut off the braids of Chinese railroad workers. The relationship between the two was reported to be in constant friction because of cultural differences. The intergroup tension heightened in the 1870s due to large-scale immigration into Indian land and economic hardship at the national level. While each was subordinated by the white-dominated capitalist system and unable to gain control over the other, both competed for the limited economic opportunities. Pacific Northwest tribes complained about the Chinese encroachment over their traditional fishing areas. In the Washington territory, both groups sought work from Europeans as hops pickers. Growers preferred Chinese for they could be hired at two-thirds of the rate of American Indians, but American Indians became angry and expelled the Chinese in 1879. Northern Paiute women who gathered and sold wood found themselves displaced at one point in time by the Chinese. In San Francisco, American Indian women and Latinas found themselves undersold by Chinese laundrymen after 1850. When Chinese appeared to gain an upper hand economically by being better able to adapt to modernization and change, American Indians responded with harassment and increasing violence. Although some of the assaults were said to be committed by whites masquerading as Indians, American Indians obviously participated in the extortion of Chinese by presenting themselves as tax collectors, invading their place of settlement, and committing at least three mass murders prior to 1880.

Intergroup competition and conflicts subsided when interactions between the two communities diminished after Chinese retreated to urban enclaves or returned to China. The exclusion of new Chinese immigration after 1882 and the limitation of Indian mobility after the 1887 General Allotment Act also significantly reduced chances for inter-action. Subsequently, the two developed a relationship of "commen-salism" or peaceful coexistence (Liestman 1999). A cordial business relationship was forged when Chinese paid Indians for rights to farm, fish, or mine on Indian lands; they also employed local Indians. Eco-nomically, Chinese occupied a middle position between American Indi-ans and whites. Socially and politically, Chinese operated as the marginalized middleman minority. Occasionally, interracial matri-mony took place between Chinese men and American Indian women. Such exogamous relations were sometimes seen as a means for Chinese to stay in the country. In Alaska and the Pacific Northwest, interracial union between Chinese, Japanese, and Filipino male workers and American Indian women was more common because of the shortage of Asian women and the location of the canneries (Friday 1994). The liai-son between Chinese, Japanese and Indian workers was often damp-ened, however, by intense competition over agricultural labor and met with resistance from the communities. Filipino workers, because of their English fluency and penchant for dances and music and the growth of small communities in southeast Alaska, were engaged in more intermarriages than their Chinese or Japanese counterparts.

Despite their common plight as subordinated minorities, the Chinese and Indians did not actively seek to establish bonds or alliances. This was mostly because of the spatial, social, and economic distance between the two communities. When alliances occurred they were "spontaneous, expedient, and short-lived" (Liestman 1999). However, the wartime internment of Japanese Americans created an unusual physical context for coalition building. Two of the officially listed Ari-zona camps were on Indian lands, belonging to Pimas and Maricopas on the Gila River and to Mohaves and Chemehuevis on the Colorado River (Drinnon 1987). The Leupp Isolation Center in Arizona was next to a Navaho reservation. Although American Indians were not con-sulted on the borrowing of the land and some resented the presence of the camp and viewed both inmates and keepers as intruders, other tribal Indians developed emphatic concerns with the plight of Japanese internees (Drinnon 1987). American Indians saw the similarity to their own removal and relocation and assisted in teaching internees farming methods and other survival techniques (Jaimes 1994).

Blacks and Asians

When commenting on whether Asian (yellow) was black or white, Okihiro (1994) noted that, "Yellow is emphatically neither white nor black; but insofar as Asians and Africans share a subordinate position to the master class, yellow is a shade of black, and black, a shade of yellow" (34). Although the white supremacist, capitalist system deliberately pitted Black workers against Asian workers, and despite the mutual ethnocentrism and prejudice frequently devolved by ideas and practices of the dominant race, Blacks have displayed a surprising degree of solidarity toward Asians in U.S. history. Nevertheless, instead of a progressive movement from conflict to cooperation, as seen in the Indian-Asian interaction, Blacks in general held ambivalent attitudes toward Asians, and the intergroup relationships fluctuated between conflict and cooperation. Rather than the western frontier, the main setting for Black-Asian interaction occurred in urban areas.

In part because of the prevailing anti-Asian sentiment in mainstream society, Blacks forged prejudicial responses to early Chinese and Japanese immigrants even before the two made physical contact. The rocky beginning was turned into a negative one by such factors as economic competition, Blacks' anxiety over their own social status, Blacks' jealousy over the preferential treatment of Asians, Asians' perceived inferiority in religious and moral standards, and Asians' perceived prejudice against Blacks (Shankman 1982; Kearney 1998). Like American Indian and Latina women, Black washerwomen found themselves displaced by Chinese laundrymen. Black maids, cooks, and butlers lost their jobs to Chinese domestic workers. Chinese, Japanese, and Filipinos were hired as scabs to defeat the Black unionizing effort in the Pullman Company. Since the late 1920s, when mass surveys were available, Chinese consistently ranked among the least desirable groups by Blacks (Shankman 1982). Black elites such as Booker T. Washington found the Chinese particularly objectionable and unfit to be assimilated into Western civilization because of their perceived deficiency in moral standards. Most Blacks in the nation, however, were not in direct contact or competition with Asians. During the brief years of the Reconstruction Era, when Chinese laborers were brought in from Cuba, California, and

China to replace freed Black slaves in the South, Blacks responded with a dual consciousness (Hellwig 1979). Whereas some welcomed the Chinese for the prospect of promoting Black labor above a menial status, others feared that the importation of Chinese would lower Black wages. Yet, both sides opposed the restrictions on Chinese immigration and naturalization. They realized that the Chinese were just a new target of racism and that any discrimination against the Chinese was to reinforce the subordination of Blacks.

Blacks responded in a similar vein to the racist attacks suffered by the Japanese in California (Kearney 1998). However, Black attitudes toward the Japanese could be summarized as at once "idealistic, pragmatic, and a bit therapeutic"(44). In addition to treating the Japanese as fellow victims of American racism, many Blacks fondly identified with the Japanese as "Asian Negroes . . . the most progressive Asian wing of the Negro race" (14). Japan's militarism displayed in the Russo-Japanese War of 1904–5 allowed Blacks to rebuke the Eurocentric claim of white supremacy, and the Japanese gained the empathy and respect of Blacks for their ability to stand up to white imperialism. Protests by the Japanese in Los Angeles to the showing of a racist movie, *The Cheat,* increased blacks' sense of comradeship with the Japanese. Prior to 1942, Blacks lived close to Japanese in many western U.S. cities. Although the two groups competed in employment and housing and some Japanese businesses denied services to Blacks, the relationship between the two groups was typified by a "friendly spirit of cooperation and sympathetic understanding" (Kearney 1998, 66). Japanese in Oakland advertised in the local Black newspaper. In Los Angeles, the head of the Japanese Chamber of Commerce was invited to speak before the Negro Businessman's League, and the local Japanese hospital employed two Black surgeons. The image of the Japanese being fair to Blacks was enhanced by reports of Black-Japanese intermarriage. In Seattle, Black, Asian, and white groups organized inter-ethnic meetings and events to bridge cultural divides throughout the interwar years (Taylor 1991).

Fearful of a Japanese-Black alliance, the FBI began to compile information on "Negro subversion" as early as 1917 (Kearney 1998). After Pearl Harbor, Black draft resisters and organizations suspected of being sympathetic toward Japanese war efforts became special targets of surveillance, investigation, and harassment despite the lack of evidence of any systematic disloyalty or subversion (Lipsitz 1998). When the internment order was issued, many Blacks felt a sense of apprehension about their own fate. Although few protested the racist action taken by the government, those Blacks who lived close to Japanese expressed a much stronger emphatic concern. A Seattle newspaper, *Northwest Enterprise,* was one of the few local presses to oppose the evacuation (Taylor 1991). Some Blacks assisted the Japanese in their evacuation. After the war, Black Californians were often the first to welcome the return of ex-internees, even though this may have meant a need to evacuate from their leased homes (Kearney 1998). A Pacific Coast Fair Play Committee was established in 1945 in San Francisco by representatives of Black, Filipino, and Korean community groups and government agencies in support of Japanese Americans (Lipsitz 1998). When the redress movement began to take off in the mid-1970s, Congresswoman Yvonne Burke of California, head of the Congressional Black Caucus, was among the first non-Asians to express support for redress. Her action was echoed by the Western Baptist State Convention, an association of 100 Black churches in California, which passed a resolution supporting redress (Maki, Kitano, and Berthold 1999).

Filipinos were another Asian group with whom Blacks were able to identify. During the Filipino-American War in 1899, Black soldiers noted that white soldiers used the same racial epithets used against them to describe Filipinos. The Filipino insurgence against U.S. imperialism set an example for Blacks to emulate. One Black soldier answered the appeal for racial solidarity from the Filipinos and became an officer in the guerrilla army (Lipsitz 1998). Nearly 500 Black soldiers elected to remain in the Philippines at the conclusion of the conflict. Another example of Black-Filipino alliance occurred in the 1930s when the Brotherhood of Sleeping Car Porters dropped their opposition to Filipino "scab laborers," who were hired in 1925 to replace the Blacks who had served for over fifty years on private cars. They called for unity with Filipinos to help secure better conditions and wages (Okihiro 1994).

During the Black Power movement of the 1960s, many Asian Americans found their racial identity through the teachings of Black spiritual leaders (Okihiro 1994). Instead of encouraging integration and assimilation, Malcolm X opened the eyes and minds of many Asians through his talk of total liberation and nationalism (Kochiyama 1994). His teachings on the importance of heritage and history influenced the direction of the Asian American movement (Wei 1993). Participants were encouraged to insist on opportunities to learn about the past and where Asians were from and to feel pride in their ethnicity. He inspired Asians in Los Angeles to set up programs to help the ex-felons, ex-addicts, and drug abusers in the community. (But his unqualified admiration for the words and deeds of Imperialist Japan and Communist Mao Tse Tung also hurt his support among other Asians). During this period, many middle-class students and community youths joined Third World liberation groups and protested along with African, Hispanic, Native, and European Americans against the imperialist war in Vietnam. The multiracial coalition established in this movement laid the foundations for the continuing struggles for racial equality and rights today.

Latinos and Asians

Similar to the American Indian–Asian relationship, Latinos and Asians share ancient connections such as in the area of Aztlan, which, to some Spanish explorers, was directly linked to Asia through a fabled waterway that existed above today's U.S. Southwest (Chavez 1989). The two groups also share many common grievances. Despite their indigenous origin in much of the American Southwest, Mexican Americans have been treated as foreigners or permanent outsiders to the United States.[2] Puerto Ricans became second-class Americans through annexation at the end of the same war that accounted for the annexation of the Philippines.[3] Both groups were accused of failing to assimilate because of the maintenance of their ethnic culture, religion, language, and concentration in certain neighborhoods and localities (Johnson 1997). Employers began to hire Mexican immigrants as low-wage, low-skilled replacement workers after the exclusion of Chinese and Japanese laborers had significantly reduced the supply of cheap labor and when agricultural economy in the West was expanding (Friday 1994; Gutierrez 1995). Like Filipinos, Mexicans also became targets for mass deportation in the 1930s during the Great Depression. During WWII, some Mexicans expressed fears of being the next targets for internment following the Japanese (Ruiz 1998).

Although Mexican Americans were socially and politically constructed as nonwhites and excluded from public places (Martinez 1998), their legal status as whites, in addition to their small population, presence of the old Mexican ruling class (ranchero elites), and similarities in physical appearances, language, religious practices, and sociopolitical institutions to those of European Americans, made the working-class Mexicans initially more acceptable to whites (Alamguer 1994). Mexicans were permitted to become citizens and join labor unions, albeit in segregated units. Their different racial position became a source of tension when a 1903 strike by Chicano street railway construction workers in Los Angeles, organized as an AFL union, was defeated by Japanese and Black strikebreakers (Stimson 1955). Nevertheless, Mexican American workers exerted solidarity with Asians in another strike during the same year. In Oxnard, California, 1000 Japanese and 200 Mexican workers, or about 90 percent of the local sugar beet work force, launched the nation's first major cross-racial labor strike against low pay, labor contractor commissions, and company store monopoly (Almaguer 1994; Okihiro 1994; Saito 1998). The nonwhite labor contractors and farm laborers formed the Japanese–Mexican Labor Association (JMLA) and overcame cultural and language barriers by holding meetings in Spanish, Japanese, and English. They received assistance from the state AFL union to win the strike, but their application for an AFL chapter was denied because Mexican workers refused to bar Asians from union membership.

Most of the incidences of Latino-Asian coalition building took place among the working class and involved other racial and ethnic groups. The multiethnic and multiracial nature of the interactions can be traced back to 1900 when Portuguese and Japanese female field workers in Hawaii organized to demand a raise and won (Ariyoshi 1976). During a major sugar plantation workers' strike in 1920, Puerto Rican and Portuguese workers showed their solidarity by joining Japanese, Filipino, and Chinese workers. In the early 1930s, Asian agricultural workers in California organized numerous strikes with Chicano, Black, and white workers (Yoneda 1971). The United Cannery, Agricultural, Packing, and Allied Workers of America (UCAPAWA) union was formed in 1937 with male and female workers of Asian, African, European, and Mexican origins from many parts of the nation. Japanese, Chinese, and Filipino cannery workers held important local positions in the West Coast chapters where meetings were often conducted in English, Spanish, Chinese, and Filipino languages (Ruiz 1987). In 1965, Cesar Chavez and his National Farm Workers Association joined the Delano grape strike started by Filipinos. This coalition led to the formation of the United Farm Workers Union (UFW). His success in enlisting broad-based support through community-based labor organizing set a new trend in union movement among nonwhites, as illustrated by the case of the Local 11 of the Hotel Employees and Restaurant Employees Union (HERE) in Los Angeles. Faced with the termination of a union contract by the new Korean ownership of the Los Angeles Hilton and Towers, Latino labor leaders called on the Korean Immigrant Workers Advocates (KWIA), which quickly used its connections to the Korean American community and the labor movement in South Korea and helped diffuse racial tension and settle the class conflict (Saito and Park 2000).

Latinos collaborated with Asians on other issues. For example, a local chapter of the League of United Latin American Citizens (LULAC) and Chinese American Parents and Teachers Association of Southern California established the Multi-Cultural Community Association to deal with racial differences among parents and persuade the school board to implement policies regarding racial violence (Saito 1998; Saito and Park 2000). A Coalition for Harmony in Monterey Park (CHAMP) was created as a multiracial coalition uniting Asians, Latinos, and whites in an effort to rescind an English-only resolution passed by the city council in 1986 (Horton 1995; Saito 1998). In New York, Puerto Ricans formed coalitions with Asians and other racial and ethnic groups to address issues of common concern such as education, labor exploitation, and racial violence. In the late 1960s and early 1970s, a coalition of Asian, Black, and Latino parents of the Lower East Side worked together to advocate bilingual education, professional development for teachers, and accountability to community interests (Jennings and Chapman 1998). The Young Lords Party banded with I Wor Kuen, a progressive group of Chinese Americans, to fight police brutality and racism in New York (Morales 1998). As reported in Chapter 2, Puerto Ricans (NCPRR) joined Asians (CAAAV) in a 1995 citywide civil disobedience to protest racial violence and police brutality. In May 1998, the New York Taxi Workers Alliance (NYTWA), a South Asian–dominated labor organization, united cab drivers from Haiti, West Africa, Saudi Arabia, and Eastern Europe with Black and white American drivers to strike against discriminatory legislation and exploitation of immigrant workers (Esser et al. 1999).

Latino-Asian solidarity was challenged as some Asian immigrants occupied the class position as employers (Saito1998; Gonzalez 1999). In 1933, 1,500 mostly Mexican berry pickers went out on strike in the fields surrounding El Monte, California, against Japanese leaseholders. The relationship between grower and worker was complicated by racial divisions in housing, school, and public facilities. The two minorities occupied different economic classes, but they shared social space in classrooms and public areas. In addition, the class conflict was complicated by international and federal forces. Although the Japanese growers were caught between rising rents levied by Anglo landowners and Mexican workers' demand for higher wages, the strikers themselves were caught between a class-based and a Mexican Consul–sponsored union. Mexico's politicians donated substantial support funds to the strikers as an attempt to develop a loyal and politically dependent emigrant community. In response, the Japanese Consul stepped in to try to broker a settlement. To complicate the matter, the local chamber of commerce appealed to President Roosevelt for arbitration under the new National Industrial Recovery Act. Class conflict once again smothered the development of Latino-Asian solidarity when Mexican workers, organized by the UFW Union, picketed farms owned mostly by Japanese Americans in the early 1970s. U.S.-born Japanese American students, based on concern over the economic exploitation of the "Third World people," sided with Mexicans in this conflict (Fugita and O'Brien 1978). These cases indicate that race relations between Asians and Latinos or any other American group have often been influenced not only by the domestic economic, racial, and political order, but also by local and transnational forces—a theme in the political experience of Asians found also in their interactions with whites recounted below.

Whites and Asians

In spite of a racially exploitative system that played off Asians against non-Asians, nonwhites against whites, and immigrants against citizens, segments of the white population managed to establish cross-racial union with Asians through interracial marriages, integrated labor unions, and organized cultural and business activities. These were the same avenues used by other nonwhite groups to form alliances with Asians. In addition to examples of multiracial cooperation involving whites mentioned in previous sections, intermarriages between Chinese men and Irish women were recorded in 1855 in the New York state census (Tchen 1999). In the 1920s and 1930s, interracial sexual alliances and liaisons took place in the taxi dance halls between Filipino men and white working-class women, which functioned as a means of resistance against racial and sexual subordination for the former and against sexual and class subordination for the latter (Parrenas 1998). In the West, the pioneer experiences of Asians and Jews were connected by economic ties; the Jews were business and domestic employers and the Chinese were customers and tradesmen (Clar and Kramer 1988). Both were clustered in businesses as makers of cigars, shoes, and clothing. Although Jews were part of the middle class, both groups were sometimes lumped together for discrimination and disdain. Unlike their counterparts on the East Coast, many Jewish elites in the West were prejudiced against the Chinese. However, at the individual level, "[m]utual help, warmth, and the ever-present Chinese amiability appeared in virtually every account of business or household relationships where they were maintained" (152).

White solidarity with Asians was also evident in the words and deeds of government officials, clergymen, educators, and other public figures who dissented from prevailing anti-Asian thought and practice (Foner and Rosenberg 1993). Although only a minority of whites was opposed to racism, ethnocentrism, nativism, and capitalist exploitation against Asians throughout history, their opposition was a courageous deviation from the prejudicial norm of the time. Reasons for their dissent ranged from a demonstration of humanitarian sympathy, to interracial friendship, to Christian ethics, to class consciousness, to a belief in equal constitutional rights, to outright protest against any anti-Asian violence. Two members of the Radical Republican Congress from Massachusetts, Senators Charles Sumner and George Hoar, advocated for Chinese naturalization and against Chinese exclusion in the 1870s. In 1892, leading reformers, clergymen, educators, and businessmen as well as 2,500 other citizens of Massachusetts petitioned Congress to repeal the Geary Act (Foner and Rosenberg 1993). During the height of the anti-Japanese movement, the Oakland-based American Committee of Justice produced a pamphlet to oppose the Alien Land Acts (Takaki 1989). Traces of support for Asians can also be found in leading groups that were formed to bridge Black-white gaps in the 1930s and 1940s. For instance, the first Catholic Interracial Council carried out protest activities, promoted school curriculum changes, and fought for fair employment practices and for the opening of hospitals to Blacks and all nonwhite physicians and nurses (Jacobson 1998). The Common Council for American Unity was established to counter sentiments of "anti-alienism" toward the foreign-born population. A prominent Chinese scholar, Lin Yutang, served on the advisory board of its journal, *Common Ground,* published between 1940 and 1949.

Although the U.S. labor movement historically opposed including Asians in unions and the AFL was at the forefront of the anti-Asian movement, other unions endeavored to incorporate Asian workers. Some admitted Asian miners out of the "unique local exigencies in negotiation with the Japanese contractors and the coal operators . . ." (Ichioka 1979, 15–6). Others did so to promote multiracial unity. The militant Industrial Workers of the World established early on an approach to unionizing Asian workers in the West and the Pacific Northwest. Through aggressive lobbying by Asian American activists such as Karl Yoneda, the Communist Party led the campaign to organize Asian and other nonwhite workers among predominantly white organizations in the 1920s and 1930s. The CIO encouraged the participation of Asians alongside workers of other races during the Great Depression. The ILWU on the Pacific Coast and in Hawaii stressed multiracial cooperation and was one of the few organizations that stood by its Japanese members in the face of legal harassment and mass evacuation following Pearl Harbor.

Patent white-Asian solidarity quickly dissipated after Japan attacked Pearl Harbor. Norman Thomas, a prodigious labor organizer, a major Socialist Party figure, and a leader of American Civil Liberties Union, was one of the earliest opponents of the evacuation. His position contrasted with that of his own party and most left-wing organizations. The Communist Party, for example, suspended all members of Japanese descent two months before President Franklin Roosevelt issued the internment order. Another notable exception was the formation of the Committee on National Security and Fair Play by a group of religious leaders and educators (Daniels 1971). Nevertheless, recent scholarship proclaims that opposition to the removal and internment of Japanese Americans was more widespread than historians generally acknowledged among white educators, socialists, pacifists, and returned missionaries, who had developed close ties to Japanese Americans through friendship, religious fellowship, or acquaintance at school (Shaffer 1998). Many American missionaries who served in Japan prior to the war formed a network of anti-internment activists. Other important centers of dissent were state universities and public schools on the West Coast. Although they constituted a very small minority of Americans, they helped to maintain a spirit of community, build a line of communication between Japanese Americans and the larger society, and prepare the Japanese for renewed participation in U.S. society after the internment. These dissenters also facilitated the removal of anti-Japanese prejudice in state and federal legislation. They combined opposition to internment with concrete acts of service such as providing internees with necessities, a few luxuries, and information. Thus, well before the passage of *Brown* (1954) or the dawning of the modern Civil Rights movement, a steady stream of whites were in coalition with Asians to help the latter claim their space in American life and politics.

This sweeping review of the past interactions between Asians and others provides strong evidence of the necessity to examine not only between-group but also within-group and beyond-group structural factors in understanding racial dynamics and the conditions of conflicts and cooperation. It suggests that the likelihood of occurrence of conditions conducive to cross-racial coalitions could be severely hampered by factors outside of the Asian American community. Different groups of Asians were engaged in various forms of relationships with other races that tended to fluctuate according to changes in group socioeconomic status and social integration as well as national immigration policy, regional economic condition, local labor market needs, and international relations. Competition and conflicts often arose out of differences in culture, class position, and social status and worsened during times of economic recession, perceived large influx of immigration, and Japan's attack on Pearl Harbor. Nevertheless, even during the most difficult times, such as WWII for Japanese Americans, each race had a segment of the population that managed to develop a collaborative relationship with Asians through linkage institutions based on common class status, religious belief, anti-racist ideology, shared neighborhoods, economic interest, or friendship and marital ties. Moreover, there was more than one pattern of relationship out of interracial contact. When contacts were sustained, particularly in the case of Latino-Asian relations, conflicts and cooperation often coexisted. Decreased competition resulting from reduced contact, as in the case of American Indian–Asian relations, may help restore peace but not necessarily trust or respect. Although increased contact may beget competition and conflict, it may also create opportunities for coalition building.

Key to achieving cooperative outcomes may be the availability of bridging organizations that "facilitate resource development, community mobilization, leadership training, political lobbying, and serve as a basis for communication and negotiation among groups" (Saito and Park 2000, 440). A case in point is the construction of Latino-Asian coalitions in labor organizing and political mobilization in suburban Los Angeles, which would not be possible without the presence of community activists (middle-class professionals or entrepreneurs in the San Gabriel Valley) who possessed "shared goals and keen understanding of their subordinate positions in U.S. society" (Saito 1998, 127). These linkage institutions helped break barriers created by racial segregation, class exploitation, and sexual subordination. In addition, both interracial coalitions and conflicts may occur in the same political context but they may refer to different strata of each group. For instance, whereas elites may be engaged in political coalition building, working- and lower-class persons may be competing for jobs, housing, and services (McClain and Stewart 1999, 150). Such competition is not uncommon in the Black-Asian and Latino-Asian interactions. The reverse can also be true when race relations are more harmonious at the grassroots than elite level, such as in the Chinese-Jewish case. A coalition may be formed out of strategic needs and interests rather than feelings of commonality or solidarity. Intergroup solidarity based on common grievances facilitate (but is neither a necessary nor a sufficient condition for), the building of coalitions. However, long-term coalitions or alliances built on increased levels of friendly contacts, a reduced sense of economic competition, and greater proximity in ideology and beliefs at the mass level across racial groups may be better able to survive the crisis of leadership when forward-looking and positive-sum solutions are shortchanged for easy but narrowly cast and conflict-prone ones.

CONTEMPORARY RACIAL TENSIONS BETWEEN ASIANS AND BLACKS, LATINOS, AND WHITES

Although cross-racial solidarity reached a new high in the Third World Liberation movement of the 1960s, the relationship between Blacks and Asians deteriorated in the following decades because of demographic, economic, and political changes occurring both within and outside of the United States. The ascendance of Japan as an economic superpower prohibited many Blacks from seeing an analogy between the two groups in their social status. Black leaders were also disinclined to forgive and forget the anti-Black opinions expressed by Japanese politicians (Kearney 1998); instead, Blacks are more inclined to identify with whites as allies. A 1991 study by the Joint Center for Political and Economic Studies found that fully 47 percent of Blacks believed that Japanese companies were more discriminatory toward Blacks than American ones. Conflicts between inner-city Blacks and immigrants escalated during the 1980s as a result of the clashing of two forces: (1) rising family reunion and refugee immigration among Asians and legal and illegal immigration among Latinos, and (2) worsening Black social and economic conditions due to plant closures in central cities, sharp cuts in public assistance programs for low-income and unemployed people, and massive job losses in the heavy manufacturing sector where blue-collar Blacks could earn better wages (Wilson 1987).

Asian immigrants, especially Koreans, have a particularly contentious relationship with Blacks because of the high concentration of Korean-run small businesses in Black neighborhoods. Whereas Korean owners regard inner-city neighborhoods as the most affordable place to open stores, Black residents view them as another wave of absentee owners after the Jewish and the Italian owners who drained resources out of the community without contributing to the local economy (Yoon 1997). The reciprocal negative perceptions of Blacks and Koreans are also shaped by prejudice, misunderstanding, distrust, and fear of being mistreated and are fueled by inflammatory media reports about intergroup differences. Many Blacks view Koreans as free riders on the Civil Rights movement and a hindrance to their social and economic mobility. Many Korean immigrants are from middle-class backgrounds, have strong aspirations for upward mobility, and have a desire to be accepted by whites. They view Blacks as the lowest in social and economic standing. Black-Korean tensions erupted in 1992 with the release of the not-guilty verdict of four white policemen who were caught on video beating a Black motorist. Blacks released their despair and rage by looting and setting fire to the mostly Korean-owned Asian businesses in South Central Los Angeles. The sources of the Black-Korean conflicts do not appear to differ much from the conflicts between Blacks and other Asian immigrant groups in urban areas (Yamamoto 1999).

Latino youths, whose community constituted half of the area population and who shared with Blacks many of the frustrations with the extant political and economic system, also looted and burned Asian businesses in the Los Angeles riots (Petersilia and Abrahamse 1994). Nevertheless, compared to Black-Asian relations, Chicano-Asian tensions have not run as high (Acuna 1996). The reduced Asian-Latino conflict may be attributed to the shared immigrant ideology (similar drive toward upward mobility), foreign-born status (thus absence of nativist scapegoating), and Latino businesses' lower vulnerability to competition from Korean immigrant entrepreneurs (Cheng and Espiritu 1989). It may also be attributed to the shared history of immigration/annexation and proximity in residential and work space in certain localities. Specifically, Asians have chosen to settle close to Chicanos and Latinos in Los Angeles (Acuna 1996). This seems to provide a fertile ground for intergroup competition over both substantial and trivial issues, but whatever frictions that exist have usually remained under the surface—owing in part to the better communication between the respective political elites and their organizations, which have had a critical mass of second- and third-generation leaders (Acuna 1996).

At the same time, when the levels of economic competition and cultural conflicts between Asian small business owners and their Black and Latino customers were on the rise, Asians slightly decreased their interactions with whites through residential ties both at the national level and in several major metropolitan areas. The influx of new Asian immigrants and their extremely diverse ethnic and class backgrounds contributed to the revitalization and expansion of urban ethnic enclaves and the establishment of new suburban ethnic towns in the 1980s (Hum and Zonta 2000). As a result, the dissimilarity index, which measures residential segregation based on census data, increased from 0.41 in 1970 to 0.44 in 1990. Nevertheless, compared to other nonwhite groups, Asians still held the highest level of residential integration with whites nationwide. This can be attributed to their higher overall socioeconomic status than Blacks and Latinos as well as the more favorable attitudes of Asians and whites toward each other. A survey of Los Angeles County residents shows that Asians preferred to live next to whites rather than to Blacks or Latinos; they were also the more acceptable neighbors to whites. A similar conclusion was drawn from a study on the mixed-race residential patterns of Los Angeles residents (Oliver and Grant 1995). The study found that Asians were more likely to share residential space with whites than Latinos. About one-fourth of Asians and one-fifth of whites in Los Angeles lived in biracial census tracts that had at least the group's share of the population in the county. The authors suspect that Asians and whites may interact on an equal status basis and have enough political and social resources to be effective partners, if new understandings can be forged through sustained levels of contact within these areas. Whether a cooperative relationship can be forged, however, may hinge on the nature of interracial contact. Although shared residential space may enhance the level of contact, this may not necessarily facilitate political coalition building if, in addition to racial prejudice and ignorance, race relations become contentious because of concerns over the rapid rise of Asian immigrants in a neighborhood and the perceived harm done to the quality of life and economic opportunities in areas such as Southern California (Lien forthcoming).

ASSESSING SOCIAL DISTANCE AT THE MASS LEVEL

How large are the degrees of social distance and political gaps between Asians and other groups? How likely is it for Asian candidates to receive support from Black, Latino, and white voters? Which racial group would be the most viable coalition partner or ally for Asians? These questions may be most appropriately answered with large-scale, scientifically collected public opinion data. However, as I caution in the Appendix, there are critical methodological issues to bear in mind when analyzing data dealing with Asians. What follows is an analysis of an assortment of multiracial datasets collected at national, state, and local levels in the 1990s, which contain a significant number of Asian respondents and are archived by the nation's two premier houses of public opinion data. Additional information from exit polls conducted by leading community organizations is used. The strengths and weaknesses of each dataset is noted in the Appendix. Because of the lack of nationally representative data, a multiplicity of datasets are analyzed to help construct a more accurate profile of the opinion gaps between Asians and others. The racial gaps are gauged with multiple indicators measuring race relations, political partisanship and ideology, candidate choice, and issue preference. A problem with analyzing multiple data sources collected with diverse methodologies is the likely inconsistencies in opinion patterns of the same phenomenon across datasets, which may be a function of changes in question wording and question sequence or differences in sampling frame and time period of investigation, as well as events taking place between surveys. The problem is most apparent in the studying of Asians, reflecting both the small sample size and extreme heterogeneity of the multiethnic community across geographic locations. The inconsistencies may also reflect the genuine fluidity of political opinions among Asians over even a short span of time. Because of these concerns, greater emphasis in the following analysis is placed on horizontal comparison across groups and vertical comparison across time, rather than on identifying a specific opinion pattern among Asians across time and space.

The degree of social distance between Asians and other groups is assessed with four indicators: racial knowledge, cross-racial friendship, racial prejudice, and perceived impacts on community. The question wording and distribution patterns in percentage terms for a selected number of measures are reported in table 4.1.

Racial Knowledge

According to a 1995 national race relations survey (*Washington Post,* Kaiser Foundation, and Harvard University 1995), only a tiny percentage of the respondents knew the population share of Asians in the nation, but the percentage among whites (3.2 percent) is higher than that among Blacks (2.7 percent) or Latinos (2.0 percent). A much higher percentage of Asians (20 percent) was able to correctly identify the percentage share of the Latino population than that of the white (4.2 percent) or Black (2.3 percent) population. A similar pattern is observed in the 1997 survey of Los Angeles City residents (LATP-LAC) where a greater percentage of whites (32 percent) than Blacks (26 percent) or Latinos (22 percent) was able to correctly identify the percentage of Asians in the city, whereas a much higher percentage of Asians (26 percent) knew the correct population share of Latinos even though they were ignorant of the population share of whites or Blacks. In the 1993 survey on Asians in Southern California (LATP-SC), a greater percentage of whites (60 percent) than Blacks (55 percent) or Latinos (38 percent) knew that the first Asians settled in California more than 100 years ago.

Cross-racial Friendship

Among respondents to the LATP-SC survey who were fluent either in English or Spanish, a higher percentage of whites (46 percent) than Blacks (34 percent) or Latinos (31 percent) reported having a close per-

TABLE 4.1   Percentage Distributions of Racial Attitudes by Race

	Asian	Latino	Black	White
LASUI, 1993–94 (adults 21 and over in Los Angeles County)				

Cross-racial Friendship:
For each group I want to know if you think they tend to be easy to get along with or tend to be hard to get along with. (Mean score in a 7-point scale with 1 being the most and 7 being the least easy to get along with.)

	Asian	Latino	Black	White
Asians	2.9	4.2	4.5	3.7
Latinos	3.6	2.8	3.7	3.6
Blacks	4.1	4.4	3.4	3.8
Whites	3.9	3.7	4.2	3.2

Racial Prejudice:
For each group I want to know if you think they tend to treat members of other groups equally or tend to discriminate against members of other groups. (Mean score in a 7-point scale with 1 being treating others equally and 7 being discriminating against others.)

	Asian	Latino	Black	White
Asians	3.5	4.6	5.3	4.4
Latinos	3.6	3.6	4.5	4.3
Blacks	4.1	4.9	4.0	4.7
Whites	4.5	4.8	5.4	4.1
N	1,055	1,020	1,103	835

LATP-SC, 1993 (adults in Southern California)
In your opinion, which groups or which kinds of people in Southern California are the most prejudiced? Do you think whites are the most prejudiced, or Asians, or Blacks, or Latinos? Is there another group that you think is almost as prejudiced, or not?

	Asian	Latino	Black	White
Asians	22	19	41	17
Latinos	10	15	13	17
Blacks	25	33	10	45
Whites	54	53	60	39
No group in particular	15	13	18	17
N	221	199	144	646

LATP-LAC, 1997 (adults in city of Los Angeles)
In your opinion, which racial or ethnic groups in the city of Los Angeles are the most prejudiced? Do you think whites are the most prejudiced, or Asians, or Blacks, or Latinos, or some other group, or don't you think any group is the most prejudiced? Is there another group that you think is almost as prejudiced?

	Asian	Latino	Black	White
Asians	11	20	24	10
Latinos	6	13	11	11
Blacks	18	28	11	34
Whites	21	37	41	26
No group in particular	42	31	32	34
N (weighted)	161	526	195	668

Source and *Note:* N represents base sample size. See Appendix for the full name of each acronym and information on survey methodology for each dataset.

sonal friend who is Asian. Among Asians, 68 percent reported having a close personal friend who is white, compared to 57 percent having a close Latino friend and 54 percent having a close Black friend. In another survey taken about the same time among residents of Los Angeles County, many of whom were immigrants not fluent in English (Bobo et al. 1998), Asians were again considered most easy to get along with by whites and least easy to get along with by Blacks. Latinos, however, were considered most easy, and Blacks least easy, to get along with by Asians.

Racial Prejudice

According to the LASUI survey (Bobo et al. 1998), Asians were considered by whites to be least likely, but by Blacks to be most likely, to discriminate against members of other racial groups. By contrast, Asians considered whites to be the most, and Latinos the least, likely group to discriminate against members of other racial groups. In the LATP-SC survey, a much higher percentage of Blacks (41 percent) than Latinos (19 percent) or whites (17 percent) considered Asians to be the most prejudiced group in Southern California. A much higher percentage of Asians (54 percent) considered whites to the most prejudiced group; only 10 percent of Asians considered Latinos to be as prejudiced. In the LATP-LAC survey, again, a higher percentage of Blacks (24 percent) than Latinos (20 percent) or whites (10 percent) considered Asians to be the most prejudiced group; a slightly higher percentage of Asians considered whites to be more prejudiced (21 percent) than Blacks (18 percent). In fact, in both the LATP-SC and LATP-LAC surveys, whites received the highest mentions of being the most prejudiced group by respondents within each nonwhite community. Among both Latinos and whites, Asians received fewer mentions of being the most prejudiced among other out-groups. Finally, considering the scope and direction of percentage change between the two LATP surveys of respondents in each racial group who either thought a certain group was particularly prejudiced or did not think any one group tended to behave as so, there is clear evidence of improved race relations between 1993 and 1997 in this extremely ethnically diverse region.[4]

Perceived Impacts on Community

According to the LATP-SC survey, a higher percentage of Blacks (38 percent) than Latinos (33 percent) or whites (21 percent) considered

Asians to be getting more economic power than is good for Southern California. Among Asians, 34 percent considered whites to be getting too much economic power compared to the 7 percent who felt Blacks were. A quarter of Black respondents (26 percent) felt Asians had a negative impact on life in Southern California, which is higher than the percentage of Latinos (20 percent) or whites (16 percent) who felt Asians had a negative impact. When asked if their neighbors would be upset by a substantial increase in the number of Asians moving into their own neighborhood, a higher percentage of Blacks (40 percent) than whites (34 percent) or Latinos (29 percent) responded affirmatively to this. In the LATP-LAC survey, Blacks did not have a higher tendency than others to mention Asians as getting more economic power than other groups in Los Angeles. A large percentage of Asians (50 percent), Latinos (39 percent), and Blacks (34 percent) mentioned that whites had more power than others. However, 36 percent of Blacks also mentioned Latinos as getting too much economic power.

These indicators of social distance illustrate a state of race relations that continues to be mangled by historical and contemporary structural forces. They suggest that, despite gradual social changes after 1965 and signs of improvement in recent years, race relations among the nation's four major racial groups are hardly harmonious or reciprocal. Those Americans racialized as white in the 1990s knew the most about, made the most friendly contacts with, and were least concerned about the economic impact of Asians. They considered Asians the least prejudiced and easiest to get along with among nonwhites. Asians, nevertheless, considered Latinos the least prejudiced and most easy to get along with among out-groups. Asians were also far more knowledgeable about the demographic share of Latinos than other groups. In return, Latinos showed the least concern about the influx of Asians into their neighborhoods. They considered Asians less prejudiced than Blacks or whites. However, Latinos also considered Asians to be less easy to get along with than whites and they were more concerned than whites about the economic and cultural impacts of Asians on the local community. Blacks' views of Asians are the exact opposite to whites'. Blacks were more likely than Latinos and whites to consider Asians as most prejudiced and least easy to get along with. They were most concerned about the impacts of Asians on local economy and culture. Although Asians also found Blacks most difficult to befriend, they did not find Blacks to be most prejudiced nor were Blacks considered an economic threat to them.

How can Asians get along with others given the scope of racial tensions? An answer to this may be provided by examining factors that shape racial attitudes about Asians. Two indicators of social distance found in LASUI data and reported in table 4.1 are analyzed with multivariate regression procedures. (Results from these and other multivariate analyses are not shown but are available from the author.) Respondents' assessment of the degree of easiness to get along with Asians and their evaluation of Asians' tendency to discriminate against other groups are the two dependent variables. The ordinary least squares (OLS) results show that, although each non-Asian group, especially Blacks, has a higher tendency to consider Asians as being harder to get along with, this antagonism can be reduced by greater participation in social and political organizations,[5] after controlling for differences in nativity, citizenship, education, home ownership, age, length of residence in community, marital status, gender, and English language fluency. Similarly, those who reported attending at least once a year meetings held by their membership organization(s) are predicted to be less likely to perceive Asians as discriminatory against other races, once the above-mentioned controls plus the degree of easiness in getting along are taken into account. Regardless of racial origin, participation in the formal electoral process, such as becoming registered voters, may increase the perceived difficulty of getting along with Asians; this factor, however, is rendered insignificant in predicting perceived discrimination of Asians once attitudinal differences in assessing easiness in getting along with Asians are controlled. This finding suggests that a study that focuses on racial attitudes of the electorate may overstate racial tensions in regions with large numbers of immigrants and underestimate the possibility of cooperation across groups.

CONFIGURING THE CONTOURS OF POLITICAL GAPS AND BRIDGES BETWEEN ASIANS AND OTHERS

The political gaps between Asians and other racial groups are also evaluated with four indicators: political partisanship, ideology, candidate choice, and issue preferences.[6] The percentage distributions of these indicators are reported in tables 4.2 to 4.5.

TABLE 4.2 Percentage Distributions of Political Partisanship by Race

	Asian	Latino	Black	White
National				
Race Poll, 1995 (adults in 48 contiguous states)				
Generally speaking, do you usually think of yourself as a:				
Democrat/Republican/Other/No	26/24/46/4	41/20/34/5	63/5/26/7	27/30/36/7
N	343	237	443	791
(among Other/No) Do you lean more toward:				
Democrat/Republican/No	36/36/28	39/23/38	58/6/36	32/38/31
N	173	100	148	341
VNS, 1996 General Election (voters in 50 states)				
Do you usually think of yourself as a:				
Democrat/Republican/Other	34/39/26	61/21/19	72/12/14	34/39/28
N (weighted)	182	741	1,660	13,599
VNS, 1998 General Election (voters in 42 states)				
Do you usually think of yourself as a:				
Democrat/Republican/Other	41/31/28	49/26/26	75/7/18	32/40/29
N (weighted)	141	603	1,156	11,381
State				
VNS-CA, 1996 General Election (voters in California)				
Do you usually think of yourself as a:				
Democrat/Republican/Other	32/48/19	61/23/17	69/13/18	37/42/21
N (weighted)	124	354	194	2,327
LATP-CA, 1996 General Election (voters in California)				
Do you usually think of yourself as a:				
Democrat/Republican/Other	44/33/22	71/17/12	84/4/12	38/45/17
N (weighted)	117	210	135	1,545
LATP-CA, 1998 Primary Election (voters in California)				
Are you registered to vote as a:				

Democrat/Republican/Other	36/48/16	72/18/10	79/7/15	39/51/10
N (weighted)	162	530	618	3,104
LATP-CA, 1998 General Election (voters in California)				
Are you registered to vote as a:				
Democrat/Republican/Other	45/37/18	66/21/13	66/21/12	41/47/12
N (weighted)	239	415	426	2,082
VNS-CA, 1998 General Election (voters in California)				
Do you usually think of yourself as a:				
Democrat/Republican/Other	37/31/32	67/18/15	70/11/19	36/43/21
N (weighted)	100	391	195	2,085
Local				
LATP-SC, 1993 (registered to vote in Southern California)				
Which political party are you registered in?				
Democratic/Republican/Other/No	39/38/7/16	59/24/2/15	83/5/4/8	41/44/4/11
N	150	124	137	610
LASUI, 1993–94 (registered in Los Angeles County)				
Generally speaking, do you usually think of yourself as a:				
Democrat/Republican/Other/No	22/31/10/34	54/16/13/16	81/4/7/6	42/36/15/6
N	310	243	951	690
ALC, 1994, General (voters in San Francisco Bay Area)				
Which party are you registered to, if any?				
Democratic/Republican/Other	62/22/16	84/4/12	73/14/13	68/17/15
N	893	412	833	1,655
APALC, 1998, General (voters in Southern California)				
Which party are you registered to, if any?				
Democratic/Republican/Other/No	42/34/3/21	79/13/2/6	81/9/3/6	46/42/5/6
N (approximately)	1,420	700	192	560

Source and Note: See table 4.1, page 150.

TABLE 4.3   Percentage Distributions of Political Ideology by Race

	Asian	Latino	Black	White
National				
Race Poll, 1995:				
Would you say your views in most political matters are:				
(V)Liberal[a]/Moderate/(V)Conservative	25/45/31	29/32/39	38/36/27	24/40/36
VNS, 1996 General Election				
On most political matters, do you consider yourself as:				
Liberal/Moderate/Conservative	24/58/18	26/49/24	29/51/21	18/47/36
VNS, 1998 General Election				
Liberal/Moderate/Conservative	33/43/24	26/50/25	29/54/18	17/50/33
State				
VNS-CA, 1996 General Election				
Liberal/Moderate/Conservative	19/55/26	26/46/28	27/51/22	20/45/35
LATP-CA, 1996 General Election				
In most political matters, do you consider yourself as:				
Liberal/Moderate/Conservative	23/44/33	32/45/23	36/46/18	17/47/36
VNS-CA, 1998 General Election				
Liberal/Moderate/Conservative	21/45/34	25/52/24	27/56/17	21/48/31
LATP-CA, 1998 Primary Election				
Liberal/Moderate/Conservative	23/41/36	26/44/30	24/53/23	18/40/42
LATP-CA, 1998 General Election				
Liberal/Moderate/Conservative	21/44/35	24/48/28	28/41/32	22/43/35

Local

LATP-SC, 1993 (adults)

How would you describe your views on most matters having to do with politics? Do you generally think of yourself as:

(V)Liberal/Moderate/(V)Conservative/None	29/29/36/5	30/26/38/6	38/30/29/3	27/31/41/1
(Among the registered)	27/35/35/3	36/25/37/2	38/32/28/3	26/32/42/5

LASUI, 1993–94 (adults)

We hear a lot of talk these days about liberals and conservatives. Here is a 7-point scale on which the political views that people might hold are arranged from extremely liberal to extremely conservative.

Where would you place yourself on this scale?

(V)Liberal[b]/Moderate/(V)Conservative[b]/None	24/27/35/10	27/19/29/24	38/30/27/5	29/33/34/4
(Among the registered)	22/29/39/9	31/30/33/6	39/30/27/3	30/32/36/2

LATP-LAC, 1997 (adults in city of Los Angeles)

How would you describe your views on most matters having to do with politics? Do you generally think of yourself as:

(V)Liberal/Moderate/(V)Conservative/None	30/23/28/21	30/20/37/12	32/21/36/11	39/27/29/5

Note: See relevant Base *N* for each dataset in tables 4.1 and 4.2.

[a](V) means "very."

[b]Includes leaners.

TABLE 4.4   Percentage Distributions of Candidate Choice by Race

	Asian	Latino	Black	White
National				
Race Poll, 1995 (voters in 48 contiguous states) 1992 Presidential Vote				
Democrat (Clinton)[a]	45 (85/16/34)[b]	52 (77/8/50)	86 (94/33/75)	37 (78/7/34)
Republican (Bush)	41 (7/79/44)	32 (11/77/23)	7 (3/58/12)	42 (8/77/33)
Independent (Perot)	13	16	5	20 (14/14/32)
N	152	95	281	530
VNS, 1996 (voters in 50 states) 1996 Presidential Vote				
Democrat (Clinton)[a]	43 (78/15/38)	72 (91/26/61)	81 (93/39/69)	43 (81/12/41)
Republican (Dole)	48 (12/83/43)	21 (6/68/13)	12 (4/54/18)	46 (12/81/38)
Independent (Perot)	8	6	4	9
VNS, 1998 (voters in 42 states) 1998 U.S. House Vote				
Democrat	53 (90/3/53)	59 (87/23/43)	88 (96/22/75)	42 (85/9/45)
Republican	43 (10/97/31)	35 (12/72/50)	11 (3/78/23)	55 (14/90/51)
State				
LATP-CA, 1998 Primary Election (voters in California) U.S. Senate Vote				
Democrat (Boxer)	33 (62/6/42)	56 (66/25/28)	76 (84/34/60)	34 (67/8/33)
Republican (Fong)	49 (31/63/31)	10 (8/20/11)	8 (4/35/17)	26 (11/38/19)
VNS-CA, 1998 General Election (voters in California) U.S. Senate Vote				
Democrat (Boxer)	55 (87/15/63)	72 (85/26/60)	85 (94/38/78)	46 (85/15/48)
Republican (Fong)	44 (13/81/38)	23 (11/67/29)	13 (6/63/15)	50 (13/82/44)
N (weighted)	100	391	195	2,085
LATP-CA, 1998 General Election (voters in California) U.S. Senate Vote				
Democrat (Boxer)	48 (87/6/40)	69 (89/15/53)	64 (88/7/36)	47 (86/14/43)
Republican (Fong)	51 (13/90/61)	24 (8/84/11)	34 (12/93/45)	48 (12/83/36)

—, U.S. House Vote				
Democrat	55 (94/12/50)	72 (92/17/52)	65 (93/8/14)	45 (83/12/39)
Republican	34 (3/68/43)	23 (6/82/20)	11 (2/36/14)	48(11/84/20)
—, California Gubernatorial Vote				
Democrat (Davis)	65 (88/22/86)	71 (91/18/48)	71 (97/10/37)	50 (87/19/50)
Republican (Lungren)	34 (11/77/14)	23 (8/82/9)	21 (1/89/10)	45 (11/79/29)
—, California Lieutenant Governor Vote				
Democratic (Bustamante)	49 (78/18/38)	73 (91/27/50)	72 (91/12/74)	44 (80/15/33)
Republican (Leslie)	41 (12/75/50)	17 (4/68/7)	16 (2/63/14)	45 (10/80/25)
Local				
LATP-SC, 1993 (voters in Southern California) 1992 U.S. Presidential Vote				
Democrat (Clinton)[a]	46 (71/10)	58 (76/10)	84 (74/33)	39 (64/9)
Republican (Bush)	44 (10/59)	28 (8/65)	6 (6/0)	39 (11/63)
Independent (Perot)	10 (5/8)	14 (10/10)	10 (8/33)	21 (11/19)
N	104	85	117	525
APALC, 1998 (poll voters in Southern California), U.S. Senate Vote				
Democrat (Boxer)[a]	40 (66/12)	82 (91/39)	89 (98/1)	49 (77/17)
Republican (Fong)	58 (33/88)	13 (6/59)	10 (1/74)	47 (21/80)

Source and *Note*: See tables 4.1 and 4.2.

[a]Denotes the winning candidate.

[b]Entries in parentheses are percentages among Democrats, Republicans, and others, respectively.

TABLE 4.5   Percentage Distributions of Issue Opinion and Ballot Initiatives by Race

	Asian	Latino	Black	White
Race Poll, 1995				
Should Congress do or not do (% favoring congressional action)?				
Reform the welfare system	84	84	84	92
Limit tax breaks for businesses	34	53	57	58
Cut personal income taxes	63	65	59	65
Reform medicare	75	71	67	69
Limit affirmative action	50	41	35	58
Put more limits on abortion	31	54	37	38
N	352	251	451	802
Affirmative Action				
Race Poll, 1995				
Generally speaking, do you think affirmative action is a good thing or a bad thing for the country, or doesn't it affect the country much?				
A good thing	57	59	76	43
N	321	211	423	719
LASUI, 1993–94				
Some people feel that because of past disadvantages there are some groups in society that should receive special job training and educational assistance. Others say that it is unfair to give these groups special job training and educational assistance. What about you? Do you strongly favor, favor, neither favor nor oppose, oppose, or strongly oppose special job training and educational assistance for [group]? (% strongly favor/favor)				
Asians	62	62	59	49
Latinos	58	78	79	58
Blacks	58	70	92	61
Women	65	78	88	59

Some people feel that because of past disadvantages, there are some groups in society that should be given preferences in hiring and promotion. Others say that it is unfair to give these groups special preferences. What about you? Do you strongly favor, favor, neither favor nor oppose, or strongly oppose special preferences in hiring and promotion to [group]? (% strongly favor/favor)

Asians	34	36	42	18
Latinos	27	40	58	21
Blacks	28	41	73	22
Women	34	51	71	25
VNS-CA, 1996: Proposition 209 (bans affirmative action)				
Liberal/Moderate/Conservative (% against)	55 (65/63/28)	70 (83/70/54)	73 (72/79/58)	38 (71/38/18)
N (weighted)	139	375	207	2,462
LATP-CA, 1996: Proposition 209 (bans affirmative action)				
Liberal/Moderate/Conservative (% against)	61 (83/59/50)	72 (87/77/44)	74 (57/80/87)	37 (68/40/16)
N (weighted)	113	219	140	1,554
Bilingual Education				
LATP, 1998 Primary: Proposition 227 (bans bilingual education)				
Liberal/Moderate/Conservative (% against)	43 (60/47/23)	63 (80/59/51)	50 (66/50/33)	32 (60/34/18)

Source and *Note*: See tables 4.1 and 4.2.

Political Partisanship

This opinion gap is assessed with twelve datasets collected at national, state, and local levels querying respondents' political party preferences or party registration between 1993 and 1998. Whereas the observed partisanship distributions among whites, Blacks, and Latinos are relatively stable across time and space, the same cannot be said of Asians. The percentages fluctuate greatly even with surveys taken on the same day, same question wording, and within the same election context. A case in point are the figures for the 1996 general election exit poll in California. Whereas the Voter News Service (VNS) survey finds Asian voters to be more Republican than Democrat (48 percent to 32 percent), the LATP survey finds the reverse to be true (44 percent Democrat to 33 percent Republican). Regardless, the rank ordering of the racial gaps in partisanship is clear, be it among Democrats or Republicans. With few exceptions, the partisanship gaps are smallest between Asians and whites; they are greater between Asians and Latinos; the gaps are widest between Asians and Blacks. This suggests that Asians and whites are most likely to form a voting bloc for the same political party candidates in any partisan election. Also, although Asian Democrats may not be in the majority anywhere on the mainland except in the San Francisco Bay area, there appears to be a trend leaning toward the Democratic Party in the late 1990s. Specifically, figures for the 1998 general elections collected either at national, state, or local level all show a Democratic edge from 6 percent to 10 percent over Republican identifiers among Asians. This may present opportunities for Asians to form a closer partisan tie with Latinos and Blacks as well as challenges to coalition building between Asians and whites within the Republican Party.

Political Ideology

The ideological gap across racial groups is assessed with datasets nearly identical to those used to study partisan patterns. Although the evidence is somewhat mixed depending on the geographic coverage and type of respondents surveyed, results from a national study of adults as well as from the surveying of California state and local voters or registered voters suggest that Asians are more likely to find their ideological allies among whites than among Latinos and least likely among Blacks. However, racial gaps in political ideology between Asians and the two nonwhite groups are much smaller compared to the gaps in partisanship. This suggests a greater room for political maneuvering for issue-based than for partisanship-based coalition across racial groups. Also, if results from the Los Angeles area surveys among adults can serve as a guide, Asians and Latinos can be closer ideological allies and have more potential to form ideologically based issue coalitions than Asians and whites or Asians and Blacks would. In general, Asians are ideologically more conservative than liberal, which is also true among whites and mostly true among Latinos, but not so among Blacks.

Candidate Choice

Based on the distribution of political partisanship, Asian voters are more likely to choose major party candidates that are favored by white than by Latino or Black voters. This prediction is born out in nearly all the surveys conducted at national, state, and local levels among voters for national offices and reported in table 4.4. In the 1998 California U.S. Senate race where an Asian male Republican (Fong) ran against a white female Democrat (Boxer), a much higher percentage of whites voted for Fong than percentages of Latinos or Blacks. Nevertheless, Asians were found to vote closer to Latinos than whites in 1998 elections such as in their national vote for U.S. House of Representatives, their state vote for California governor, and at the local level in their vote for California state assembly races where Asian Democrats (Nakano and Wong) were candidates.[7] The leaning toward Democratic partisanship observed among Asians may account for this increased solidarity with Latino voters.

Racial differences in voting for a political candidate may be a function of a number of factors other than political partisanship or gender. They also may be influenced by a respondent's sociodemographic (age, marital status, education, and income) and political (ideology, union household, and attitude toward the ruling administration) background. When these factors are controlled in a logistic regression analysis of California voters' support for Fong's bid to the U.S. Senate using the LATP-CA general election data, Asian voters are predicted to yield the highest support to Fong, followed by white voters. Other conditions being equal, Blacks voters are likely to yield greater support for Fong than Latino voters. Regardless of race, support for Fong is greater among males, Republicans, conservatives, the better educated, nonunion householders, and those who disliked President Clinton's sex affairs. It is not affected by a voter's age, income, or marital status. Analysis of the 1998 primary election using data collected by LATP also finds white voters most likely to support Fong after Asian voters. However, different from the general election results, Latino voters are more likely than Black voters to vote for Fong. Gender, age, partisanship, and ideology are useful predictors for this primary vote, but income, education, marital status, and union household are not.

Issue Preference

The issue gaps across races vary in width depending on the nature of the issue queried (see table 4.5). According to the Race Poll, Asians did not differ much from other racial groups in their opinions toward taxation, medicare, and welfare reform issues; a smaller percentage of Asians supported congressional action to reform tax breaks for businesses and to put more limits on abortion. Asians were at about equal distance but in a different direction from whites and Latinos on the issue of reforming affirmative action policy. Nevertheless, a majority of Asians believed that affirmative action was a good thing for the country and their opinion was much closer to Latinos than to whites or Blacks. When Asians in Los Angeles County were asked of their support for offering special job training and educational assistance to historically disadvantaged groups, the opinion of Asians was almost identical to that among Latinos and most different from that among whites. This pattern is reversed, however, when Latinos, Blacks, and women are the recipient groups. The level of support among Asians was most similar to that among whites, which was lower than that among Blacks or Latinos. The same racial pattern is repeated but with a lower overall level of support when respondents are asked to consider giving special preferences in hiring and promotion to historically disadvantaged groups.

In 1996, voters in California were asked to decide on an initiative (Proposition 209) that "prohibits the state, local governments, districts, public universities, colleges, and schools, and other government instrumentalities from discriminating against or giving preferential treatment to any individual or group in public employment, public education, or public contracting on the basis of race, sex, ethnicity, or national origin." Although the proposition was passed by a margin of 55 percent to 45 percent, analyses of state-wide exit poll data collected by VNS and LATP show that a majority of voters in the three nonwhite groups all voted against the proposition. The Asian vote was lower but closer to the Latino than the Black vote and all on the opposite side of the white vote. Yet, when the vote within each group is broken down by ideology, white liberals voted against the ban at a level that was higher than the liberals in at least one nonwhite group. White moderates and conservatives, however, all voted opposite to the issue preference of their nonwhite counterparts. To understand the role of race independent of likely confounding factors such as gender, age, education, income, partisanship, and ideology, the VNS-CA data are analyzed with logistic regression procedures estimating the likelihood of voting against Proposition 209. The result shows that, compared to Asian voters, Black voters are most likely, followed by Latino voters, to oppose the ban on affirmative action, whereas white voters are less likely to do so. Regardless of race, opposition to the ban is more prevalent among women, the young, the better educated, Democrats, and liberals, but not necessarily among the poor.

A related policy issue that California voters decided upon in June 1998 was the proposition to ban bilingual instruction and permit only English instruction in public schools (Proposition 227). It was passed by a margin of 61 percent to 39 percent among all voters. Analysis of the LATP primary election exit poll shows that 43 percent of Asians voted against the proposition. That percentage was larger than among whites but smaller than that among Latinos or Blacks. In percentage point terms, the racial gap on this issue is smallest between Asians and Blacks and widest between Asians and Latinos, even though an equal percentage of Asian and white liberals (60 percent) voted against the initiative. Like the vote for candidate Fong or against Proposition 209, the role of race in a voter's position on Proposition 227 may be a function of a number of factors dealing with one's political orientation and sociodemographic background. Logistic regression results estimating opposition to banning bilingual education suggest that, other conditions being equal, the probability of Latinos to vote "no" to Proposition 227 is much higher than that of Asians, which is higher than that of whites but about the same as that of Blacks. Regardless of race, those who are female, of lower income, better educated, Democrat, liberal, and from a union household are more likely to oppose the initiative.

This empirical assessment of political gaps between Asians and others using survey data collected throughout the 1990s suggests various configurations of possibilities to build political bridges. Asians are found to have a greater resemblance to whites than to Latinos and least to Blacks in terms of the distributions of political partisanship. A similar order of racial gaps can be found in political ideology and candidate choice among voters. However, data gathered from adult residents in Southern California reveal a closer union in ideology between Latinos and Asians. Analyses of exit poll results in 1998 also show an increased likelihood of solidarity in candidate choice between the two nonwhite groups. Moreover, Asians and Latinos have greater commonality in levels of support for the principle of affirmative action and the offering of special job training, educational assistance, and even preferences in hiring and promotion to Asians. Nevertheless, when non-Asians are the targeted group, Asians are closer to whites in terms of the level of support. When the significance of racial gaps is assessed with multiple regression procedures controlling for possible confounding factors in sociodemographic background and political experiences, an Asian Republican male candidate is estimated to receive greater support from white than Latino or Black voters. The result may be different if the candidates' race and gender are of a different combination.[8] When race-related issues such as affirmative action and bilingual programs in public schools are the focus of examination, an Asian voter is more likely to vote like a Latino voter than a white voter. The probability of an Asian to vote against the banning of bilingual programs is found not to be significantly different from a Black voter, even though his or her likelihood of voting against the banning of affirmative action is significantly lower than that of a Black voter.

Finally, public sentiment toward the issue of cross-racial coalition building may be directly assessed by a question asked in a 1997 survey of Los Angeles city residents (LATP-LAC): "Do you think minorities can make more progress by concentrating on strengthening their own communities or can they make more progress by trying to integrate themselves into and build coalitions with other races and ethnic groups?" A higher proportion of Asians (68 percent) than Latinos (61 percent), whites (59 percent), or Blacks (42 percent) chose the integration and coalition-building option. The significance of racial gaps in public support for this orientation is estimated with logistic regression procedures controlling for gender, age, education, income, marital status, ideology, and assessment of progress made by the city's racial and ethnic groups in peacefully coexisting with others after the 1992 riots.

Compared to support among Asians, support among Blacks is significantly lower, that among Latinos is marginally lower, and that among whites is not significantly different. Regardless of race, respondents who show more concern about race relations by perceiving not much or no racial progress in the city are more likely to support coalition building; differences in age, income, ideology, and marital status do not seem to matter.

The greater reluctance of Blacks in building cross-racial coalitions may be related to their stronger sense of community. In the LASUI dataset, a higher percentage of Blacks (39 percent) are found to show a lot of concern for other members of their own race in the nation than the equivalent percentage for Latinos (30 percent), whites (22 percent), or Asians (15 percent).[9] Controlling for sociodemographic and acculturation differences does not remove the distinctiveness of the Black sense of common identity. This inverse relationship between sense of community and support for coalition building suggests that a potential barrier for building coalitions between Asians and others may lie within the community itself. Ironically, different from the earlier discussion, the within-group barrier may arise not from a lack of, but rather an excess of, panethnicity. Notwithstanding, other conditions being equal, each respondent's sense of common fate can be increased with a greater level of participation in social and political organizations. Registering to vote, on the other hand, does not have an independent impact on this orientation.

CONCLUSION

This chapter reviewed the variable positions of Asians in U.S. race relations, coalition-building possibilities, and barriers Asians have faced when dealing with non-Hispanic whites, Blacks, Latinos, and American Indians. This review was made through the lenses of historical interactions and mass opinion data collected in the 1990s. Asians were placed structurally in a precarious middle position, rather than fixed at a certain subordinate level, which can be used both to reinforce the dominant position of whites and to defy the subordination of nonwhites. Paradoxically called both the "foreigner within" and the "model minority," Asians as the middleman minority, like other minority groups, have often been used as a pawn in U.S. power politics. Their opportunities to form broad-based and lasting coalitions with other racial groups have been deterred by a structural condition that encourages racial mistrust, competition and conflict, and limited accommodation for nonwhites. In spite of these tendencies and barriers, Asians were able to form cooperative relationships with American Indians, Blacks, Latinos, and white liberals out of common interests and needs as well as shared concerns of racial grievances and aspirations for liberty and equality. Global economic restructuring, shifts in political ideology, and transformations in sociodemography due to changes in international migration patterns in the post-1965 era have introduced new challenges to race relations in a multiracial/multiethnic society. New grounds for interracial coalition building between Asians and others at the mass level have also emerged because of increased opportunities for personal and organizational contacts, improved economic and social status, greater adaptation to and integration in U.S. political culture, as well as the continued need for all to address issues of social justice and political empowerment.

Depending on the political context and issue areas, Asians can be expected to form coalitions with different racial groups or all groups. However, in contemporary electoral politics, racial bridges are easier to build between Asians and whites based on interpersonal friendship, shared partisanship, ideology, and, provisionally, candidate choice. Coalitions between Asians and Latinos and Blacks can be established based on their shared concerns over race-related social redistributive issues at the local level, even though Latinos and Blacks have distinct issue concerns and different social distance to Asians. Short of a significant transformation in race relations and opportunity structure in U.S. society and societies across the Pacific, the long-term prospects of coalition building will need to be assessed at multiple levels and interpreted in situational, relative terms within the larger racial context where whites remain the privileged race and Asians are expediently positioned either as the racial middlemen, foreigner within, or model minority. In this context, between-group solidarity may be easily shaken by perceived threats to group interests and perceived opportunities for individualistic but not collective advancement. Within-group solidarity, on the other hand, may not necessarily facilitate the formation of cross-racial union. Nevertheless, multivariate results also indicate that participation in group-based activities may reduce racial tensions between Asians and others and increase the sense of common identity or panethnicity for each community. This suggests that, in both historical and contemporary settings, a critical vehicle for combating racial tensions and for constructing a more integrated society in multiracial America lies in the formation of and participation in social and political organizations. A direction for future research is to examine the generalizability of this thesis in other multiracial settings in the nation. Future research should also compare the creation, existence, and sanctity of panethnic coalitions between Asians and other racial groups. This should be explored at both organizational elite and mass levels, in various historical periods, and under various political and social contexts.

5   What Ties That Bind?

*Comparing Political Attitudes and Behavior Across
Major Asian American Groups*

"ALL ASIANS are not the same," commented a Washington-based journalist on NBC's "Meet the Press" show, who reminded another program regular of the complexity of Asian American involvement in campaign fund-raising and nuclear espionage cases.[1] Whereas the former involved several Chinese American businessmen alleged to have channeled illegal campaign money into the Democratic Party from Taiwan and other places, the latter involved a Taiwanese-born American scientist suspected of collecting nuclear secrets for the People's Republic of China. To better reflect this situation, the journalist might as well have proclaimed, "All Chinese are not the same." Chinese Americans do not share the same political origins or maintain relationships with the same political parties. In fact, intraethnic conflicts arising from partisan, ideological, and class differences associated with past alliances in their ethnic homeland among the Chinese have been a major source of division in American chinatowns and Chinese American communities (Lyman 1974; Lai 1976; Kwong 1979, 1987; Wang 1996; Lin 1998). Because Taiwan is considered a renegade government by the People's Republic of China, the journalist's attempt to prevent the lumping of all Chinese or Asians into one political camp is a rare and commendable one, something to be extolled by the embattled ethnic community in the aftermath of past controversies. Yet, recently a group of Chinese American leaders asked us to forget about this intraethnic diversity. Moreover, they hoped to downplay whatever interethnic differences exist between Chinese and other Asian American groups when it comes to participation in American politics.

Organizers of a national, nonpartisan political action called the 80-20 Initiative wished to get 80 percent of Chinese Americans and all other Asian Americans to vote for the same political party candidates in the 2000 presidential election. The assumption was that if Asian Americans residing in such key states as California and New York could unite behind candidates in either one of the major political parties at an eight

170

to two ratio, the community would be accorded with a political clout instrumental to the removal of glass ceilings and the acquisition of greater political and social equality. They noted that the ballot-box approach is the model used by Irish, Polish, and Italian immigrants, as well as by Jews, Blacks, women, and Latinos to gain power in American politics. For these Chinese Americans, the unequivocal lesson taught by these minority groups in their marches from the margins to the mainstream is that size of the community does not matter, lack of unity does. They are convinced that the quest for political empowerment must begin with the formation of a grand coalition within the multiethnic Asian American community. Setting aside the issue of intraethnic differences among each ethnic group, and granting that their theory linking political unity to political empowerment is correct, how feasible is it to conceive or construct a voting bloc among Asian Americans at the dawn of the twenty-first century? Do Asians of diverse ethnic origins tend to think alike regarding their experiences in America and their views on important community issues? More fundamentally, what is the contour of Asian American panethnicity at the mass level?

As delineated in previous chapters, the Asian American community is not a product of natural cohesion rooted in the commonness in home language, beliefs, customs, or values, but of panethnic political coalition building promoted by community activists and organizational elites who were concerned about the issues of racial subordination, economic exploitation, and cultural deprivation that affect Asians and other people of color. It is not a concept congeneric to the communities of Asian immigrants in America but a political awakening that sprouted in the antiwar, Black Power, women's liberation, and other post-1965 social movements among the young and U.S.-born generation. The formation of pan-Asian consciousness and identity was immediately challenged because of drastic shifts in the community's population structure. This resulted from the 1965 immigration reform as well as changes in the nation's sociopolitical structure due primarily to global and domestic economic restructuring and neoconservative policy orientation that emerged in the 1970s and became entrenched in the following decade. In addition, the lifting of legal barriers to voting, education, employment, and intermarriage to nonwhite Americans in and after the mid-1960s has permitted a greater number of Asians to perceive total assimilation as a viable option in their American experience. As a consequence, a pessimistic account of the sanctity of the pan-Asian community and identity may conclude that they exist only in the imagination. On the other hand, an optimistic account, one that permeates the majority of Chapter 2, would emphasize the opportunities for panethnic community construction existing in the same social, economic, and political context that has undermined the community's quest for unity and empowerment. As shown, the disintegration of urban economy, deterioration in race relations, and the rise of anti-Asian violence and political scrutiny in recent years have spurred the formation of new pan-Asian oriented organizations and the transformation of existing ones. Asian activists and organizational elites have been able to form panethnic coalitions within the multiethnic community, but to what extent and on what basis can one anticipate the construction of panethnic solidarity among the mass?

In order to gauge the magnitude of ethnic boundaries and shared concerns among Asian Americans, this chapter begins with a brief account of the historical incidences and contemporary challenges and opportunities of cross-ethnic coalition building. It uses data from the U.S. Bureau of the Census to illustrate the gaps in population characteristics among six major Asian American groups and the possible ramifications on the political unity of the multiethnic community. Adult opinions of four Asian ethnic communities in Southern California were compared and contrasted to identify cross-ethnic patterns in immigrant adaptation experiences and community concerns. Next, a series of public opinion data collected by both mainstream and community organizations was reviewed in terms of ethnic differences in political and social participation, partisan orientation, candidate choice, and ballot initiative vote. Finally, the unique meaning of ethnicity, independent of other factors was interrogated with multivariate regression procedures using multiethnic datasets extracted from the voter supplement files of the Current Population Survey (CPS), 1994–1998 and Multi-City Study of Urban Inequality, Los Angeles (LASUI), 1992–1994.

CONCEIVING CROSS-ETHNIC UNITY AMONG ASIANS: HISTORICAL INCIDENCES AND CONTEMPORARY CHALLENGES AND OPPORTUNITIES

Like the process of building interracial coalitions at the mass level, the formation of panethnic political unity among individuals of various

Asian ancestries is conceived to be an interactive effect of individual and group-based factors as well as of historical and sociopolitical forces on both the domestic and international fronts. Generally, panethnic solidarity may be more likely to form if there were historical precedents of intergroup cooperation and the presence of bridging institutions such as panethnic organizations and interethnic couples. Perceived similarity in social, economic, and political status as well as commonality in political attitudes and behavior across ethnicities may also encourage the formation of a common sense of pan-Asian identity. For the immigrant population, the sharing of both positive and negative evaluations of the adaptation experience may be another likely source of coalition. Together, these between-group factors may provide a foundation for constructing political unity across Asian American communities. However, as suggested in the previous chapter, the likelihood of having such formation may depend greatly on the norms and practices of the U.S. racial and capitalist system. It may also be affected by the internal cohesiveness of each ethnic population, which varies greatly because of differences in homeland history and culture, length of immigration, mode of entry, and adaptation patterns.

Early Asian immigrants generally arrived in a sequential manner after a previous group had fallen out of favor. Upon arrival, the predominantly male workers were usually kept in segregated units with poor working and living conditions and low pay and were subject to the "divide and rule" policy of white management (Akamine 1993). In the 1880s, when Japanese workers first arrived on the mainland they were forced to compete against the Chinese workers in mines, on farms, and on the railroads along the Pacific Coast and in Midwestern states (Yoneda 1971). Once Asians had a chance to settle down and subsequent generations became eligible for citizenship, those in Hawaii were confronted with a society and systems that forced economic, political, and cultural dependency (Okihiro 1991). Although from a historical perspective it is easy to see the common ties in the mode of entry and experience of discrimination shared by these Asian immigrants, groups often practiced "ethnic disidentification" to avoid being misidentified and suffering similar mistreatment (Espiritu 1992). Japanese immigrants worked to distance themselves from the "lowly Chinese" soon after they landed in America (Ichioka 1988). During WWII, Chinese, Filipino, and Korean Americans found it necessary to wear ethnic clothing and identification cards or buttons to differentiate themselves from the Japanese (Takaki 1989). Given the prevailing racial and social order discouraging minority coalitions, few accounts of interethnic cooperation among Asians were reported prior to the late 1960s. Most dealt with working-class struggles for economic betterment, many of which involved cross-racial participation.

At the turn of the century, when the contract labor system ended in Hawaii, the first recorded incident of interethnic cooperation took place in 1900 at the Puehuehu plantation where 188 Chinese and Japanese field and mill workers struck together to protest the holding of part of their wages and won (Ariyoshi 1976; Takaki 1983). During the 1909 Japanese strike, Chinese merchants provided food on credit to evicted Japanese laborers and their families (Chan 1991a). The first major interethnic strike occurred in 1920 and involved mostly Filipino and Japanese workers or about 77 percent of the Oahu's workforce (Ariyoshi 1976; Takaki 1983; Akamine 1993). Japanese and Filipino workers had planned to act together, but 2,700 Filipino workers walked off the job prematurely; they were joined reluctantly by 6,000 Japanese laborers. A small number of workers of other racial and ethnic origins also participated. The planters responded by evicting strikers and their families from plantation housing and hiring scabs to keep production going. Those Japanese supporting the strike housed and fed evicted Filipinos in addition to the evicted Japanese (Chan 1991a). In California, the Japanese section of the Agricultural Workers Industrial Union conducted more than twenty strikes in the early 1930s involving over 5,000 Japanese and tens of thousands of Filipino, Mexican, Black, and white workers. In 1936, the California Japanese Agricultural Union conducted a successful strike that was joined by Mexican and Filipino celery workers. After switching its affiliation in 1937 to the Congress of Industrial Organizations (CIO), the Alaska Cannery Workers Union in the San Francisco Bay area became so integrated that all meetings were conducted in English, Spanish, Chinese, and Filipino languages (Yoneda 1971). In the early 1940s, the International Longshoremen's and Warehousemen's Union (ILWU), in the promotion of racial equality, also conducted all local meetings in English, Ilocano, and Japanese (Akamine 1993). In 1945, the head office expelled a local chapter in Stockton, California, for refusing to re-admit Japanese Americans workers after the internment. In 1946, the Japanese and Filipino workers of Hawaiian ILWU joined other workers on a seventy-nine-day multiethnic strike and triumphantly won a raise in the minimum wage, a job classification system, and a ban on discrimination based on race, political belief, or union membership. These incidences of interethnic coalition were exceptions rather than the norm, and they were based mostly on the interests of the immigrant working class.

Today, the majority class status of the community has shifted from the working to the upper middle class; however, the average family income in 1989 for some ethnic groups such as Cambodian, Laotian, and Hmong ($18,126, $23,101, and $14,327, respectively) fell far short of the U.S. average ($30,056), let alone the Asian average ($41,583). The increasing gaps in income is just one indicator of the trend towards diversification and fragmentation among the Asian American population mentioned in Chapter 2. Even limited to among the six largest Asian subgroups, the spectrum of ethnic gaps uncovered in the 1990 Census casts doubts about the viability of assembling a politically coherent community. As shown in table 5.1, the six groups that account for about 85 percent of the Asian and Pacific Islander population differ from each other in practically every aspect of population characteristics. For instance, because they were the earliest group of Asian workers to arrive in America in significant numbers and because of the continuous threat of political instability or economic hardship in separate parts of their native homeland, the Chinese American population is larger than the sum of the Asian Indian and Korean American populations, yet more than two-thirds of its members in 1990 were born outside of the United States. The Japanese American population, due mainly to the relative diplomatic strength of its native homeland in the past and economic strength in the present, as well as the traumatic internment experience during WWII, has the highest median age and percentage of U.S. citizenship and the lowest percentages of the foreign-born and naturalization. Because of the strong U.S. influence in the Philippines, the Filipino American population has the highest naturalization and English proficiency rates as well as the highest percentage of people in management among the employed. The English proficiency rate of foreign-born Asian Indians is also very high, reflecting again the influence of Western colonization on India. Asian Indians also stand out among all groups in terms of their exceptionally high educational achievement and share of professional occupations. It is the Japanese American population, however, that achieves the highest median family income and

Table 5.1   Distribution of Population Characteristics Across Major
Asian American Groups, 1990

	Chinese	Filipino	Japanese	Korean	Indian	Vietnamese
N (×1,000)	1,649	1,419	866	797	787	593
Median age	32	31	37	29	29	26
Percent citizens	61	70	76	57	50	54
Percent foreign-born	69	64	32	73	75	80
Percent naturalized	43	54	26	40	34	42
Percent recent immigrant (entered between 1980 and 1990)						
	39	32	18	41	44	49
Percent who rated English proficiency as "Not Well" or "None"						
among foreign-born	31	7	24	28	9	29
among U.S.-born	5	2	3	7	4	13
Percent of education levels (among persons 25 years old and over)						
Less than 9th grade	17	10	6	10	7	20
9th–12th grade	10	7	7	10	8	19
High school graduate	15	16	26	25	12	18
Some college	18	27	27	21	15	26
Bachelor's degree or greater	41	39	35	35	58	17
Percent in managerial/professional occupation, respectively (among employed persons 16 and older)						
	15/21	18/19	10/16	12/14	14/30	6/12
Percent unemployed	5	5	3	5	6	8
Percent families/persons below poverty level, respectively						
	11/14	5/7	3/6	15/14	6/10	24/28
Median family income, 1989 (in dollars)						
	41,316	46,698	51,550	33,909	49,309	30,550
Per capita income, 1989 (in dollars)						
	15,133	13,709	19,761	11,374	18,054	9,057

Source: U.S. Bureau of the Census (1993c). *1990 Census of Population, Asians and Pacific Islanders in the United States,* Tables 1, 3–5, and special tabulations reported in Shinagawa (1996) and Jiobu (1996).

per capita income. By contrast, because of the freshness of the refugee experience and high fertility rate, the Vietnamese population ranks the lowest in terms of the same socioeconomic indicators and median age; they are the highest in terms of the percentages of families and persons living under poverty, being foreign-born, of recent arrival, and with limited English proficiency among the U.S.-born.

The lack of historical precedents of intergroup cooperation and the presence of vast socioeconomic and demographic gaps along ethnic lines lend support to the view that Asian Americans should not be conceived of as a single, monolithic political community (Nakanishi 1991, 1998a; Tam 1995). On the other hand, a focus on the availability of and growth trend in bridging institutions such as panethnic organizations and interethnic marriages would advance the argument that Asians of diverse origins can be conceived of as belonging to one umbrella community united by common issue concerns and family ties. As noted, pan–Asian American organizations, which have been critical in forging panethnic consciousness and identity, have experienced an impressive growth rate since the early 1980s in reaction to situational needs and the desire for coalitions and empowerment. The dramatic rise of inter-Asian marriages in the share of all intermarriages involving Asians from 1980 to 1990 is revealed in an analysis of the census data in California, where the rate for Asian men grew from 21 percent to 64 percent and that for Asian women grew from 11 percent to 46 percent over the decade (Shinagawa and Pang 1996). In that state, about a quarter of the married U.S.-born Asian men and women in 1990 had a spouse that was from a different Asian ethnicity. The equivalent rate for foreign-born Asian men and women was 17 percent and 14 percent, respectively. Among the six major ethnicities, U.S.-born Korean American women had the highest interethnic marriage rate of 47 percent in 1990; whereas less than 12 percent of both Chinese-born and South Asian–born women reported being married to another Asian. Obviously, the frequency of interethnic marriages may vary according to nativity, ethnicity, gender, region, and sociological cohorts, but a similar rising trend is also observed at the national level. Shinagawa and Pang attribute this trend toward pan-Asian union in marriage patterns to the growth in size, concentration, similarity in socioeconomic class status, and acculturation of the Asian American population as well as the increase in the establishment of social and personal networks and sense of shared identity and racial consciousness in the post-1965 era.

Support for the viability of constructing a politically meaningful entity from an otherwise disparate population is found in the theory of racial formation and the process of racialization (Omi and Winant 1994). Attributed in part to the apparent commonality in selected demographic profile characteristics across major ethnic groups as defined by the U.S. government and found in recent censuses, Asians from all origins have been conveniently placed into a distinct set of social positions relative to other racial groups. One such position relates to socioeconomic status. In 1990, although not all Asian subgroups exceeded whites in socioeconomic achievement, even the least advantaged of the six major Asian ethnic groups compared favorably to the nation's other major nonwhite groups in educational achievement, family and per capita income earnings, and unemployment rate. This image of success is contrasted by two other positions of Asians introduced in previous chapters. Namely, relative to whites, Asians suffer from a deficit of political participation in electoral politics either at elite or mass level, except in Hawaii. Furthermore, because Asians have a much higher percentage of the population that is foreign-born (compared to either white or other nonwhite groups), they are portrayed as the alien component of the U.S. population that could not count on assimilation in the past, is expendable in the present, and may be seen forever as a threat to mainstream culture, identity, and national security. The first position reinforces the "model minority" image that has been associated with Asian Americans since the 1960s. While this may project an illusion of assimilation and facilitate public acceptance of Asian Americans into the mainstream, it can also encourage dismissal of the needs of the less advantaged subgroups while unnecessarily subjecting all Asians to hate crimes and other racial and ethnic violence. The latter two positions contribute to the continuing marginalization of Asians in U.S. mainstream politics—an experience reminiscent of the historical treatment of discrimination, exploitation, and exclusion common to Asian ethnic groups who entered prior to 1965 and one that is unlikely to be removed completely in the foreseeable future regardless of recent social progress and group achievement.

The coexistence of profound internal diversity among Asian Americans and the possibility of unity due to cross-ethnic union and racialization highlights the *contingent* nature of the Asian American identity, which does not exist as a fixed concept but is meaningful only in relation to other social phenomena and the larger political context. Depending on the frame of reference, the population may be paradoxically characterized both as a prototype of immigrant success and as a staple of minority failure to achieve incorporation. The incongruence in racial positions of Asians being at once superachievers in the socioeconomic sphere, underachievers in political participation, and perpetual outsiders to the mainstream culture illustrates the *ambivalent* nature of being Asian in U.S. racial order and politics. These two dynamic features of the Asian American identity can present both opportunities and challenges to the construction of political unity and a pan-Asian bloc vote. On the one hand, they suggest that panethnic solidarity and mobilization can be manufactured and maintained by the interaction of voluntary forces such as the selection of marriage partners and organizations with which to affiliate and involuntary forces such as societal stereotyping and government categorization. On the other hand, individuals with diverse backgrounds may reach different political preferences based on their own experiences, interests, and evaluations of the importance of the pan-Asian community and undercut, in turn, the likelihood of pan-Asian solidarity and empowerment. If the former is a centripetal force and the latter is a centrifugal force in panethnic organizing, then both may be toppled over by situational forces such as the emergence of strong ethnic organization and leadership, and major shifts in social and political trends. Braving the confluence of these contending forces, how much do individual Asians of various ethnic origins differ in terms of immigrant adaptation experiences and specific community concerns, sense of identity with the pan-Asian community, political and social participation likelihood, and political partisanship and vote choices in the 1990s? These indicators of political behavior, informed by author's past research on the subject (Lien 1997b, 1998a, 1999, 2000), are analyzed in the order presented to facilitate a more systematic and empirical evaluation of the bloc vote potential of Asians. Because of serious data issues involved in the studying of Asians through survey research, readers are advised to consult the Appendix carefully so as to avoid making fallacious or premature conclusions from the findings reported below.

COMPARING ETHNIC VARIATIONS AMONG ADULT ASIANS IN IMMIGRANT ADAPTATION

The adaptation experiences of Asian immigrants in becoming American—their assessment of life in the United States, the treatment they receive as members of a nonwhite minority, their attachment to the homeland culture, and their concerns about the status of their own ethnic community—are reported in table 5.2 for four ethnic groups in Southern

TABLE 5.2   Percentage Distributions of Adaptation Experiences and Community Concerns Among Four Asian Communities in Southern California[a]

	Chinese	Filipino	Korean	Vietnamese
Base *N*	773	750	749	861
Interview dates	May 1997	December 1995	February–March 1992	April–May 1994
Percent of interviews in primary language	55	46	91	89
Percent foreign-born	86	84	98	98
Main reason for immigration (among the foreign-born)				
family reunion	38	47	51	26
education	25	3	21	7
job/business opportunities	15	42	16	8
political freedom	12	3	2	54
Satisfaction with community of residence in the United States				
entirely/mostly	64	69	57	69
somewhat	24	18	16	15
U.S. life compared to expectation (among the foreign-born)				
better	41	66	41	57
as expected	37	27	30	24
Personal experience of discrimination				
great deal/fair amount	10	10	10	9
some, not much	47	36	33	31
not at all	41	53	51	58
Sources of discrimination (among those who experienced discrimination)[b]				
job/promotion	30	56	20	39
business transactions	27	18	16	12
government	11	8	10	7
school	9	12	13	17
neighborhood	7	16	N.A.	17
strangers	28	36	27	26
language/cultural differences	22	13	3	19
Importance of ethnic enclave[c]				
highly or fairly important	41	N.A.	75	78
not or fairly not important	56	N.A.	15	20
Use of ethnic language at least half of the time				
at home	79	60	88	86
among children at home	55	N.A.	67	74
in business transactions	29	N.A.	51	61
media consumption	N.A.	22	76	62
Most important problem facing the ethnic community in Southern California today (accept up to two responses)				
crime/street violence	16	7	37	25
gangs	6	17	7	35
race relations	11	5	18	2
poor schools	6	1	4	3
inadequate job opportunity	3	5	1	6
unemployment	3	7	6	13

Table 5.2 *continued*

	Chinese	Filipino	Korean	Vietnamese
recession	2	2	38	5
losing culture	3	10	*	2
lack of community spirit	4	13	*	2
no problem	8	7	1	13
Primary reasons holding back own ethnic group in Southern California				
none	33	N.A.	3	12
language barrier	20	N.A.	48	34
racism/prejudice	12	N.A.	19	6
cultural difference	10	N.A.	17	12
lack of interest	6	N.A.	7	5
not sure	13	N.A.	3	11

Source: Los Angeles Times Poll #396, #370, #267, and #331. Original data were collected in Southern California and released to the author through the Roper Center for Public Opinion Research.

Note:* indicates less than 1 percent. N.A. = "not available."

aThe Korean survey only interviewed residents of Los Angeles County.

bEntries for each category are the sum of mentions from three prompts as a percentage of eligible respondents.

cFor Chinese, this is Chinatown in Los Angeles; for Koreans, Koreatown in Los Angeles; for Vietnamese, Little Saigon in the Westminster/Garden Grove section of Orange County.

California. The percentage of foreign-born ranges from 84 percent among Filipinos to 98 percent for Koreans and the Vietnamese. While respondents in three of the four groups named family reunion as the primary reason for coming to America, a greater percentage of Koreans than other groups immigrated mainly for that reason. Seeking an education was the second main reason for Chinese and Koreans, but for Filipinos, it was the opportunity to find work and run businesses. For the Vietnamese, the most important reason for immigration was political—to be free from political persecution. Regardless of the main reason for immigration, the majority of respondents in each ethnic group were very satisfied with the community in which they lived and found their life in the United States as good as, if not better than, expected. This is particularly true for Filipinos. Only one-tenth of the respondents in each group reported experiencing more than a small amount of discrimination. Although close to half of the Chinese respondents reported having experienced some, but not much, discrimination, the majority of Filipino, Korean, and Vietnamese respondents did not report any personal encounter with discrimination at all. Among those who encountered at least some discrimination, the top two sources for each group were either related to hiring and promotion or from strangers; Filipinos reported a significantly higher amount of job-related discrimination than other groups. Reflecting their recent immigration background, both the Koreans and Vietnamese highly appreciated the existence of ethnic enclaves and maintained closer contacts with their ethnic cultures than the Chinese or Filipinos through the use of their native language at home and in business settings and the ethnic media.

The high satisfaction level of life in America for these immigrants may shape their issue priorities. When queried about the most important problems facing their own ethnic community, the respondents in each group all suggested problems relating to the maintenance of social order such as crimes, street violence, and gangs. However, there were certain issues that were considered more salient for some groups than for others. Such issues were gangs and crime for the Vietnamese, economy and race relations for Koreans, ethnic group identity for Filipinos, and quality of education for the Chinese. Asked to name the primary reasons holding back their own ethnic group, Chinese, Korean, and Vietnamese respondents all considered the language barrier as the greatest obstacle to group success, followed by racism for Chinese and Koreans, and cultural differences for the Vietnamese. The most frequent response for Chinese and second most frequent response for Vietnamese respondents, however, was that the groups were not held back by anything at all.

In a nutshell, despite considerable interethnic differences, communities of Asians in Southern California still share much in the immigrant adaptation experience. Although the majority of members in each ethnic community arrived for different reasons and did not share the same level of attachment to ethnic culture or concern about the barriers in language and culture, they concurred on a highly positive evaluation of life in America as well as the prime importance of keeping their ethnic community free of crime- and gang-related problems. Unlike the experience of their predecessors, who faced blatant racism and discrimination during the era of exclusion, Asian immigrants in the 1990s reported very little incidence of personal discrimination, and when it occurred, it was more from employers and strangers than from government, schools, or neighbors.

ETHNICITY AND SENSE OF COMMON IDENTITY AMONG ASIANS

If perceived racism and discrimination is a prerequisite for group consciousness and political action (as studies of American Blacks have suggested) the findings on Asians reveal that only a very small portion of the population in each ethnic community may be mobilized on such grounds. However, the lack of perceived discrimination against the self does not necessarily mean that Asians do not have a sense of shared identity or common fate with each other. When confronted with the question on panethnic concerns, only a minority of Asian respondents in the LASUI study reported no such concerns (see table 5.3). The majority of respondents in each ethnic group agreed that whatever happened to the Asian American community at large would somehow affect one's own life; but the percentage of those who believed that it should matter a great deal varied widely across groups. It ranged from 24 percent among Koreans to 5 percent among the Japanese. The Korean Americans' experience in the wake of the Los Angeles riots may explain the greater sense of common identity expressed by respondents in this ethnic community.

How much is ethnicity a factor in structuring panethnic concerns among Asians? Differences in the ability of Asians of diverse ethnic

TABLE 5.3 Percentage Distribution of Panethnic Concerns Among Asian Americans

	Chinese	Japanese	Korean	Southeast Asian	Other	Total
Do you think what happens generally to Asian people in this country will have something to do with what happens in one's life? If yes, will it affect lot, some, or not very much? (% who agreed or disagreed)						
Yes	72	71	87	66	80	77
a lot	12	5	24	9	15	15
some	50	39	58	49	51	52
not much	10	26	5	8	14	10
No	28	30	13	34	20	23
N	410	94	357	86	86	1,033

Source: LASUI, 1993–94 (adults 21 and over in Los Angeles County).

backgrounds to think together as a community may reflect not only the influence of ethnic culture but also individual differences in socioeconomic status, demographic background, and the multidimensional experiences of immigrant adaptation. To estimate the significance of ethnicity among Asians, these individual differences are controlled in an ordinary least squares–based regression analysis with the dependent variable being a four-point scale of panethnic concerns. When only the ethnicity of each respondent is entered into the equation, Koreans are found to be more likely and Japanese less likely to possess a sense of common identity than those U.S.-born Asians who reside in English-only households. If differences in demographic background (nativity, age, gender, marital status, and length of residence in the community), socioeconomic status (education and homeownership[2]), and adaptation stages (English fluency, participation in organizations and groups, status of voter registration) are controlled for among the sample of Asian respondents, the result shows that, compared to other Asians in the survey, being Japanese conveys a weaker sense of identity toward other Asians in the nation, but being Korean is no longer different in this opinion. Regardless of ethnic origin, having registered to vote or participated in organizational or group-based meetings, in addition to being married and younger in age, may increase one's sense of concern about other Asians; being male or foreign-born may also have similar effect, but the significance level for each is borderline. However, having more years of education, living for a longer time in the Los Angeles area, being more fluent in English, or owning a home did not seem to impact the shaping of panethnic consciousness among Asians. Together, the multiple regression analysis suggests that, other conditions being equal, ethnicity may disappear as a barrier to the structuring of a pan-Asian identity for most but not all ethnic groups. For adult Asian residents in the Los Angeles County, those born in Japan or who speak Japanese at home may be less likely to express similar political concerns and participate in cross-ethnic coalitions with other Asians because of the distinct community history, structure, and politics of Japanese Americans.

ASSESSING ETHNIC GAPS IN POLITICAL AND SOCIAL PARTICIPATION

The scope of ethnic gaps in political and social participation among Asians is assessed with both national data on voting participation within the first two immigration generations and regional data on participation in organizations and groups. As shown in table 5.4, the rates of U.S. citizenship ranged from a low of 42 percent for the Vietnamese in 1994 and Asian Indians in 1996 to a high of 68 percent for Filipinos in 1996. Compared to other groups, Filipinos consistently achieved the highest citizenship rate in the elections studied and Asian Indians scored the lowest in two out of three elections. Among citizens who registered to vote, the Japanese scored the highest rate in both 1994 and 1998 elections and the Vietnamese scored the lowest rate in all three elections. Regarding the turnout rates among the registered, the Japanese again scored the highest and Koreans scored the lowest in all three elections. Despite the wide variation in participation rates across ethnicities, the voting registration and turnout rates among U.S. adults and

TABLE 5.4   Percentage Distribution of Voting and Registration, 1994–1998, Among Asian Americans

	Chinese	Filipino	Japanese	Korean	Indian	Vietnamese
November 1994 Election						
Citizens (%)	50	65	54	43	43	42
Registered (%)	23(46)	34(52)	40(73)	20(45)	24(56)	17(40)
Voted (%)	16(32)	25(39)	36(65)	12(27)	19(45)	13(31)
among registered	70	75	88	59	81	79
Weighted N (×1,000)	1,017	873	398	293	472	470
November 1996 Election						
Citizens (%)	53	68	54	47	42	59
Registered (%)	30(56)	44(64)	30(55)	25(53)	27(64)	30(49)
Voted (%)	23(43)	35(52)	26(48)	17(36)	22(52)	26(45)
among registered	76	81	88	68	79	89
Weighted N (×1,000)	1,287	1,231	424	574	614	659
November 1998 Election						
Citizens (%)	50	64	64	52	44	61
Registered (%)	23(47)	34(53)	37(57)	20(39)	25(57)	18(30)
Voted (%)	15(31)	22(34)	28(44)	9(17)	15(34)	9(15)
among registered	65	64	77	43	59	51
Weighted N (×1,000)	1,458	1,450	477	605	654	714

Source: See table 3.3.

Note: All populations are age 18 and over. Only adults who are of the first or second generation, which covers 88 percent of Asians surveyed in 1994 and 1998 and 90 percent in 1996, are included. Entries in parentheses are rates among citizens.

citizens were uniformly lower for Asian subgroups than for their non-Hispanic white counterparts reported in table 3.3. The only exception was the rates for citizens of Japanese ancestry in 1994, which were not repeated in the next two elections. However, once adult citizens of Asian ancestry were able to cross the hurdle of the voting registration requirement, the Chinese and Koreans consistently had lower turnout rates than whites; the Japanese were the only Asian group that achieved higher turnout rates than whites in all three elections.

The significance of ethnicity in political participation among Asians can be further clarified with multivariate regression procedures controlling for one's socioeconomic status (income, education), demographic background (gender, age, nativity), social connectedness (marital status, length of residence, employment status, union membership), and political context (midterm or presidential election year, residence in Hawaii or in California). With dichotomous dependent variables such as voting registration and turnout, logistic regression results from analyzing merged datasets of elections between 1994 and 1998 show that, when only dummy variables representing ethnicity are in the equation, U.S. citizens of Japanese, Asian Indian, and Filipino ancestry are more likely, whereas those of Vietnamese ancestry are less likely, to become registered. Among the registered, being Japanese or Filipino may be associated with greater turnout, but being Korean may signify less turnout. When control variables are added to the equation, they help explain away a lot, but not all, of the ethnic gaps in participation.[3] Specifically, other conditions being equal, only citizens of Chinese ancestry are estimated to register at lower rates and only registered Asians who are of Korean origin are expected to have lower turnout rates than other Asians. Registration among Asian American citizens is more likely to occur among those who are older, better educated, have higher family income, live longer in the same residence, or belong to labor unions. Their registration rates can be negatively influenced by foreign birth and midterm elections but not by gender, marital status, or residence in Hawaii or California. The probability of registered Asians to vote can be increased by being older, better educated, married, more stable in residency, and living in Hawaii or California. It is not influenced, however, by one's income, gender, nativity, or union membership status.

The degree of ethnic differences in group-based participation is gauged with a list of seven questions asked in the LASUI of respondents' participation in one or more of the meetings of each organization of which they were a member in the previous twelve months. The types of membership organization queried include neighborhood or tenant's groups or block associations, PTA or school-related groups, social clubs or sports teams, political organizations, church-related groups, ethnic or cultural organizations, and business or professional organizations. As shown in table 5.5, the Japanese reported a higher level of participation than any other Asian ethnic group in all but church-related activity, which Koreans appeared to dominate. Nevertheless, those Asians who were born in the United States and resided in English-only households scored the highest level in five out of seven items asking about group-based participation. By contrast, Southeast Asians reported the lowest level of activism in every type of organization or group queried. Compared to whites, Asian participation was low in all types of organizations except ethnic and cultural ones. Yet, the highly acculturated Asians participated either on par with or higher than whites in social clubs/sports teams, ethnic/cultural groups, and business/professional organizations.

A multivariate regression procedure similar to the one used to estimate voting participation is applied to specify the unique role of ethnicity in shaping an Asian adult respondent's likelihood of participating in American social institutions. The dependent variable is an additive index based on the seven questions on group participation (adjusted $\infty=0.67$). The control variables include demographic background (nativ-

TABLE 5.5   Percentage Distribution of Group-based Participation Among Asian Americans

	Chinese	Japanese	Korean	SE Asian	Other Asian	White
Church	25	19	32	5	23	25	36
PTA	16	17	14	9	21	15	23
Business/Professional	14	18	9	2	29	13	29
Clubs/Sports	8	21	10	4	43	13	31
Ethnic/Cultural	12	18	6	2	17	10	10
Neighborhood	7	7	3	0	9	5	21
Political	2	4	2	1	8	3	10
N	416	97	357	86	87	1,043	835

Source: LASUI, 1993–94.

ity, age, gender, marital status, and length of residence in the community), socioeconomic status (education and homeownership), and social and political adaptation (English-language fluency, frequency of attending religious services, political ideological strength, and status of voter registration). For this continuous dependent variable, OLS regression results show that, when only ethnic origin, but not control variables, were entered in the equation, being either Chinese, Japanese, Korean or Southeast Asian may decrease one's propensity to participate in social group events more than being an acculturated Asian of any origin does. However, with the addition of control variables, only Korean and Southeast Asian respondents may be associated with a lower propensity to participate.[4] Among the sociodemographic variables, only education has an impact on participation. In contrast, indicators of greater social and political adaptation, such as more frequent attendance of religious services, registering to vote, and holding stronger American political views may significantly increase one's likelihood to participate in group-based social activities.

CROSS-ETHNIC PATTERNS AMONG VOTERS AND REGISTERED VOTERS IN PARTISANSHIP AND VOTE CHOICE

Of the many aspects of Asian American politics, the partisan orientation of Asian American voters is an element that has generated the most interest and some answers. Despite the methodological constraints discussed above, many have concluded that the partisan loyalty of Asians is evenly divided between the Democratic and Republican Parties and that about a third are not affiliated with either party. Some support for this statement can be found in table 5.6, which lists the partisanship distribution by ethnicity from two Southern California surveys and six community exit polls conducted in three regions. However, the majority of evidence seems to suggest that there is no one clear pattern across the board. The lack of consistency can be attributed to methodological differences such as the involvement of different parameters of voters, study location, time frame, and ethnic makeup. Regardless, as a rapidly growing immigrant community, the political partisanship of Asians who vote and Asians who are registered to vote appears to be strongly influenced by local culture. Although analysis of a 1984 California survey shows that Asians may identify more with the Republican Party

TABLE 5.6 Percentage Distributions of Political Partisanship Among Asian Americans

	Chinese	Filipino	Japanese	Korean	Vietnamese[a]	South Asian[b]	Total
LATP, 1992–97 (registered to vote in Southern California)							
Democrat/Republican/Other	30/33/37	40/38/22	N.A.	44/47/9	24/61/14	N.A.	N.A.
N	378	375	N.A.	134	250	N.A.	N.A.
LASUI, 1993–94 (registered to vote in Los Angeles County)							
Democrat/Republican/Other	15/33/52	N.A.	43/24/33c	11/35/54	13/8/79c	42/35/23	22/31/47
N	125	N.A.	21	65	24	69	304
APALC, 1998 (voters in Southern California)							
Democrat/Republican/Other	38/38/23	49/35/16	57/36/7	57/30/9	25/41/24	N.A.	42/34/23
N	516	525	321	303	294	N.A.	2,100
ALC, 1996 (voters in San Francisco Bay Area)							
Democrat/Republican/Other	59/28/14	66/31/3	94/6/0	85/12/13	43/36/21	N.A.	62/26/12
N	N.A.	N.A.	N.A.	N.A.	N.A.	N.A.	550
ALC, 1994 (voters in San Francisco Bay Area)							
Democrat/Republican/Other	61/23/16	60/22/18	68/16/16	71/5/24c	42/48/10	N.A.	62/22/16
N	288	441	38	24	35	N.A.	893
AALDEF, 1996 (voters in New York City)							
Democrat/Republican/Other	48/20/32	N.A.	N.A.	64/19/18	N.A.	74/11/16	54/20/27
N (approximately)	2,056	N.A.	N.A.	457	N.A.	490	3,264
AALDEF, 1994 (voters in New York City)							
Democrat/Republican/Other	40/24/35	37/37/27	N.A.	53/20/27	N.A.	56/21/22	43/24/33
N	881	38	N.A.	71	N.A.	109	1,105
AALDEF, 1993 (voters in New York City)							
Democrat/Republican/No	38/23/30	24/38/26	N.A.	30/36/24	N.A.	62/16/13	N.A.
N (approximately)	1,206	82	N.A.	114	N.A.	189	1,630

Source: Assorted. See Appendix for the full name of each acronym.

Note: N.A. = "not available."

[a] For LASUI data, this column refers to those from Vietnam, Cambodia (Kampuchea), Burma, Thailand, Malaysia, or Indonesia, or those residing in households that use some language from these countries.

[b] This refers to South Asians or those who can trace their ancestral origin to India, Bangladesh, and Pakistan. For LASUI data, this column stands for "Others" or Asians who are born in the United States and reside in English-only households.

[c] Percentage breakdown for N ≤ 25 is provided only for reference purposes.

because of foreign policy concerns (Cain, Kiewiet, and Uhlaner 1991), the partisanship of Asians may be influenced as well by political trends such as the partisan affiliation of a sitting president and perceived effects of actions taken by the majority party in Congress regarding the interests of immigrant and minority communities. The occupancy of the White House by a Democratic president from 1992 to 2000 and the switch to a Republican-controlled Congress after the 1994 elections—which then passed welfare reforms to cut immigrant and minority benefits—may push some Asians out of the Republican Party and into the Democratic Party.

Three partisan patterns are apparent in this analysis. First, certain regions may have a more homogenous political outlook than others. Of the three regions, Bay Area voters are much more liberal, with each ethnic group having a Democratic majority except the Vietnamese. Second, the dominant partisan identity of an ethnic group may vary from one region to another. For example, the Chinese voters in the Los Angeles area were more Republican than their counterparts in San Francisco or New York City, but Filipino voters were not. Third, a trend of conversion toward the Democratic Party in recent years may have taken place in certain communities. This trend is most prominent among Korean voters during and after the 1994 elections. A similar shift towards more Democratic identification can also be observed among Chinese and Filipino voters, but Chinese voters in areas outside of the Bay Area may still identify more with the Republican Party.

Still, a significant proportion of Asian voters were not affiliated with either of the major parties in the 1990s. Again, the degree of nonpartisanship varied by region and ethnicity. It was much lower for every group in the Bay Area than in other regions, because of the strong Democratic identity in the region. In the New York area, the degree was smallest for South Asian voters and largest for Chinese voters. In Southern California, the 1998 APALC survey found single digit nonpartisanship rates for Japanese and Korean voters. As much as 50 percent of Chinese and Korean registered voters in the LASUI data, though, did not report any partisan affiliation in 1993–94.

If the disparate outlook of political party identity gives little hope for the construction of a pan-Asian vote, an assessment of votes cast for candidates and ballot initiatives appears to offer a much brighter prospect (see table 5.7). In elections held between 1994 and 1998 in Southern Cal-

TABLE 5.7 Percentage Distributions of Vote Choice Among Asian-American Groups

	Chinese	Filipino	Japanese	Korean	Vietnamese	South Asian	Total
Candidate Choice							
APALC, 1998 (voters in Southern California) between Davis (D) and Lungren (R) for Governor							
Democrat/Republican	61/37	60/39	66/31	72/27	63/36	N.A.	64/35
N	516	525	321	303	294	N.A.	2,100
APALC, 1996 (voters in Southern California) between Clinton (D) and Dole (R) for President							
Democrat/Republican	66/30	52/43	56/28	59/31	44/50	N.A.	54/41
N	N.A.	N.A.	N.A.	N.A.	N.A.	N.A.	900
ALC, 1996 (voters in San Francisco Bay Area) between Clinton (D) and Dole (R) for President							
Democrat/Republican	76/21	71/29	79/5	88/0	53/40	N.A.	75/20
N	N.A.	N.A.	N.A.	N.A.	N.A.	N.A.	550
ALC, 1994 (voters in San Francisco Bay Area) between K. Brown (D) and Wilson (R) for Governor							
Democrat/Republican	60/40	68/29	82/18	62/21	38/62	N.A.	66/32
——, between Feinstein (D) and Huffington (R) for U.S. Senator							
Democrat/Republican	74/23	69/29	92/8	71/9[a]	68/32	N.A.	73/23
N	288	441	38	24	35	N.A.	893
AALDEF, 1998 (voters in New York City) between Schumer (D) and D'Amato (R) for U.S. Senator							
Democrat/Republican	67/33	N.A.	N.A.	69/31	80/20	69/31	66/32
N (approximately)	945	N.A.	N.A.	210	N.A.	270	1,500
AALDEF, 1994 (voters in New York City) between Cuomo (D) and Pataki (R) for Governor							
Democrat/Republican	45/53	36/61	N.A.	55/45	N.A.	66/33	47/51

(continued)

Table 5.7 *continued*

	Chinese	Filipino	Japanese	Korean	Vietnamese	South Asian	Total
——, between Dinkins (D) and Giuliani (R) for Mayor, 1993							
Democrat/Republican	22/77	10/81	N.A.	29/71	N.A.	46/51	24/74
N	881	38	N.A.	71	N.A.	109	1,105

Ballot Initiative Opinion

Proposition 209 (bans affirmative action), % against

	Chinese	Filipino	Japanese	Korean	Vietnamese	South Asian	Total
APALC, 1996	72	71	73	85	79	N.A.	76
ALC, 1996	80	79	89	100	67	N.A.	80

Proposition 210 (raises minimum wage), % for

	Chinese	Filipino	Japanese	Korean	Vietnamese	South Asian	Total
APALC, 1996	65	70	54	67	71	N.A.	66
ALC, 1996	65	62	83	83	60	N.A.	67

Proposition 187 (bans benefits to illegal immigrants), % against

	Chinese	Filipino	Japanese	Korean	Vietnamese	South Asian	Total
ALC, 1994	73	69	91	88	61	N.A.	79

Source: See table 5.6.

Note: N.A. = "not available."

[a]Percentage breakdown for N ≤ 25 is provided only for reference purposes.

ifornia and the San Francisco Bay Area and the 1998 election in the New York area, each ethnic group gave a majority vote to the Democratic candidates for the top federal and state offices. The only exception was the Vietnamese vote for U.S. president in Southern California in 1996 and for California governor in the Bay Area in 1994. In the New York gubernatorial contest of 1994, only South Asian and Korean voters cast a majority vote for the Democratic incumbent Mario Cuomo. These two groups of voters, however, had banded together with other Asian groups to vote Republican in the mayoral election held the previous year and sent Rudolph Giuliani to victory in 1993.

The political preferences of Asian American voters bear a most homogeneous outlook when examined in terms of the ballot initiative opinion in California in the elections of 1994 and 1996 (see bottom half of table 5.7). A large majority of voters across ethnic groups were unanimously against Proposition 209 (the banning of government-initiated affirmative action programs), in particular Korean voters. The majority of Asian voters of all ethnic backgrounds also supported Proposition 210 (the raising of the minimum wage) in 1996, in particular Filipino and Vietnamese voters in Southern California and Korean and Japanese voters in the San Francisco Bay Area. They sent a strong signal of opposition to Proposition 187 (the denial of education, welfare, and medical services to undocumented immigrants), and voters of Japanese and Korean origin particularly opposed it. In each ethnic group, the percentage of those holding the liberal position was higher in the Bay Area except for that of the Vietnamese vote and the Filipino and Chinese vote on Proposition 210. The coexistence of disparate partisanship and much more coherent and liberal vote choice among Asian voters suggests that many were willing to cross the party line and yield support for the candidates and issue positions favored by leading panethnic civil rights organizations.

Given the high incidence of noncitizenship and the low rate of voting in nearly all ethnic groups, the opinion of Asians expressed through the ballot box may reflect only a fraction of the community opinion. Voters' opinions can be influenced by the campaign context (e.g., mobilization of interest organizations, framing of issues, candidate quality, party competitiveness, emergence of tie-breaking political events) and may not necessarily represent the opinion of the community at large where numerous others are in the process of becoming naturalized Americans.

In the surveys of the four Asian communities in Southern California, 84 percent of Chinese, 81 percent of Vietnamese, 67 percent of Filipino, and 42 percent of Korean respondents who were noncitizens at the time of interview expected to become U.S. citizens in the next few years. Results of chi-square tests of difference in opinions between citizens and noncitizens within each of the communities reveal that, in all four groups, citizens are more likely than noncitizens to report personally experiencing discrimination and having close friends that are of other races. Both Filipino and Korean American citizens are more likely than their noncitizen counterparts to report high levels of satisfaction with their community of residence, whereas no significant difference exists among Chinese and Vietnamese respondents. Only Chinese and Filipinos were asked of their ideological orientation. In both communities, the percentage of noncitizens reporting uncertainty or inattention is more than double the percentage among citizens. A higher proportion of Chinese American citizens (25 percent) self-identify as being somewhat more conservative than their noncitizen counterparts (12 percent). In contrast, a greater percentage of Filipino American citizens (22 percent) self-identify as being somewhat more liberal than their noncitizen counterparts (13 percent). The LASUI survey also reveals a similar tilt toward conservatism among Chinese American citizens, although U.S. citizens of Japanese descent appear to be more moderate and those of Korean descent appear to be slightly more liberal than their noncitizen counterparts.

CONCLUSION: TIES THAT MAY BIND

Today's Asian American community is arguably the most heterogeneous nonwhite community in the United States. It is a community that consists of individuals who not only differ in history and origin but vary greatly in sociodemographic background. Attributed mostly to past discrimination in U.S. labor migration and immigration policies as well as to variations in homeland political and economic conditions, this internal diversity can present an enormous challenge to community organizing and achieving political empowerment. However, compared to other U.S. racial groups, Asians collectively bear certain paradoxical group positions that cannot be fully substantiated by census statistics for each of the subgroups. Depending on the racial group and sociopolitical domain in reference, Asians can be characterized simultaneously as superachievers, underachievers, and strange outsiders. This contingent and ambivalent racial group status of Asians in America can be a barrier to the structuring of political consensus across communities when each Asian may make a different political choice based on his or her assessment of the group status and importance of community. On the other hand, the process of racialization can also be instrumental to the forging of panethnic unity when it is able to influence an individual Asian's decision to marry or associate with other Asians (which is occurring more frequently) through pan-Asian unions and organizations.

Given the confluence of these forces, what social and political ties are there to bind together Asian Americans of diverse origins? Focusing on ethnic origin as the unit of analysis and, after a perusal of extant data sources, this study finds that, with few exceptions, Asian voters in the three major metropolitan areas of Los Angeles, San Francisco, and New York in the 1990s often supported the Democratic candidates and liberal issue positions. This consistency is remarkable considering that the political partisanship among those who voted or registered to vote across Asian subgroups was rather disparate, indefinite, and sometimes rare. Asian voters not only differ in the same political party affiliation across ethnicities, but the contours within each ethnic group may vary by region and political context. And yet, once mobilized, communities of Asians have shown an ability to forge a common sense of identity and vote in a bloc. Analysis of the opinion of voting-age Asians in Southern California also reveals a cross-ethnic consensus on the positive assessment of the adaptation experience and common concern for maintaining the order of the community, regardless of immigration motives and levels of acculturation and ethnic attachment.

When respondents in Los Angeles were asked about their degree of concern for Asians elsewhere, the majority in each ethnic group expressed a high degree of concern for other Asians. Nevertheless, the Japanese were found to show a weaker sense of concern when individual differences in sociodemographic background and immigrant adaptation stages are controlled. This finding of the Japanese distinction is not repeated when their levels of social and political participation is the subject of analysis. Although the Japanese in Los Angeles participate in organizations and groups at a higher overall level in percentage terms than any other Asian ethnic group and they report the highest percentages in registration among citizens and turnout among the registered in national elections between 1994 and 1998, the significance of Japanese ethnicity disappears in multivariate regression results. Instead, when other conditions are equal, persons with Korean ties are found to have lower propensity to turn out to vote and participate in group-based activities. Persons of South Asian origin are also less likely to join groups or organizations, but the study estimates that it is American citizens of Chinese ancestry who are least likely to become registered. Apparently, the role of ethnicity in political attitudes and behavior among Asians is not consistent across groups or domains of investigation.

Still, based on the observations reported above, it seems that although ethnic differences are often deep and cannot be neglected, it may be quite feasible to imagine the construction of a panethnic vote if given proper mobilization and context. It appears that the anti-immigrant and -minority sentiment in the latter half of the 1990s provided community organizational elites who were central to the renaissance of the Asian American movement with a context to structure the vote toward the Democratic Party candidates and liberal agendas. Yet, the answer to the prospect of political unity among Asian Americans is not transparently self-evident. For one, the nature of a bloc vote for Asians, like the nature of their racial status and identity, should be considered as situationally defined and politically constructed. There are possibilities but no certainties. The possibilities may be enhanced with the presence of responsible leadership within and outside the government framework as well as panethnic-minded, community-based institutions and groups. The general lack of such political infrastructure among Asian Americans nationwide may present formidable challenges to mobilization beyond ethnic boundaries. Second, if the immigrant opinion in Southern California is any guide, there may be an inherent contradiction between the assimilationist, socially conservative orientation of the immigrant population and the majority liberal orientation of the U.S.-born community organizational elites, as discussed in Chapter 2. The challenge of bridging this opinion gap to create political organizing may become increasingly more difficult because of the rise of transnational issues. Third, the finding of common ties reported here can only be tentative because of the multitude of methodological issues associated with surveying Asian American political opinions. Because of the foreign-born and urban characteristics of the majority of the respondents in these surveys, the results may underestimate the ethnic differences in behavior and opinions for Asians who live elsewhere. The degree of bias because of this may not be known until the availability of better survey data.

Finally, even if a pan-Asian political unity can be reasonably expected within a certain context, this may not automatically translate into a political asset. Although the intent of this chapter is to assess the bloc vote potential of Asians, it is perhaps worth noting that the greater threat to the prospect of political empowerment for Asian Americans today is not divided participation but nonparticipation. Until more community resources are invested in helping eligible Asians gain citizenship, register to vote, and get out to vote, there may be little interest for the powers that be to heed the contributions and needs of the growing population. Furthermore, although bloc voting is desirable, the lack of it is not necessarily a barricade in the road to empowerment. Given the tiny voter base and the diversity within the population, an alternative strategy to demanding single-party affiliation of the pan-Asian population is to encourage bipartisan accountability to the various concerns of the multiethnic community. While unity may be the goal of political elites who desire to access power, diversity in the mass should be considered a strength as well when making bargains and forming coalitions. The following chapter discusses the degree of ease for Asian American women to form class- and gender-based coalitions with Asian men and other groups of men and women.

6 Linking Race, Ethnicity, Class, and Gender

Asian American Women and Political Participation

"Women have long known themselves to be at the center."
—Gary Okihiro (1994, 92)

A STUDY of Asian Americans and political participation cannot be complete without addressing the role of women as well as the issue of gender and its intersectionality with race, ethnicity, and class. Immigrant and U.S.-born Asian women have been indispensable to the building of communities in America through their hard work both inside and outside the home. Yet, they have been mostly invisible in the history, literature, and sciences of their adopted land. A marginalized population within a historically marginalized minority community, Asian women have never been a serious factor in studies about American politics. The voices of Asian women have been muted for a number of reasons, the first being that few women accompanied the early Asian immigrant groups. This was largely because of restrictive homeland cultures that discouraged women from participating in activities outside of the home and because the American demand was for male workers. When women did arrive in the United States, they were denied, as were their male counterparts before them, the freedoms of interracial marriage and property rights as well as equal access to schools, professions, courts, voting booths, and other sociopolitical institutions. Even after stepping outside the home, many women were forced to work behind the scenes as clerks in backroom offices, where they were less likely to be noticed and promoted to more prominent positions. Within the Asian American community itself, until recent decades women were often denied regard or personal freedoms by their male counterparts. Finally, until quite recently, the tendency within the discipline of Asian American Studies has been to celebrate the history of working-class men while overlooking the constitutive role that women played in preserving and transmitting Asian cultures

(Okihiro 1994) and enabling social class mobility and economic success (Yanagisako 1995).

In spite of common social borders that may bond Asian women to their male counterparts, as well as to women of other racial and ethnic groups, Asian women have often been alone in their journeys, battling against the intersection of racial, sexual, cultural, and class oppression. Like Asian men in America, Asian women historically have been forced to confront a system permeated with pervasive and covert forms of racism, sexism, and colonization that limited their opportunities for social, economic, and political participation (Cheng and Bonacich 1984; Mazumdar 1989; Lowe 1996; Espiritu 1997). Additionally, Asian women are challenged by the patriarchal attitudes that have been pervasive in societies of both East and West. Furthermore, Asian women may have had special socialization disadvantages in the United States because most of them originated from cultures in which the proper roles and opportunities for women were especially restricted (Chow 1987). Chinese-, Japanese-, and Korean-born women, for instance, confronted gender and generational hierarchies within their own households (Hune 2000). The interactive effect of racism and patriarchy in a competitive capitalist economy has often relegated women of color, including Asians, to lower class status through exploitation, segregation, and subordination (Glenn 1985). Yet, for a socioeconomically disadvantaged new American group such as the Vietnamese, both men and women need to work so as to put rice on the table. This may simultaneously undermine the traditional form of patriarchy, because of men's declining economic power, and provide the circumstances for women to achieve gender equality because of their assumption of greater economic responsibilities and decision-making power in family and community affairs (Kibria 1990).

The following sections describe the multifaceted transformations of Asian American women from images of prostitutes, picture brides, housemaids, and war brides to professionals, corporate managers, and elected officials. From Afong Moy to Representative Patsy Mink, Asian women have not only persevered, but become indispensable partners in uplifting the socioeconomic and political status of the community in America. This chapter poses two empirical questions relating to women of color: How well are they able to participate as equal individuals to their male counterparts both inside and outside of the Asian American community?, and How different are their voices from those of Asian men and the men and women of other racial and ethnic groups?

EXCLUSION AND IMMIGRATION OF EARLY ASIAN AMERICAN WOMEN

In the early years of Asian immigration, there were far fewer women than men in the immigrant population. Highly skewed gender ratios were reported in census reports and other writings for each Asian group (Cordova 1983; Chan 1991a, 1991b; Hing 1993; Okihiro 1994; Yung 1995). In 1890, for instance, there were twenty-seven men for every woman of Chinese origin in the United States. Before the Japanese government intervened through the Gentlemen's Agreement to encourage female emigration, about twenty-four times more men than women of Japanese origin were counted in the 1900 Census. The gender ratio for the Filipinos was slightly more balanced, but men still outnumbered women by a ratio of fourteen to one in 1930. Besides these three major groups, about 10 percent of Koreans immigrating to Hawaii in the early 1900s were women, but fewer than a dozen out of the 2,000 Asian Indians who arrived on the West Coast before WWII were women. The result of the scarcity of women in the early history of Asian immigration was the belated formation of families and the sluggish growth of a balanced community (Japanese Americans after 1907 were the exception to this pattern). This was aggravated by the anti-miscegenation laws in the mainland states, which, in turn, may have delayed the entrance of Asians into American electoral politics.

The scarcity of women was common in the early immigration history of all groups to America. For Asians, it was due in part to the sojourner mentality of early immigrant men, to the reported hardship in the long journey across the Pacific, and the raucous frontier environment. Another crucial factor was the rigid cultural traditions that bound women from venturing outside of their homes (Mazumdar 1989). More importantly, labor recruiters preferred single or unattached male workers who would be willing to accept low wages and could be relocated or disbanded with ease once their labor was no longer in demand. Perhaps most concretely, though, Asian women were denied entry both explicitly and implicitly by U.S. immigration laws, and the judicial interpretations and administrative enforcement of those laws

(Chan 1991a). Intra- and interethnic differences also existed among groups of Asian women whose immigration was influenced by cultural, economic, and political circumstances and conditions in both their Asian homelands and the receiving U.S. regions. Thus, for instance, more Chinese women went to Hawaii than to California and more Japanese women went to both Hawaii and California than their Chinese counterparts (Takaki 1990).

The first U.S. immigration law against Asian women was established in 1875 soon after the arrival of a tiny but notable group of mostly poor and uneducated Chinese women whose chief means of survival was meeting the physiological needs of the bachelor society. Although some of the earliest single women of Chinese (and later, Japanese) origin migrated to the United States out of free will, most of them came bonded (Cheng 1984; Tong 1994). They were sold, kidnapped, or tricked into climbing up the "gold mountain" (a Chinese nickname for San Francisco, eluding to the wealth one may accumulate from mining), but ended up serving in an institution that grew inevitably out of the skewed gender ratio of a frontier society. Life was hard; many coped by using drugs. To leave the trade, a few committed suicide, some escaped with their suitors into the interiors of California and other western states, but many more found a way out by marrying Chinese men, an arrangement made either by themselves or by mission rescue homes (Tong 1994). The undesirable visibility of single Chinese women as prostitutes contributed to the rise of anti-Chinese hysteria in the 1870s and gave Congress one more reason for passing the Chinese Exclusion Act of 1882 (Mazumdar 1989).

The Act, which was repealed in 1943, not only suspended the immigration of Chinese male laborers, it effectively prevented the immigration of laborers' wives and any single Chinese woman, while leaving the (re)entry status of U.S.-born women and wives and daughters of U.S. residents and citizens undefined. Thus, an initial form of political activity for many Asian women during this time period was to fight for their own admission into the United States through the courts (Chan 1991a). Even wives of Chinese merchants, who were exempted from the Act along with diplomats and students, sometimes had to count on litigation to earn their entry permits after being detained and interrogated like other Chinese immigrants on Angel Island in San Francisco Bay. Because the Act and its interpretation favored the merchant class and their wives over those groups of lower class status, it facilitated the establishment of small businesses by the merchants as well as the growth of the middle class among Chinese Americans (Chan 1991a). This is one of the many instances in which U.S. immigration restrictions and preferences historically dictated the shape of the Asian American community (Hing 1993).

Except for a small group of wealthy merchant wives, all groups of Asian women toiled in the family or at work to help establish and solidify the economic and cultural basis of the immigrant community. In the days prior to the 1940s, when wage work outside the home was not an option, they either worked alongside their husbands in the fields or practiced self-employment by running boarding houses, laundries, barber shops, fruit stands, and restaurants in their homes, which catered to the needs of the bachelor society. This was in addition to their responsibilities of raising a family (Chu and Ling 1984; Yang 1984). When Asian men were driven out of the labor market or out of their own businesses due to economic competition and racism, women provided the indispensable means of economic survival by working in some of the lowest positions in agriculture, garment factories, canneries, and domestic service (Mazumdar 1989). Although women's wage labor outside the family might have helped them gain them a measure of independence, the dual responsibility as providers of household income and unpaid attendants in domestic spheres could also be a source of great oppression (Glenn 1986).

TRANSFORMATIONS SINCE WORLD WAR II

The watershed moment of Asian women's history arrived during WWII. Because of the shortage of labor, President Franklin Roosevelt issued the nation's first affirmative action order in 1941 to ban racial discrimination in defense industries. Many Asian women—particularly of Chinese and Filipino origins—responded eagerly to this historic opportunity to show loyalty to the country they called home by taking on U.S. defense jobs or serving with Asian men in the armed forces. Out of patriotism to the United States and kinship for their homeland, foreign- and U.S.- born Asian women volunteered, by selling war bonds, donating blood, caring for and entertaining soldiers, and participated in other war relief activities (Kwong 1979; Cordova 1983; Lee 1984; Yung 1995).

The war also lowered racial and gender barriers in certain professions for Asian and other groups of minority women. A broad range of jobs opened up in the civil service, professional fields, and factories outside of ethnic enclaves. Although access to high-paying jobs was still not possible, for the first time some Asian women were able to gain white-collar clerical work. This triggered the creation of a new stereotype of Asian women as obedient "office wives." Nonetheless, their war efforts diminished racial prejudice, ended occupational and residential segregation, and provided employment and educational opportunities so that future generations of Asian American women could achieve greater social and political mobility.

Although the wartime internment produced substantial net losses for Japanese American women and men, even that traumatic experience produced some positive aspects in terms of the transformation of women's roles and relationships within the community (Matsumoto 1984). For instance, camp life introduced first- and second- generation women to the concept of equal pay and the opportunities to take English classes and Japanese art and handicrafts lessons, to meet men without family arrangements, and to form friendships with women from other backgrounds. When young Nisei women were given the chance to leave the camps in order to satisfy the nation's need for labor in the domestic, agricultural, and manufacturing sectors outside the American West, they helped to build a more inclusive community by tearing down residential and occupational segregation (Amott and Matthaei 1991).

The end of WWII marked the beginning of a trend toward more open immigration and the easing of the steep gender imbalance among non-Japanese Asian immigrant groups. An amendment to the War Brides Act in 1947 allowed U.S. servicemen who were citizens or who became citizens to bring their non–U.S. born wives and children to the States. Both Filipino men who enlisted in the U.S. Navy and Chinese American war veterans took this opportunity to become naturalized so as to look for wives in their homelands (Pido 1986). With the removal of anti-Asian racial restrictions by the McCarran-Walter Immigration and Nationality Act of 1952, many Asian women from Japan, Korea, and the Philippines who were married to American GIs entered as nonquota immigrants. The historic gender imbalance was gradually corrected through the elimination of the national quota system and the assigning of admission preferences to family reunions in the 1965 Immigration Act, thereby increasing the immigration of Asian women.

More importantly, through a series of congressional actions such as the repeal of the Chinese Exclusion Act in 1943 and the passages of the Luce-Celler Bill and the 1952 Immigration Act, Asian male and female immigrants were finally allowed to apply for citizenship, and thus gained access to the right to vote and the freedom to pursue legal, political, economic, and educational rights previously unavailable to them because of their alien status. In addition, unlike their predecessors, who faced exclusion and rampant discrimination, this new wave of immigrant men and women generally benefitted from the improved civil rights environment of the post-1965 era. Under President Johnson's "Great Society" program, many newcomers were able to receive federally funded, community-based assistance in learning the English language and job skills and obtaining medical care. Because of the diversity guidelines and timetables set by President Nixon's affirmative action policy, employers in the public and private sectors sought both native-born and foreign-born women of Asian origin. From exclusion to inclusion, Asian women have made great strides participating in community building in the American setting; but how well are they able to participate as equals to Asian men and to other American women in the economic and political arenas? This question is empirically assessed in the following sections with census data and public opinion surveys.

THE SOCIOECONOMIC STATUS OF ASIAN AMERICAN WOMEN AND MEN

One way to measure the progress made by Asian women is through their socioeconomic achievements. A comparison of selected socioeconomic characteristics between 1960 and 1990 among Asian American and U.S. men and women shows both pointed advancement and continuing challenge in gender equity (see table 6.1). In 1960, Asian males were better educated, had higher rates in labor force participation, held better jobs, and received better pay than females in any Asian American population. However, Filipinas scored better than their male counterparts in educational achievement and percent holding professional or technical jobs; yet, they were as low in percent holding managerial or proprietary positions as the men. The gender gap between Chinese men and women was the smallest of all populations. Both Chinese males and females were among the most educated compared to all other popula-

TABLE 6.1   Socioeconomic Characteristics of Major Asian American
Groups by Gender, 1960 and 1990

	Chinese	Japanese	Filipino	Korean	Indian	Vietnamese	U.S. total

1960

Percent Male/Female with 4 years of college or more (among persons 14 years and older)

	Chinese	Japanese	Filipino	Korean	Indian	Vietnamese	U.S. total
	17/13	12/6	5/11	N.A.	N.A.	N.A.	8/4

Percent Male/Female in labor force (among persons 14 years and older)

	79/44	80/44	83/36	N.A.	N.A.	N.A.	77/35

Percent Male/Female as managers, officials, and nonfarming proprietors (among employed persons 14 years and older)

	15/5	10/2	2/2	N.A.	N.A.	N.A.	11/4

Percent Male/Female as professional or technical workers (among employed persons 14 years and older)

	18/17	15/12	6/24	N.A.	N.A.	N.A.	10/13

Median income for all males with income in 1959

	$3,471	$4,304	$3,053	N.A.	N.A.	N.A.	$4,103

Median income for all females with income in 1959

	$2,067	$1,967	$1,518	N.A.	N.A.	N.A.	$1,357

Ratio of female to male median income for all persons with income in 1959

	.60	.46	.50	N.A.	N.A.	N.A.	.33

1990

Percent Male/Female with a bachelor's degree or more (among persons 25 years and older)

	Chinese	Japanese	Filipino	Korean	Indian	Vietnamese	U.S. total
	47/35	43/28	36/42	51/23	66/49	22/12	23/18

Percent Male/Female in labor force (among persons 16 years and older)

	73/59	76/56	79/72	74/56	84/59	72/56	74/57

Percent Male/Female in managerial occupations (among employed persons 16 years and older)

	18/13	24/12	12/9	17/8	19/8	6/7	15/10

Percent Male/Female in professional occupations (among employed persons 16 years and older)

	27/15	23/17	13/19	18/10	39/19	14/8	13/15

Median income for males with income in 1989 (among males 15 years and older)

	$31,746	$37,334	$26,094	$28,256	$36,185	$24,258	$29,237

Median income for females with income in 1989 (among females 15 years and older)

	$23,277	$24,133	$21,690	$18,760	$21,590	$18,771	$19,570

Ratio of female to male median income for persons 15 years and older with income in 1989

	.73	.65	.83	.66	.60	.77	.67

Source: U.S. Bureau of the Census (1963, Tables 7, 8, 11–13, 16–18, 34–36; 1964, Table 100; 1993a, Tables 253, 277; 1993b, Table 123–129; 1993c, Tables 1, 3–5).

Note: Figures for Chinese, Japanese, and Filipinos in 1960 were based on the 25 percent sample data. N.A. = "not available."

tions in the table. They also comprised the only Asian group that had a higher rate than other Americans in the top occupational positions. However, among Asian populations, the Japanese male possessed the highest amount of median income in 1959, which was higher than the U.S. average but slightly lower than the white average of $4,319. Because they were usually more educated, held a greater proportion of professional or technical occupations, and faced less severe gender-based exploitation, each of the three groups of Asian women surpassed the median income of average U.S. and white women in 1959.

These statistics reveal not only the differential impacts of past discriminatory policies and homeland political developments on each ethnic group but also the differential benefits each may have reaped from the unprecedented industrial growth, peace, and prolonged prosperity in the post-WWII years. The Chinese and Japanese benefitted by making great strides in their Americanization process. Limited by a rigid racial order, they focused on acquiring education as a strategy to succeed and were finally permitted to move into the professional and technical fields because of the demand for such workers within the social and economic parameters of the period (Takahashi 1997). Their stories helped create the model minority myth of Asian Americans—even though the claim could hardly be substantiated by census statistics, especially from the perspective of Filipinos. The lower status of Filipinos, as compared to the Chinese and the Japanese, resulted from their belated entry as migrant workers, the lingering legacy of a colonized homeland, an imposed economic and cultural dependency, and the lack of exposure to trade and business operations back in the Philippines (Cabezas, Shinagawa, and Kawaguchi 1986–87; Min 1986–87; Revilla 1998).

Three decades later, despite the dramatic transformation in community demographic structure (as depicted in Chapter 2), there is a remarkable degree of continuity in the relative socioeconomic status across groups of Asian men and women. For instance, in 1960, Filipino men were less educated, but other groups of Asian men and all groups of Asian women were better educated, than other Americans of their gender. In 1990, except for the newest arrival group (the Vietnamese), all groups of Asian men and women in the table were much higher in educational achievement than the average American men and women. The rate of labor force participation for Asian men and women of major subgroups continued to be equal to or higher than the U.S. average. In terms of occupational prestige, Filipino men had a lower rate of holding managerial or professional positions than average U.S. men in 1960. In 1990, Vietnamese joined Filipinos as the two major groups of Asian men who had a lower rate of employment in top-ranked occupations. Among women in 1960, only Chinese had a higher rate than other Americans in the top occupational positions; in 1990, Japanese were the only other group that had a higher rate in managerial positions, whereas Korean and Vietnamese had a lower rate in professional positions than the average American. In terms of earned income, Asian men again surpassed Asian women in all ethnicities; but both males and females of Korean and Vietnamese origin and Filipino men had a lower median income than what was earned by their average U.S. counterparts.

In the end, despite the much-touted socioeconomic achievement of Asian Americans in the latter half of the twentieth century, the population has never been homogeneous nor free from racial subordination and gender exploitation for all ethnicities, with the newest arrival groups experiencing the most severe forms of socioeconomic disadvantage. This was true in both 1960 and 1990. Moreover, the gender gap in median income between Chinese American men and women did not recede as quickly as the U.S. average, and it even grew wider between Japanese American men and women. Furthermore, the two Asian groups that had the most equal gender ratio in income (Filipino and Vietnamese) are also the groups whose men earned less median income than the U.S. average, despite their education. For them, racial oppression experienced by men created the facade of greater gender equity in income class within each ethnic community.

The interrelationship between race, gender, and class regarding Asians can be further clarified with controls over education, employment status, and occupational type. According to the March 1998 Current Population Survey, about 39 percent of Asian women and 46 percent of Asian men aged twenty-five and over attained at least a bachelor's degree in education (see table 6.2). These rates were much higher than those of their non-Hispanic white counterparts. Yet, the rates among Asian women (11.3 percent) and men (6.3 percent) who had never entered high school—due mostly to adverse conditions in Asia— were also higher than white women and men (4.7 percent) in 1998. The median earnings of year-round, full-time workers aged twenty-five and over were significantly higher for Asian women ($29,120) than for white

TABLE 6.2   Gender Differences in Socioeconomic Characteristics
Between Asians and Whites in 1998

	Asian		Non-Hispanic White	
	%Women	%Men	%Women	%Men
Educational Attainment (among persons 25 years and older)				
0–8th Grade	11.3	6.3	4.7	4.7
High School Graduate	23.7	22.2	44.9	40.9
Some College	19.8	19.7	26.3	25.0
Bachelor's Degree or greater	38.7	45.8	24.1	29.3
Earnings in 1997 of Year-Round, Full-time Workers (among persons 25 years and older)				
Median Earnings	$29,120	$35,528	$26,732	$37,893
Among High School Graduates	$19,261	$26,600	$21,766	$31,727
Among those with Bachelor's Degree or greater	$37,338	$45,400	$36,757	$52,104
Earnings in 1997 of Year-Round, Full-time Workers with Bachelor's Degree or More (among persons 25 years and older)				
Executive/Administration/ Managerial	$42,463	$60,693	$43,028	$62,119
Professional Specialty	$46,546	$51,591	$37,343	$55,696
Administrative Support/Clerical	$30,892	$28,094	$26,016	$35,653
Sales	$26,199	$40,106	$38,334	$50,685

Source: U.S. Department of Commerce, Bureau of Census (1999a, Tables 2, 3, 6, 7, 8, 11).

women ($26,732) in 1997, but the reverse was true among men. For every $100 earned by white men, Asian men made $94 in 1997. That earned income ratio drops to $87 for Asian men when comparison is made among college graduates and to $84 when it is made among high school graduates. When similar controls over education are applied to women, Asian women who held a bachelor's degree or more did not make a significantly different amount of money compared to white women of similar background in 1997; however Asian women who held a high school diploma made 88 percent of what their white counterparts earned. These suggest that racial gaps in income may be reduced by education, but that this is more easily accomplished within the female population.

When the occupation of college-educated earners is controlled, differences in income between Asians and whites disappear for both men and women who held the most prestigious occupational positions. Although well-educated Asian women who held professional specialty and administrative support jobs earned significantly higher income and those who held sales positions earned significantly lower income than their white counterparts, Asian men were found to make marginally lower income in the professional category and significantly lower income in each of the two other categories. These results suggest that, among the highly educated, occupational prestige can help ameliorate racial differences in income, but Asian women fared much better than Asian men in this.

An important reason for the relative prosperity of Asian American women is the greater gender disadvantage suffered by white women, in addition to the greater racial disadvantage experienced by Asian American men. For year-round, full-time, white workers aged twenty-five and over, women made only about 70 percent of men's median earnings in 1997. The gender ratio is about the same for both college and high school graduates. In comparison, education improved the earnings made by their Asian counterparts. Asian women with at least a college degree, made 82 percent of what Asian men of similar background made, which was 10 percentage points higher than the ratio among high school graduates. When occupation is controlled among year-round, full-time workers aged twenty-five and over and with at least a college degree, both Asian and white women made about 70 percent of what was earned by their male counterparts. The gender ratio in income improved to 90 percent for Asian women in the professional category; it slid down to 67 percent for their white counterparts. Highly educated Asian women in the administrative support positions made no less than their Asian male counterparts, whereas white women with similar backgrounds and positions made only 73 percent of the income made by their male counterparts. In contrast, the gender ratio in income for highly educated women in sales positions was better among whites (76 percent) than among Asians (65 percent). However, the most telling and persistent feature of these statistics is that, regardless of their educational attainment and occupational prestige, neither Asian women nor Asian men nor white women were able to receive nearly equal return in earned income compared to their white male counterparts.

Clearly, an assessment of the socioeconomic class status of Asian women cannot be conducted without taking into consideration the racial and gender dynamics in the American system. Compared to white women, greater proportions of Asian women twenty-five years of age and over had either never entered high school or received at least a bachelor's degree in 1998. Compared to Asian men, Asian women were not as well educated or well rewarded in earnings for their education and work. Nevertheless, gender disparity in education and earnings was less severe for Asian than white women. This is explained by both the greater racial disparity between Asian and white men than women as well as by the greater gender disparity between whites than Asians of comparable background. Once they acquired college degrees, Asian women were better able than Asian men to receive similar earnings for their education to comparably educated whites who worked year-round and full time. Although the general socioeconomic status of Asian American women and men has been improving, these observations about the gendered and racialized labor market economy are generally consistent with previous findings on the status of Asian American women and provide evidence of the persistence of sexual and racial subordination (Woo 1985, 1989; Xu and Leffler 1992; Ong and Hee 1994; Ortiz 1994; Espiritu 1997; Lien 1998b).

For persons with transnational, transcultural, or both backgrounds, an assessment of their socioeconomic status is complicated by the ethnic group differences endogenous in the histories and experiences of these men and women both before and after immigration. An analysis of the 1990 Census Public Use Micro Samples data comparing earnings among three Asian groups in California and Hawaii finds that, controlling for differences in human capital, Filipino men earned significantly less than Chinese and Japanese men, especially for the foreign-born and in California; however, foreign-born Filipino women in California received higher rates of return for education than other Asian women (Mar 1999). This finding of the extreme heterogeneity in the experience of Asians in the regional labor markets echoes observations made earlier in the chapter about the interlocking relationships of the class status of Asian American subgroups with issues of race, ethnicity, and gender. To comprehend the significance of gender relative to other agents of influence in shaping the political attitudes and behavior of Asian women as a whole and by ethnic subgroups, this section begins with a brief description of their participation history in the American political setting.

ASIAN AMERICAN WOMEN AND POLITICAL PARTICIPATION:
CROSSING BOUNDARIES AND BORDERS

Historically, Asian women and men have been denied formal means of participation in American politics. This was first due to their limited entry into the United States, then by the denial of their legal right to become naturalized upon petition, and still later by social segregation and economic exploitation. The lack of political and legal rights, however, did not mean that they were acquiescent in the face of oppression. Like Asian men, whose presence dominated the majority of the Asian American history presented in Chapter 1, Asian women have been engaged in numerous incidents of individual and collective political action to fight against ethnic-, race-, and gender-based repression and for democracy and freedom in both the United States and their ancestral homelands. Some of the first acts of resistance are seen in the women's decision to seek personal freedom, economic security, and self-improvement by leaving their homelands (Hune 2000). Besides immigration litigation and wartime volunteer activities mentioned earlier, at least three other major spheres of political participation are documented by Asian American scholars—labor strikes, homeland independence and wartime relief efforts, and social movements—before Asian women entered U.S. electoral politics in a significant manner in the 1980s (Chan 1991c; Wei 1993; Okihiro 1994; Yung 1995; Ling 1998).

As Asian women became more integrated into the American workforce and contributed to a greater share of the family income, the balance of gender power within some families started to shift from subordination to partnership. Even though women seldom kept all of the wages they earned, their earning power and access to social networks outside the family often helped ameliorate the imbalance of power within the household. The shift in gender relations within the household was not always beneficial to women, as some men tried to affirm their traditional status and authority through violent means (Lin and Tan 1994; Kim 1995). Nevertheless, through their workplace training and exposure, many grew to be more aware of their deprived positions and learned ways to articulate and protect their interests. Between 1909 and 1925, Filipinas in Hawaii, brought in at first to calm striking Filipino male workers, were active in nine strikes against low wages and long hours (Sharma 1984). In 1938, after many frustrating attempts to negotiate steady employment and higher wages, Chinese women garment workers employed by the National Dollar Stores organized their own union chapter and went on strike for 105 days. Although little was gained in terms of increased wages and job security, the experience marked their first stand against labor exploitation. The strike raised the women's political consciousness and demonstrated their organizing skills (Yung 1995). These are just two of the many incidents in which women played a commanding role in the history of the Asian American labor movement.

Asian American women also had an active history of participation in the independence and nation-building struggles of their ancestral homelands (Chan 1991c). Chinese American women, for example, raised funds for Dr. Sun Yat-sen's revolutionary cause and for war and famine reliefs in the years after 1911. They solicited donations, contributed handcrafted items to fund-raisers, wrapped bandages, sewed garments for refugees, and knitted socks and scarves for those on the battlefield (Yung 1995). Similar efforts were made by the Korean women in California and Hawaii who formed associations both in the wake of the 1919 Mansei Uprising and in the 1930s, when Japan invaded Manchuria and North China (Yang 1984). They raised funds for the Korean independence movement, trained emergency nurses for anti-Japanese actions, boycotted Japanese foods, and engaged in relief work for needy Koreans. Even the handful of Asian Indian women in the United States donated their gold bangles to finance the 1914–15 Gadhar movement against the British (Mazumdar 1989). During the Japanese invasion of China (1931–1945), many Chinese immigrant women, in response to appeals from the nationalist leadership in China calling for sisterhood and nationalism, joined the Women's New Life Movement Association to raise money for war relief efforts. Second-generation girls also assisted in organizing rallies and boycotts of goods made in Japan, and conducting "Bowl of Rice" fund-raising events (Lee 1984). Particularly noteworthy was the Chinese Women's Patriotic Association (made up mostly of merchants' wives and their American-born daughters), which conducted a variety of highly successful fund-raising activities between 1933 and 1943 such as auctions, bazaars, charity balls, and the sale of goods donated by local businesses (Kwong 1979).

One reason Asian women actively participated in homeland independence and relief affairs was because they saw a connection to their own cause of liberation in America (Okihiro 1994). Between the latter half of the nineteenth century and early part of the twentieth century, when women activists in China resisted foot-binding, polygamy, and prostitution, Chinese and other Asian women in America also sought an end to these oppressive practices and for a woman's right to health care, education, gainful employment, and social and political participation (Yung 1995). They formed and joined women's organizations such as Chinese Young Women's Christian Associations to learn slices of mainstream American life. Because of this participation, by the early 1930s, Chinese women in San Francisco began to register to vote, campaign for political candidates, and contest legislation against immigrants and noncitizens. Their participation helped ameliorate racial exclusion and social segregation.

In the late 1960s and early 1970s, the understanding of the transnational linkage across women of color took the form of the development of a Third World identity (Okihiro 1994). Women constituted a vital but independent component of the first wave of the Asian American Movement (Wei 1993). These women were forced to form their own organizations because of undisguised sexual oppression from some of their revolutionary-minded male comrades who often assigned them auxiliary and trivial roles (Espiritu 1992; Wei 1993). Some also felt compelled to divorce themselves from the mainstream women's movement because of the latter's preoccupation with self-improvement and gender equality while neglecting issues that deeply affected racial minority and lower-class women (Ling 1989). In addition, many Asian feminists experienced marginalization within the U.S. left because of the obliviousness of white antiracists to the persistent and virulent oppression faced by non-Black people of color as well as the stereotypical image of Asian women as "exotic" (Pegues 1997). Unlike their non-Hispanic white counterparts, many Asian American feminists did not advocate independence from the family or working outside the home. Because of their experiences working in a racially stratified labor market to supplement men's income, many women relied on the family network as a retreat from their daily battles against myriad forms of oppression. In addition to mainstream organizations' concerns over pay equity, domestic violence, and division of labor at home, Asian American women's organizations also addressed issues of fraud and sexploitation of mail-order brides, prostitution in U.S. military bases abroad, equal wage rights of garment workers, human rights of Third World women and child laborers, racial stereotypes, and environmental justice affecting women of color, among other issues (Amott and Matthaei 1991).

With the demise of the first Asian American movement, large organizations consisting of primarily middle-class, professional, East Asian women specializing in educational and service projects grew and flourished in the 1980s (Wei 1993). Their participation in these organizations and the networking opportunities they gained from them permitted a growing number of Asian women to extend their professional knowledge and concern for children's education and family and community welfare to the quest for public office. According to Chu (1989), most of these women did not have career plans to enter politics, nor did they have mentors or role models to teach them the necessary skills of lobbying, networking, and coalition building. Most did not have extraordinary backgrounds, but they did have supportive families and an extensive experience of involvement in community affairs. Many of them did not run for office until after their children were out of high school, and the decision to run for office was often sparked by a crisis. Their electoral success can often be attributed not to the presence of a large ethnic constituency, but to their individual tenacity, personal contacts, uniqueness in physical appearance, and the positive stereotype of being a competent, capable, honest, and nonthreatening Asian woman. However, for many more women, their social group backgrounds worked against them and prevented them from running or receiving endorsements from political parties or other major organizations and community groups. As a result, Asian men have held many more political offices than Asian women. Yet, as shown in Chapter 3, those women who were able to break through the cultural, racial, and sexual barriers often became true trailblazers, entering into some areas of politics far ahead of Asian men.

At the grassroots level, sexist incidents such as the banning of progressive South Asian women from participating in traditional cultural events by male community leaders continued to serve as a reason for organized protests in the 1990s (P. Shah 1997). Nevertheless, in reaction to new challenges in the social, political, and global economic realms, a new wave of the Asian American women's movement has also emerged as part of the new labor movement featuring community organizing across races, generations, national borders, and industries. One of the forerunners of this movement was the Garment Workers Justice Campaign, launched by Asian Immigrant Women Advocates (AIWA) in 1992. It effectively organized national support among workers, students, and community activists through education, public disruption, media events, and a four-year-long boycott against designer Jessica McClintock (Delgado 1996). Its success secured back pay for the exploited sweatshop workers and protection for government workers, and transformed the capacity and style of operation of the AIWA, which developed a network of research assistants and connections with other women's, labor, church-based, student, and community organizations. It also helped nurture a new generation of leadership among both immigrant and U.S.-born Asian women. Out of the contemporary conditions of global capitalism, the new Asian American feminist movement has been able to transcend identity politics and make "connections among the politics of labor, health, environment, culture, nationalism, racism, and patriarchy" (S. Shah 1997, xix). Testimonies to the successful cross-racial and -border organizing between Asian and Latina women are groups like the Support Committee for the Marquiladora Workers and Borders Workers Regional Support Committee (Lowe 1996).

CURRENT STATUS OF POLITICAL PARTICIPATION: IS THERE A GENDER GAP AMONG ASIANS?

Past research on gender gap issues in mass political participation has dealt mainly with differences in the extent of participation and in the distribution of ideological orientation and opinions on issues. Women and men may differ in these matters because of different socialization experiences and opportunity structures. Although various speculations have been advanced about the contours of the gaps, many agree that there is increasingly little difference in the rates of voting and other forms of participation between American women and men, and there is no clear division in ideological outlook and certain opinion positions. These findings, like most of American political science research, have been based predominantly on the observations of behaviors of non-Hispanic whites rather than Asian or other Americans.

Until 1980, sixty years after the ratification of the Nineteenth Amendment on women's suffrage, American women still registered and voted less than men. However, the gender gap in terms of voting participation in presidential elections appears to have been substantially reduced since 1980 (Baxter and Lansing 1983; Conway 1991; Conway, Steuer-nagel, and Ahern 1997; Seltzer, Newman, and Leighton 1997). This gradual reformulation of the gender gap in the past several decades may have been facilitated by the feminist movement, government activism, and the greater participation and autonomy of women in social and economic life (Poole and Zeigler 1985; Carroll 1988).

In terms of governmental participation beyond voting, recent studies find that men still hold a small but definite edge over women in activities such as making campaign contributions, contacting government officials, running for public office, volunteering in community affairs, and affiliating with political organizations (Schlozman, Burns, and Verba 1994; Schlozman et al. 1995). Similarly, a longitudinal study reports that women are slightly less likely than men to persuade others how to vote or to contribute their time and money to a political party or candidate (Rosenstone and Hansen 1993). Rosenstone and Hansen postulate that the gaps in gender may be associated with the lack of mobilization of women by political parties. Scholzman and others attribute the gaps to the differences in resources, particularly those dealing with money (1994). They note that gender differences may be relatively muted among the more socioeconomically advantaged citizens. Nevertheless, none consider the gaps in participation as being huge or unbridgeable.

Many observe that gender gaps remain real, if not widened in recent years, in reaction to an environment of growing conservatism in national political leadership (Wirls 1986). From the 1960s through the 1980s, women were more liberal than men in political ideology, partisanship, and vote choice (Sapiro 1983; Mansbridge 1985; Shapiro and Mahajan 1986). Women were also more liberal on certain social issues such as health, welfare, employment, and programs to aid minorities. However, they tend to be more conservative when it comes to issues dealing with traditional values, such as school prayer, drug use, pornography, sex education, and government defense spending (Shapiro and Mahajan). Female participants may also assign more priority to certain issues by giving more weight to educational and abortion issues than their male counterparts do (Schlozman et al. 1995).

Can the contours of the gender gap observed in the white majority be generalized to racial and ethnic minority groups? So far, according to the limited number of studies on Blacks and Latinos, the answer appears to be a mixed one. Perhaps boosted by the consciousness of the "dual oppression" of both sexism and racism, Black women typically participate at higher levels than their male counterparts (Verba and Nie 1972; Shingles 1981; Baxter and Lansing 1983; Jennings 1993). Although the gender advantage of Black female participants disappears in analysis of the turnout for the 1984 elections when factors such as income, homeownership, and political interest are controlled, Black females are more likely to be partisan, show more interest in political campaigns, and register to vote more than Black males (Tate 1993). Yet, other studies of Black and Latino participation in elections of the 1980s find little difference between men and women on a variety of subjects such as political ideology, partisan identification, vote choice, and opinions on social welfare and other issues (Welch and Sigelman 1989). Black and Latina women are as likely as their white counterparts to be Democratic Party identifiers and vote for Democratic candidates. When male-female differences exist, the gap tends to be modest and the largest difference is in the political ideology between white men and women.

How do Asians compare in terms of the significance and size of gender gaps in political attitudes and opinion? Asian women in America, as discussed in previous sections, have fought against sexism, racism, colonization, and capitalist exploitation and for inclusion and homeland liberation throughout history. Like Asian men, whose presence dominated political participation (as depicted in Chapter 1), Asian women have also had an extensive but unsung story of political participation spanning ethnicities, immigration generations, ideologies, and styles. Today's Asian American women have come a long way in attaining an overall level of education and income status that is comparable to or even surpassing that of non-Hispanic white women. Their relatively superior socioeconomic position to other groups of women presents an interesting opportunity to study the interplay of race and gender when economic class is not predominantly low for a group of nonwhite women. In light of the affinity between higher socioeconomic class and greater participation in voting and other electoral activities in the United States, the aggregated socioeconomic success of Asian American women may cast doubt on the continued significance of their race and gender in terms of political participation. Yet, the preceding account on income data indicates that, although contemporary Asian American women are still not equal to their male counterparts in terms of education and earned income, both genders share the experience of receiving fewer dollars in return for their education and work compared to their white, male counterparts. The issue of racial and gender discrimination is particularly severe for those Asians who never entered college. When class is controlled, the common experience of racial exploitation may help forge a political outlook among Asians that downplays gender differences. Nevertheless, neither men nor women may be able to overcome the hindrance to their abilities to translate socioeconomic resources into political action that is imposed by the lingering effects of restrictive U.S. immigration and naturalization policies, limited socialization processes among immigrant adults, conservative group cultural norms, and mainstream political mobilization bias, among other factors. As a result, being an Asian man or woman may be associated with a lower likelihood of participation.

Furthermore, although Asian women have fought independently of men to gain a measure of emancipation from sexism in America and abroad, their gender consciousness may not be as established or salient to that held by their counterparts in other races. As told, the formation of a panethnic group identity and consciousness among Asians has been made difficult by the growing heterogeneity in race, class, religion, language, and immigration generation across Asian ethnic groups in recent decades. As members of a multiethnic community, the dynamics of racial formation may serve as a source of fusion among groups of Asian women, but the differential history and socialization experience regarding gender roles in each ethnic community may also create a source of friction among them. Other conditions being equal, gender may not be as prominent a determinant of political attitudes and opinions for Asians than for other races, even though there may be interethnic group differences within the pan-Asian community.

Finally, when gender is significant, it may structure the political opinions of Asian women in ways different from both white and other nonwhite women. A gender-based solidarity between Asian and white women may be made difficult by the interconnectedness of the issue of gender to issues of race, class, and culture. A race-based solidarity between Asian and other women of color may be more viable because of the sharing of the triple oppression of race, class, and gender. The personal or family immigration background of Asian American women may facilitate the forging of alliances with other immigrant women of color such as Latinas. However, differences in education, income, socialization, acculturation, group consciousness and identity, and other factors may also set apart their political choices from those of other immigrant and U.S.-born women. The situation of Asian American women at the nexus of these social boundaries and national borders makes it rather intriguing to predict the unique significance of gender in structuring their political attitudes and behavior at the mass level. In the balance of the chapter, expanding upon many of the empirical analyses by race and ethnicity discussed in previous chapters, multivariate regression procedures are used to help sort out the direction and weight of gender relative to other competing influences in different spheres of political participation. To test the unique contributions found in the dual identities of being female and nonwhite, interactive terms multiplying the effects of race/ethnicity and gender are entered along with dummy variables indexing the independent effects of each racial/ethnic and gender group in the restricted model. Additional terms controlling for possible confounding effects of socioeconomic status, social connectedness, and political context are included in the full model (see Lien 1998b for details).

EMPIRICAL EVIDENCE OF GENDER GAPS IN POLITICAL AND SOCIAL PARTICIPATION

The unique effect of being Asian and female on voting participation is examined based on analyses of the Current Population Survey (CPS) data, 1990–98 (as reported in Chapter 3). When only race, gender, and their interactions are entered in the regression model of citizens' likelihood to become registered voters, Asian women are found to be no different than Asian men in their propensity to register to vote, even though the latter are significantly less likely than non-Hispanic white males to become registered. The same observation applies to Latinos and American Indians, but not to Blacks. Black women demonstrate a higher likelihood to register than Black men, even though the latter are less likely to do so in comparison to whites. Controlling for differences in sociodemographic factors does not change the role of gender among Asians, but it increases the racial gap between Asian and white males.[1] This is a phenomenon contrary to what would be expected from studying the behavior of other nonwhites. Latino and American Indian men's underparticipation compared to white men can be ameliorated or explained away by the control variables. For Blacks, women continue to participate at a higher level than their male counterparts, but Black men are also more likely to register than their white counterparts after adding controls.

Gender plays a similar role in predicting voter turnout among the registered Black, Latino, and American Indian voters. The exceptions are that Indian men were not less likely to turn out in both 1990 and 1994 and that, other conditions being equal, Black men were still associated with lower turnout likelihood in 1992. For Asians, gender differences in turnout levels are not significant, but neither are racial differences between Asian and white males significant in three of the five elections (1990, 1994, and 1996). The addition of control variables, again, increases rather than reduces the racial gaps. Similar findings of this curious phenomenon are reported in Lien (1997a, 1998b, 2000) and Cho (1999b). They lend support to the idea that sociodemographic variables have a different role in structuring political participation for Asian women and men than for their counterparts in other racial groups. Because adult citizens of Asian descent tend to come from an immigrant background and carry a different socialization experience than their U.S.-born counterparts, their education, skills, and other personal characteristics traditionally considered as participation assets among the American electorate may be accrued outside of the U.S. systems and cannot be directly translated into participation resources.

Among Asian American citizens of the first two immigration generations, results using merged CPS data from 1994 to 1998 show that, when only ethnicity, gender, and their interactions are in the logistic regression model predicting voting registration, women in each ethnic group have the same likelihood to register as their male counterparts. However, males of Japanese and Asian Indian origins may have a higher propensity, and Vietnamese males a lower propensity, to become registered. When variables controlling for differences in sociodemographic background, social connectedness, and political context are added to the equation, none of the dummy variables representing effects of ethnicity, gender, and their interactions are significant in influencing the likelihood of registration. In models predicting turnout among the registered, again, gender is not a source of division, even though Japanese and Asian Indian males may initially have a higher propensity to turn out than other Asian males. This difference disappears when control variables are added, except that registered Korean males are less likely to turn out than other Asians. A similar finding of the smaller and mostly insignificant gender divide within each Asian subgroup relative to ethnic gaps across males of each Asian community can be reported for other spheres of political participation, as is described later in this chapter.

One shortcoming of the CPS data is that they were gathered only from English-speaking respondents. This may mitigate the effects of race, ethnicity, and gender on the attitudes and behavior of the non-English-speaking population. Findings about the roles of race and gender may also be influenced by the race and sex of interviewers in face-to-face situations. However, an analysis of political and social participation using the Multi-City Study of Urban Inequality (MCSUI) data in Los Angeles (which meticulously addressed these issues in the research design) reports a similar pattern of racial and gender roles to that identified in the national CPS data. Namely, citizens who are Asian and female are not less likely than citizens who are Asian and male to become registered, even though Asian men are much less likely to do so than white men. The negative and significant sign of slope coefficient associated with Asian males does not disappear when a list of control variables addressing differences in sociodemographic background and social and political adaptation (the same as those used in the multivariate procedures predicting political participation reported in Chapter 4) are applied. Nevertheless, contrary to the census data, the size of this slope coefficient reduces from -1.01 to -0.74 between the restricted and the full model. The addition of controls, however, is able to explain away the differences in registration between Latino and white men.

Among both citizen and noncitizen respondents in Los Angeles, Asian women are found to be significantly less likely to participate in group-based meetings than their male counterparts who, in turn, are less likely to participate than their white counterparts. Black and Latino men are also lacking in social participation compared to white men, but there are no gender differences between Black and Latino men and women. The negative and significant sign associated with Asian females disappears when control variables are added. These controls reduce, but are unable to remove, the relative deficit in the level of social participation associated with being male and Asian, Black, or Latino as compared to their white male counterparts. Among Asian respondents, gender is not a significant factor for each ethnic subgroup, but being Chinese, Korean, or Southeast Asian can be associated with less participation. The ethnic gaps are rendered insignificant for Chinese and marginally significant for Koreans and Southeast Asians after adding controls.

EMPIRICAL EVIDENCE OF GENDER GAPS IN POLITICAL ORIENTATION AND VOTE CHOICE

Significant gender gaps among adult Asians may exist in political partisanship and support for affirmative action as a national policy but not in political ideology. These are findings from both the restricted and full regression models using the Race Poll data. Namely, compared to an Asian man, an Asian woman may show less Democratic identification and weaker support for affirmative action policy, even after controlling for differences in education, income, age, region, information level, ideological strength, and perceived role of government. Asian men are predicted to be more likely than white men to be Democratic identifiers and supporters of affirmative action, but this significance disappears in the full model. Comparatively, Black and Latino men or women are all more likely to identify with the Democratic Party than their white counterparts. Both Latino men and women are equally more likely to support affirmative action than white men or women. However, Black women, more so than Asian women, are predicted to have a lower degree of support for affirmative action than their male counterparts who, in turn, have a more favorable attitude toward the policy than their white counterparts. White women comprise the only group that is expected to exert more support than their male counterparts for the Democratic presidential candidate and to think more favorably of the affirmative action policy. Black women are equally as likely as Black men to possess a liberal ideology; their level of identification as political liberals is unparalleled to those held by Asian, Latino, and white men or women.

The unique opinion pattern toward affirmative action of adult Asian and Black women found at the national level is not echoed by results analyzing the Proposition 209 vote among California voters in the 1996 general election. Using the VNS exit poll data, women of Asian, Black, and Hispanic origin are all estimated to be as likely as Asian, Black, and

Latino men who, in turn, are more likely than white men to oppose the abolition of affirmative action. This is true in both the restricted and full models. Virtually the same opinion pattern can be reported for the vote against Proposition 227 (abolish bilingual education) among California voters in the primary election of June 1998, except that the attitudes of Asian men or women are similar to those of white men or women.

Finally, the evidence of gender gaps among voters is examined through their choices of a political candidate. The national Race Poll data found only white women, but not other groups of women, were more likely to support candidate Bill Clinton in his first presidential bid than their male counterparts. The same is true among respondents in the LATP survey of Southern Californians. Gender differences among voters supporting Matt Fong for the U.S. Senate are evident in the 1998 primary but not the general election. Asian women had a lower, and Latina women had a higher, propensity to vote for Fong than their male counterparts did. The gender gap among Asians is rendered insignificant after taking into consideration sociodemographic and political party identification and ideological differences. Latino men, however, remained less likely to vote for Fong than Latinas. Not surprisingly, support for Fong was much higher among Asian than any other group of men, both before and after adding controls. Although a respondent's gender made no difference in the vote for Fong in the general election for all four racial groups, the results predict white voters to be as supportive of Fong as Asians are, and, other conditions being equal, Black male voters can also be expected to provide as high a level of support as Asian male voters.

These findings suggest that, in both the extent and direction of political and social participation, gender gaps within each nonwhite group are smaller than racial gaps between whites and nonwhites. Gender gaps between Asian men and women, however, are not necessarily smaller than gender gaps between the men and women in other nonwhite groups. Nevertheless, within each Asian ethnic group, women tend not to differ much from men in their participation likelihood and orientation, if given equal access to participation resources. When differences in the possible correlates of voting, registration, and group-based participation are controlled, race remains important in suppressing the participation of Asians and Latinos, whereas gender within each race is not significant in determining the level of participation. The evidence of gender gaps is stronger in political orientation, candidate choice, and issue preference models. However, the opinion gaps are smaller among voters than among adults who may or may not be citizens. Greater political integration apparently has the effect of reducing gender differences in political opinions.

CONCLUSION

This chapter opened with a review of the emergence of Asian women in American society and politics. From exclusion to special provisions for admission to open admission, this nation's immigration policies have played an important role in determining the size and shape of the female immigrant community. Once admitted into the United States, Asian women often labored alongside their male relatives either at home or in the fields for economic survival and also labored to promote the social mobility of the Asian American community. When World War II provided women the opportunity to work outside of home, many plunged into jobs in the defense industries, the white-collar sector, and the armed forces, where they served multiple functions. However, bigger breaks came during the next twenty years when Asians were granted the right to petition for immigration and naturalization, and thus, the right to vote in elections and have equal access to employment opportunities in the United States.

In the post-1965 era, men no longer far outnumber women in the Asian American community. Along with the influx of highly educated, well-skilled, Asian-born female workers, many less-educated female relatives of American citizens and permanent residents of Asian origin as well as traumatized refugee women of Southeast Asian origins have arrived in the United States. This development tends to diversify the class and gender structure of the ever-expanding, immigrant-dominated Asian American community. However, today's Asian American women, at the aggregate, generally enjoy an economic life that surpasses the economic lives of other groups of women in the United States. Their economic success is more than a fortuitous coincidence of opportunity and ability. It is true that many of today's Asian American women arrived or came of age at a time when this nation became more open and equal. Asian American women also now tend to spend more years in school after graduating from high school and are increasingly able to earn better income as full-time workers with college or advanced degrees. But the appearance of their relative success reflects as much on the preferences of the post-1965 U.S. immigration policies for highly skilled workers as on the myriad forms of oppression suffered by Asian American men and all other groups of American women. Moreover, the greater gender equity in income associated with certain ethnic groups can be attributed to exploitation and (neo)colonization that originated in both Asian homelands and America. And, those Asian women who are not able to receive a higher education may still face triple oppression based on race, gender, and class as they try to receive equal income returns.

The brief discussion of their political participation history shows that the struggles of Asian women more than mirror the saga of their male counterparts. Their participation in resisting immigration exclusion via the courts, organizing labor strikes, and creating social movements to eliminate racial, gender, and class oppression has been an integral part of the efforts in building a more politically credible community in America. Their participation in domestic community building, including forming and joining women's organizations, and homeland independence and wartime relief movements, cultivated their interests, sharpened their skills, and established the networks needed to enter American electoral politics, where many became trailblazers in local and state offices. Their participation within the U.S. left and in community-based labor organizing across social boundaries and national borders provided new hopes for coalition building at the organizational level in a globally interdependent, capitalist system.

Encouraging prospects for coalition building at the mass level are provided by multivariate statistical results that tend to show that gender gaps in political attitudes and behavior are mostly a white phenomenon and that race and, to a lesser extent, ethnicity rather than gender are the greater barriers to solidarity for each of the groups. Although contemporary Asian American women are at least as disadvantaged as other nonwhite women in terms of their likelihood of participation in electoral politics, their political experiences at the crossroads of race and gender are shaped more by ethnicity than gender. The few gender gaps among Asians (seen in the adult females' lower likelihood to participate in group-based activities and in female voters' lower predicted support for candidate Fong) can be eradicated once dif-

ferences in socioeconomic resources, cultural adaptation, social connectedness, and political orientations are taken into account. Although
gender differences in party identification and attitude toward the affirmative action policy among Asian adults cannot be removed after these
controls, the opinion gaps may cease to exist among the politically more
integrated segment of the population, such as the registered voters.

These research findings underline the centrality of race when considering the political experience of nonwhite men and women. They
echo the call for recentering race into the study of gender made by many
feminists of color. Nevertheless, findings on the marginalization of gender because of the dual oppression in race and class also highlight the
importance of studying and presenting these categories of difference as
relationally constructed. Therefore, to conclude that race is more significant than gender in structuring political attitudes and behavior should
not be interpreted as denying the persistence of gender oppression or,
by the same token, capitalist exploitation. However, findings on the various gender gaps between whites and nonwhites and among different
nonwhite groups do present a challenge to the prevailing conceptual-
ization of presenting race, class, and gender as Black/white, lower
class/middle class, and male/female dichotomies. In this sense, this
study supports Espiritu's (1997) call to move beyond dualism in studying the dynamics of race, class, and gender.

Finally, given the multiple methodological issues in conducting survey research on Asians, results reported here can only be considered
tentative, and much more research is needed to explore the potential
uniqueness of the political experiences of Asian American and other
groups of women. Moreover, in terms of addressing concerns over the
contradictions in feminist methodology, this empirical approach may
not be sufficient to discover the "hidden determinants of oppression"
(Gorelick 1996). It is therefore imperative to conduct more research
examining a wider range of political behavior using various research
design, theory, and timeframe of analysis. More research is also needed
to further investigate the coalitional opportunities for Asians and across
groups of women and men in other spheres of political participation
and policy making areas.

Conclusion

"Is this America?" So opens Gish Jen's (2000) letter to the *New York Times* editors. "To think of Wen Ho Lee in his nine months of solitary confinement is to think not of Horatio Alger, but of Kafka." Why should Wen Ho Lee's story be different from that of any other hardworking immigrant to America? What distinguishes the experience of Asian Americans from that of other racial and ethnic groups? Lee, a naturalized citizen from Taiwan who was fired from the Los Alamos National Lab for being suspected of stealing nuclear secrets for China, was released from jail after admitting to one out of fifty-nine counts of mishandling classified data and being sentenced to the 278 days that he had served. Essentially, Lee negotiated his freedom by admitting to a crime of downloading data from a secure to an unsecured computer, a practice that was routinely violated by his colleagues and former FBI director John Deutch but went unpunished until the Lee case. Lee's release came after a federal district court judge indignantly concluded that the government had arrogantly unleashed its full force of powers to mislead the court and to keep Lee incarcerated (Sterngold 2000). His freedom also came after the Chinese and Asian American communities had waged a surprisingly strong campaign against racial and ethnic profiling. Many believed that Lee was singled out because of his Chinese ethnicity, a scenario reminiscent of the Chinese exclusion cases more than a century ago.

As a way of conclusion, this chapter briefly compares elements surrounding the *United States of America v. Wen Ho Lee* (1999) and a case discussed in Chapter 1, *Fong Yue Ting v. the United States* (1893) to illustrate the continuity and change in both Chinese and Asian American communities and in America itself.

First, the similarities. Both cases dealt with the national government's attempt to deprive non-native-born Chinese Americans of equal rights and protection out of a convergence of forces that included racial anxiety, partisan and labor politics, intergovernmental disputes, and international relations. The 1893 case was in reaction to the Geary Act, which extended and expanded Chinese exclusion (McClain 1994). By presuming every Chinese's residence in the States to be illicit unless proven to the contrary with a certificate, the Act threw the burden of proof on the Chinese suspects—the same situation faced by Lee during lengthy pre-trial detention. The Geary Act forbade bail to Chinese who were denied entry and who applied for habeas writs in federal courts; Lee was also denied access to bail and his plea was repeatedly refused. The punishment of arrest and deportation for those who did not have a certificate of residence was considered cruel and unusual; Lee's condition of solitary confinement with one hour of exercise each day (while wearing shackles) can also be described as cruel and unusual. In both cases, the Chinese were assisted by highly competent white attorneys and by strong non-Asian local support. The community's reaction was also similar in that litigation was only part of a multipronged national campaign that included a call for civil disobedience (noncompliance with the registration order in *Fong* and boycotting the national labs in *Lee*), mass meetings or rallies, community fund-raising and public education campaigns, lobbying Congress, and the formation of new organizations to address the issues.

Second, the differences. Amid salient anti-Chinese sentiment of the late nineteenth century, *Fong* was a test case prearranged with federal authorities to challenge the constitutionality of the Geary Act; it went expeditiously through the court system in nine days. A clause of the Geary Act even limited, for the first and only time in this nation, the right to testify in federal court to white witnesses. In the *Lee* case, the community, including Lee himself, was caught unprepared. Reflecting in part the perception that the racial environment in the late twentieth century had greatly improved, Lee did not find it necessary to hire an attorney until his daughter insisted upon it. And the community, which had grown much bigger and more diversified in place of origin, class status, gender ratio, and whatnot over the century, was very slow to react. Only few people in the beginning, and still not many at the time of his release, considered *Lee* to have any relevance to their personal or professional lives. Regardless of technological changes, such as the convenience of the Internet, which greatly facilitates information exchange and communication across geopolitical boundaries, power within the Chinese American community became dispersed enough that homeland government-controlled organizations were not interested in nor capable of weighing in on *Lee*.

Political divisiveness related either to domestic or homeland issues further contributed to the fragmented reaction of the community. Instead, women, especially Alberta Lee and Cecilia Chang, the executive director of the Wen Ho Lee Defense Fund, played a leading role in the campaign for liberty and justice for Lee. They were joined by academic elites of multiple ethnicities in the only two national Asian American organizations that, shepherded by University of California Ethnic Studies professor Ling-chi Wang, passed resolutions to launch the boycott movement. Last but not least, a coalition of civil rights organizations, rather than a single group like CERL, banded together under the Coalition Against Racial and Ethnic Stereotyping (CARES) to protest Lee's incarceration and mistreatment.

Third, the outcome. In a 6–3 decision on the *Fong* case, justices on the U.S. Supreme Court ruled against *Fong* and denied any application of the Bill of Rights to Chinese residents, including many who had resided in the United States for as long a period of time as some of members of Congress who had passed the Geary Act. Racial antagonism was too high a bar to cross, despite all the skills, resources, and good will from both within and outside the community. The defeat, however, did not discourage the Chinese from litigation. Within five years, they were able to win two U.S. Supreme Court cases, which found portions of the Geary Act to be unconstitutional and affirmed the birthright citizenship of the U.S.-born (*Wong Wing v. United States* 1896 and *Wong Kim Ark v. United States* 1898). The plea bargain deal in *Lee*, though it helped set him free, was unjust by forcing him to become a convicted felon with no right to sue the government for racial and ethnic profiling. It remains an open question, at the time of this writing, whether the system will ultimately work for the liberty and justice of all. What is known for certain is that the Asian American community (or at least certain members of the community), in conjunction with members from other communities, will not give up in this and other fights for equality, justice, and empowerment. The American dream is too much of an enticement to give up.

Both then and now, Asian Americans have not been docile victims of racial discrimination, but dogmatic actors and resisters, too. And, as documented throughout this book, our participation mattered. A beleaguered minority can sometimes win through its own determination, strategic planning, and resistance as well as through the righteousness of those inside the system. Several things remain to be answered: Would it have mattered more had more individuals and groups, especially the resourceful ones, participated, or participated early enough, in each of the campaigns? How much can we expect elected and appointed officials or other nongovernmental leaders to speak out for the disadvantaged within the community? How effective can community organizing based on ethnic identity or panethnicity be, given the multiple layers of cleavages, including intraethnic and transpacific ones? Are there viable alternatives to a civil rights–based panethnic coalition? These are some of the questions that I have in mind as I ponder a closing for this book. They are more than I have answered, or could have possibly answered, in a small volume. Consider this as laying the groundwork and a call for future undertakings.

Appendix

Researching Asian American Political Behavior
with Sample Surveys: A Methodological Report

In the realm of modern political science, survey research is the most common way to scrutinize political behavior. The approach involves administering questionnaires to a sample of respondents selected from some population. Public opinion surveys are particularly useful in describing the characteristics of a large population. They permit the development of operational definitions from literature review and the testing of hypotheses in a systematic matter. They provide an efficient and objective means to answer the classical questions of who, what, when, where, why, and how much. However, survey research also has many weaknesses. One of the complaints of the survey approach is that it can fragment the complexities of life into discrete, clean-cut, and unitary variables that do not reflect political or social reality. Another concern is that it is superficial and seldom represents the context of social life. Surveys cannot measure social action—they can only relay self-reports of recalled, hypothetical, or prospective action. Surveys may also suffer from a lack of validity because of the need for standardized questionnaires (Babbie 1989). Nevertheless, with all of its limitations, survey research still constitutes "the most direct, and thus most valid, way of finding answers" when studying political behavior (Dennis 1991, 52).

An empirically based and systematic analysis of political opinion across the nation's major racial groups and Asian American subgroups requires the availability of scientifically collected and politically relevant survey data. However, empirical evidence about the comparative political attitudes and behavior of Asian Americans to other racial groups is scanty at best and limited in the number of respondents, geographic coverage, and type of questions asked. Publicly accessible survey data, which are useful to estimate the political preferences of Asian subgroups, are even harder to find and do not exist beyond the regional level. One purpose of this section is to provide a general review of the nation's major archival data on public opinion research and their relevancy to the study of Asian American political behavior. In general, these data can be grouped into four types. They vary widely in terms of usefulness in studying the political attitudes and behavior of Asian Americans, but they share a common deficiency in that they are inadequate to assess the contours of Asian American political opinion either in the aggregate or by ethnic groups. Reports about the direction of the national Asian vote can be unreliable and misleading. Their ability to answer the basic research questions about the shape of the national political community is restricted in multiple ways, either in topical interest, sampling methodology, interviewing language, or ethnic or geographic representation. Nevertheless, as a collective, they may provide invaluable baseline information on the Asian American political opinion, particularly when assessed at the local level and viewed from a comparative group and time trend perspective.

The first and the largest category of archival political data is one that contains *either no Asians or a very small proportion of Asians in the sample.* Examples in this category include prominent data series such as the American National Election Study, the General Social Survey (GSS), and the national election exit polls conducted by Voter News Service (VNS) and its predecessor. It also includes the American Citizen Participation Study, 1990 (Verba et al. 1995a), the 1994 and 1998 National Black Election Panel Studies (Jackson 1993), the 1996 National Black Election Study (Tate 1998), and the 1989–90 Latino National Political Survey (de la Garza et al. 1992). Although statistically sound in survey methodology, each fails to draw a meaningful number of Asians for analysis. Nevertheless, the California section of the VNS data may be used to analyze and compare state-level results with other data sources.

The second category refers to multiracial datasets that contain an *oversample of Asians* either at the national or subnational levels. A unique dataset collected at the *national* level is the 1995 *Washington Post* Poll on Race Relations, which is to date the only multigroup national survey other than the census data discussed in this Appendix that has come close to including a large number of Asians for analysis. Nevertheless, its English-only and mainland-only methodology may introduce unexplained biases by excluding the opinions of non-English-speaking Asians and those residing in Hawaii. Also, a number of questions important to explaining immigrant political behavior such as citizenship, English-language proficiency, and length of residence are missing from the list of survey items. The search for multiracial data containing Asians is more fruitful at the *subnational* level. Particularly useful are four datasets: the 1984 Caltech Ethnicity Survey, the *Los Angeles Times* Poll (LATP) 1993 Survey of Asians in Southern California, the 1997 City of Los Angeles Survey, and the Los Angeles portion of the 1992–94 Multi-City Study of Urban Inequality (MCSUI). English is the only language used to interview Asians in the first three surveys; the fourth study uses bilingual speakers of several Asian languages (Mandarin and Cantonese Chinese and Korean) to survey the area's Chinese, Korean, and Japanese populations. It also distinguishes itself by adopting a rigorous multistage, stratified area probability sampling design (see Appendix F in the MCSUI codebook for a sample report on Los Angeles). Still, Asians were only one-tenth of the county population and the researchers found it necessary to adopt oversampling techniques to ensure the inclusion of a sufficient number of Asians. In addition, opinions among Asian and other voters in California may be assessed with exit poll data collected by the LATP and VNS for 1996 and 1998 elections. To study only the poll voters' opinions, however, is to miss the opinions of about 75 percent of voting-age Asians who could not or failed to cast their votes on any given election day in the 1990s[1] as well as to miss about 20 percent or more of voters who cast their votes by absentee ballots.[2]

The third category refers to those datasets that contain *only Asians in the sample*. In fact, each of the datasets contains only respondents from a single Asian ethnic group and they are all from the same region. Specifically, these are surveys of Korean, Filipino, Vietnamese, and Chinese residents in Southern California conducted by the Interviewing Service of America between 1992 and 1997 for the *Los Angeles Times* Poll. The poll used bilingual interviewers to ensure that the respondents were interviewed in their language of preference. With the exception of the Korean survey, which only covers Los Angeles County, these surveys include the six counties of Southern California. This data series contains many questions that may be used to study immigrant adult socialization and political adaptation. Although it does not contain information about voting, it does ask questions about citizenship status, citizenship intent, voter registration, political party registration, political ideology, activism in mainstream and ethnic affairs, and opinions on issues specific to each ethnic community and its Asian homeland(s).

The fourth data category is the series of *sample survey data collected by the U.S. Bureau of Census*. Specifically, they are the Current Population Survey Voter Supplement Files (CPS). From the statistical point of view, this is the type of data that can best represent the Asian American opinions at the national level. Unfortunately, politics and participation are not the focus of this government survey and it queries only a limited scope of voting participation. Moreover, prior to the 1990 survey, the race question does not include Asians as a possible response category. Also, English is the only language used to interview Asians.

Besides a general lack of interest and concern of government agencies, corporations, and the mainstream media in gathering opinions from traditionally marginalized social groups, a major reason for the absence of political data on Asian Americans at the national level is the practical difficulty of systematically sampling a small, bicoastally distributed, residentially dispersed, and ethnically and linguistically diverse population. As a result, it is difficult to locate enough cooperating Asians in a multigroup, English/Spanish language survey with equal probability design (each unit has equal chance of being selected) within any specified geographic unit across the nation. For instance, of the 2,904 completed interviews in the 1996 GSS, only 27 of the interviewees were Asian. Similarly, in the 1996 VNS exit polls, only 182 out of 16,637 respondents were Asian. Even if the sampling problem can somehow be mitigated by using targeting methodologies in areas of high Asian concentration (and therefore sacrificing national representativeness of the results), researchers may still be unable to address satisfactorily the difficulty of identifying and categorizing individuals with Asian Pacific surnames into appropriate ethnic groups for the purposes of ethnic sampling, interviewing, and data analysis. A discussion of the problems of omission and misidentification can be found in Nakanishi (1986, 1998a). Primarily, the surname approach may exclude Asians who have unlisted surnames or carry non-Asian surnames through adoption or marriage, but include non-Asians carrying Asian surnames. Ethnic misidentification may arise among individuals with Asian surnames that are common for more than one Asian group, such as the surnames of Lee, Young, and Chang for Chinese and Koreans, or those with surnames that are identical to those of non-Asians, such as the surnames of Lee for Chinese and Koreans, Sanchez for Filipinos, or an assortment of surnames for Samoans. The misidentification problem may be alleviated by knowledge of first names and distribution of ethnic population in each census tract.

Compared to an English-only survey, the costs of surveying Asians can be significantly higher due to the need to prepare non-English questionnaires in multiple languages and to recruit and train bilingual, Asian-language speakers. In the situation of a multilingual telephone survey, a researcher can be frustrated by the omission of unlisted households because of the necessity to rely on the listed surname rather than a random-digit dialing (RDD) approach to assemble a sufficiently large and ethnically diverse group of respondents. An additional source of frustration in this situation is the general incompatibility between random-digit dialing and the assignment of appropriate bilingual staff to conduct interviews in more than one language. Methodological difficulties like these may severely affect the quality of data and bias the information on Asians. These methodological constraints should not, however, be used as an excuse for not studying Asians. Rather, they are the very reasons for the need to collect new data using innovative and improved sampling methodologies. Before better datasets become available, they are also the mandate for looking above and beyond a single-shot survey and for using extreme caution when interpreting results from a multiplicity of datasets. Given the multitude of methodological issues already described, there may not be a single best way to gather large-scale, systematic data on Asian American political opinion. Yet, concerns about the validity and reliability of the datasets should by no means outweigh the potential gain in knowledge contributed collectively by these groundbreaking studies. Although each data source has its deficiencies, together they may provide a more complete portrayal of the political attitudes and opinions of the multiethnic community, both at the comparative race level and at the ethnic-subgroup level than any single set of existing data.

The balance of the report describes the survey datasets used in this research and discusses the specific strengths and limitations of each dataset. They are arranged by three levels of the geographic coverage of the sampling frame: national, state, and local. Despite the best of intentions and efforts, this search for available datasets was not exhaustive. It was limited to publicly accessible datasets collected and released in the 1990s that contain a significant number of Asian American participants and are stored in the two leading national archives of political and social data: the Inter-university Consortium for Political and Social Research (ICPSR) and the Roper Center of Public Opinion Research (RCPOR). Important exclusions include the 1984 Caltech Ethnicity survey, the 1986 UCLA Asian Pacific American Voter Registration Study, the California Field Polls, and a number of community media polls conducted by *Asianweek* and other news media. Datasets that are proprietary in nature or otherwise not accessible or known to the author are also excluded from discussion. However, to appreciate the dynamics of local politics in areas of high Asian concentration, and to fill in the data gap, particularly at the intra-Asian, ethnic-subgroup level, results from a series of community exit polls conducted in three metropolitan areas (of which the author has no direct access to data files) are included in the discussion. What follows is a discussion of datasets by three levels of geographic coverage.

NATIONAL

Current Population Survey Voter Supplement Files (CPS, 1990–98)

The U.S. Census Bureau's Current Population Survey (CPS) is a household sample survey conducted monthly by the Census Bureau to provide estimates of employment, unemployment, and other characteristics of the general labor force. The entire civilian, noninstitutionalized population of the United States living in households is sampled to obtain the respondents for this series of surveys. A national probability sample is used in selecting household units. The Voter Supplement Files contain the core questions included in every CPS as well as an additional series of questions on voting and registration. About 136,000 to 164,000 respondents were interviewed for each survey between 1990 and 1998. CPS added the "Asian or Pacific Islander" category to the racial identification question in 1990. The percentage of Asians among voting-age respondents ranged from 2.5 percent in 1990 to 3.7 percent in 1998.

Compared to the American National Election Study (NES), a traditional data source for political research, the CPS is better equipped to study the political behavior of multiracial Americans for several reasons. One is its much larger sample size; even small ethnic groups are well represented. The pooled dataset between 1990 and 1998, for example, includes 16,382 Asians, 37,598 Latinos, 4,564 American Indians, and

49,032 Blacks. Another is its less biased representation of low-income and nonwhite minorities in the sample. Although both data sources are guilty of missampling the minority populations, this problem is much more severe with the NES surveys (Teixeira 1992). A major CPS revision in 1994, which introduced new population controls based on the 1990 census adjusted for the estimated population undercount, may improve data quality and add confidence to the results reported here. The third reason is the smaller inflation of self-reported voting and registration rates. The differentials in aggregated turnout rates between official records maintained by state officials and the census-based estimates in the 1980s were about 7 percentage points, a gap much smaller than the double-digit differentials based on NES data. Although better socioeconomic status and exposure to pre-election polling may largely account for the higher level of reported turnout among NES respondents (Abramson, Aldrich, and Rhode 1994, 1998), the nonpolitical nature of the census survey may reduce respondents' propensity to misreport turnout (Teixeira 1992).

Despite the superiority of the census data, their quality and utility may be threatened by the following factors. First, no validation of voting is done for the CPS respondents. Second, only a small number of questions address political participation. Third, the special sampling problems of various minorities may result in a substantial undercounting of Latinos, Blacks, Asians, and American Indians on reservations but an overcounting of those in urban areas (Passel 1990; Leung and Mar 1991; Harris 1994). Fourth, besides miscounting, there may be a lack of consistency in the identification of minorities such as in the case of Latinos (Arvizu and Garcia 1996). Fifth, the CPS does not collect information on ethnic identity among Asian and Pacific Americans. However, with the major redesign implemented in 1994,[3] new questions on nativity and place of birth permit a limited opportunity for this research to analyze ethnicity by parental lineage. Finally, changes in the questionnaire, data collection, and data management made in 1994 may introduce additional errors when longitudinal analysis is attempted.

Washington Post/ *Kaiser Foundation/Harvard University Poll, 1995 (Race Poll, 1995)*

The national survey was conducted by Chilton Research Services for the *Washington Post*, Kaiser Foundation, and Harvard University in 1995. Adults residing in the forty-eight contiguous states were interviewed by phone between July 20 and August 9, 1995, as part of an Omnibus survey, a national survey that uses random-digit dialing sampling to conduct weekly surveys on a variety of topics. In the course of this interview, a race demographic (Black, white, or other) was collected. The "other" respondents originally identified in the Omnibus were then oversampled to ensure sufficiently large samples of ethnic/racial minorities. The RDD national sample and the "other" supplement failed to locate enough cooperative Asian females to analyze that group separately. An additional 100 Asian females were surveyed in September 18–28, 1995, using a list source of Asian females.

Although this may introduce additional bias to the representativeness of the survey, to the best of the author's knowledge, there is no other multigroup national survey that has come close to including a sufficient number of respondents for each nonwhite group nor come up with a reasonable solution to overcome the multitude of difficulties in surveying opinions across the four major racial/ethnic groups. The resulting sample has a total of 1,970 respondents, including 802 whites, 451 blacks, 251 Latinos, and 352 Asians. The margin of sampling error for all respondents is ±3 percent.

Voter News Service (VNS, 1996, 1998)

Known as Voter Research and Surveys until 1994, VNS is a cooperative arrangement of the Associated Press and ABC, CBS, CNN, Fox, and NBC News networks. Interviews were conducted with a probability sample of voters as they left their polling places on election day. This was conducted in all fifty states and the District of Columbia in the general election of 1996. A total of forty-two states participated in the 1998 general election exit polls. The total sample size was 16,637 for 1996 and 11,387 for 1998. Only 1 percent of the respondents in each dataset were Asians.

The state samples were selected in two stages. In each state, a probability sample of voting precincts was selected that represented the different geographic areas and the vote by party. Precincts were selected with a probability proportionate to the number of voters in each precinct. However, in certain states, precincts with large minority populations were selected at a higher rate than those without. A subsample of the state precincts was selected at a uniform rate to be part of the national sample, with the exception that minority precincts had higher probability of being selected. Within each precinct, voters were systematically sampled throughout the voting day at a rate that gave all voters in a precinct the same chance of being interviewed.

Weighting for this survey was computed by taking into account the probability of selection, a nonresponse adjustment by the observed age, race, and sex of those who were missed or refused to be interviewed, and a ratio estimate to the final vote totals. All weights were reduced by a constant so that the sum of the weights approximated the sample size.

Although the VNS adopted state-of-the-art sampling design, extreme caution should be used when interpreting the results containing Asians because of the unsettlingly high margin of error. The sampling error can be as high as 13 percent for a sample size of 100, although that figure is reduced to 4 percent for an N of 1000, and to 1.1 percent for an N of 15,000. In addition, the error margin may be influenced by other errors not associated with sampling methods but with the practical difficulties involved in conducting any public opinion survey.

STATE

Los Angeles Times *Poll, Study #420, California General Election, November 3, 1998 (LATP-CA, 1998G)*

The *Times* Poll interviewed 3,693 voters as they left sixty polling places across California during voting hours. Precincts were chosen based on the pattern of turnout in past statewide elections. Confidential questionnaires in three languages (English, Spanish, and Chinese) were administered. About 1 percent of voters used the Spanish survey and another 0.5 percent used the Chinese survey. The total sample included 251 Asians, 421 Latinos, 426 Blacks, and 2,115 whites. The margin of sampling error for all voters was ±2 percent. The error margin was ±8 percent for Asians. The sample was slightly adjusted by actual returns and demographic estimates to offset the exclusion of absentee voters and those who declined to participate.

Los Angeles Times *Poll, Study #413, California Primary Election, June 2, 1998 (LATP-CA, 1998P)*

The *Times* Poll interviewed 5,143 voters in English and Spanish as they left ninety-nine polling places across California during voting hours. The total sample included 169 Asians, 543 Latinos, 637 Blacks, and 3,162 whites. The margin of sampling error for all voters was ±2 percent. For Asians, it would be about ±10 percent.

Los Angeles Times *Poll, Study #389, General Election (California), November 5, 1996 (LATP-CA, 1996)*

The *Times* Poll interviewed 2,473 California voters in self-administered English and Spanish questionnaires as they exited forty polling places across the state. The total sample included 120 Asians, 223 Latinos, 143 Blacks, and 1,584 whites. The margin of sampling error for all voters was ±3 percent.

Voter News Service, California (VNS-CA, 1996, 1998)

For both 1996 and 1998 general elections, VNS conducted telephone surveys of absentee/early voters in California and two other states (Oregon and Washington) the week before the election; a fourth state, Texas, participated only in 1996. Households were selected using RDD, and a respondent was randomly selected within each household. Those who had either already voted absentee/early or who were likely to do so were asked questions dealing with vote choices, issues and factors that most influenced those votes, and national policies. Demographic information was collected on race, sex, age, religion, education, political party identification, and family income. No ethnicity information was collected. The telephone data were combined with the exit poll data and weighted to reflect the relative proportion of absentee/early voters and election-day voters.

LOCAL

Los Angeles Times *Poll, Study #318, Asians in Southern California, 1993 (LATP-SC, 1993)*

Between August and October 1993, the *Los Angeles Times* Poll conducted a telephone survey that included 221 Asians in the six counties of Southern California. This study adopted RDD techniques to survey Asians, but the base sample was augmented with an oversample of Asians from telephone exchanges where there are high concentrations of Asians.

Los Angeles Times *Poll, Study #395, City of Los Angeles Survey, Fifth Anniversary of the Rodney King Riots, April 1997 (LATP-LAC, 1997)*

The *Times* Poll interviewed 1,560 adult residents of the city of Los Angeles by telephone, April 13–20, 1997. Asians were oversampled to ensure a large enough size for analysis. The total sample includes 161 Asians, 526 Latinos, 145 blacks, and 668 whites. The margin of sampling error for the entire sample was ±3 percent.

Los Angeles Times *Poll of Asian Ethnic Groups in Southern California (LATP, 1992–1997)*

The series of the *Los Angeles Times* Poll datasets was collected between 1992 and 1997 by interviewing adults age eighteen and over with Korean, Vietnamese, Filipino, or Chinese surnames who resided in Southern California. Telephone interviews were conducted with 750 Korean residents in Los Angeles County as well as with 773 Chinese, 750 Filipino, and 861 Vietnamese residents of Los Angeles and five additional counties: Orange, San Diego, San Bernadino, Riverside, and Ventura. RDD techniques were used to produce about one-third of the Korean sample; the rest were drawn from lists of Korean-surnamed households countywide. Separate lists of ethnic surnames were used to draw the Chinese, Vietnamese, and Filipino samples from phone directories in the six counties. Vietnamese residents of Orange County were oversampled to produce 58 percent of the Vietnamese sample. The margin of sampling error was ±5 percent for the Korean sample and ±4 percent for the other three. Information about interview dates and languages used is reported in table 5.2.

These surveys are unique not only in their pioneering nature of systematically collecting large-scale Asian opinions from diverse ethnic communities in the same region, but that they were conducted by bilingual interviewers who spoke both English and the home language of the specific group of respondents. These two features greatly enhance the reliability of results in gathering Asian opinions at the subgroup level. The findings may be generalized to the Southern California region with weighed data adjusted by census figures on population characteristics such as sex, age, and education of the region. However, the results may be subject to limitations endemic to surveys using telephones and listed surname samples. The former not only prohibits the interviewing of those who did not have access to phones (which was 4.4 percent of the Asian households in 1998, according to a 1999 U.S. National Telecommunications and Information Administration [NTIA] report), it restricts the number of questions an interviewer can ask in a single interview lasting approximately twenty minutes. The latter restricts sampling to those individuals with listed phone numbers who bear the Asian surnames identified in a prepared surname list. This is biased against those who have unusual surnames or carry a non-Asian surname through adoption or marriage. Additionally, the five-year span in the time frame of interviews between the Korean and the Filipino samples may impair the comparability of results. The accuracy of data may be influenced by other factors such as events taking place while the survey is in the field, the wording and sequence of questions, and undetected flaws in sampling and interviewing procedures. Nevertheless, these concerns should by no means outweigh the potential gain in knowledge about opinion patterns within and across Asian ethnic groups contributed by these datasets.

Multi-City Study of Urban Inequality (MCSUI), 1992–1994: Los Angeles, Household Survey (LASUI, 1993–94)

The Los Angeles file of the MCSUI comprises of two surveys—a face-to-face survey of households and a telephone survey of employers. The Asian portion of the household survey used here contains 1,055 interviews with adults twenty-one years of age and older residing in census tracts with both low and high rates of poverty between September 1993 and August 1994. The base sample was drawn using a multistage stratified, clustered area-probability design. Asians who self-identified as Korean, Japanese, or Chinese were oversampled from areas of high ethnic concentration (higher than 10 percent of the population in each stratum) and low to medium-high income levels to obtain a large enough sample size for analysis. About 36 percent of interviews were conducted in English, 29 percent in Mandarin, 28 percent in Korean, and 7 percent in Cantonese. Among respondents, about 76 percent of Chinese, 98 percent of Japanese, 85 percent of Koreans, and 64 percent of Southeast Asians were interviewed in non-English languages. Professional translators experienced in questionnaire translation were used to prepare independent forward/backward translation for non-English questionnaires. To elicit open and honest responses to questions about racial and ethnic stereotypes, nearly all of the interviews (98 percent) were conducted by Asian interviewers recruited from Asian-language newspaper ads.

Because of the lack of self-reported ethnic origin information from Asians, a derivative method based on birthplace and home language use was used to decide the ethnicity of each respondent. Those Asians who were born in Asian countries or were currently exposed to Asian languages at home were assigned one of five ethnic groupings. Those who were born in China, Taiwan, or Hong Kong or used Mandarin or Cantonese at home were assigned into the "Chinese" ethnic grouping. Those born in Japan or who used some Japanese at home were assigned into the "Japanese" grouping. Those born in Korea or who resided in Korean-speaking households were identified as "Koreans." Those born in Vietnam, Cambodia (Kampuchea), Burma (Myanmar), Thailand, Malaysia, or Indonesia, or those who used some language of these countries at home were categorized as "Southeast Asians." Those Asians who were born in the United States and resided in English-only households were assigned into the "Other" category. This categorization system accounted for about 99 percent of all Asian respondents in the Los Angeles household survey.

Regional APA Community Exit Polls

As part of a national and longitudinal effort directed by the National Asian Pacific American Legal Consortium in collecting voting behavior information from Asian communities, a series of exit polls were conducted in three regions following each general election after November 1994. The Southern California poll was conducted by the Asian Pacific American Legal Center of Southern California (APALC). The San Francisco Bay Area poll was conducted by the Asian Law Caucus (ALC). The New York City poll was conducted by the Asian American Legal Defense and Education Fund (AALDEF).

Although the three regions accounted for only about 35 percent of the APA population in the nation, results of these polls may be considered more representative of the APA vote than those reported by the mainstream polls such as those conducted by VNS and *Los Angeles Times* Poll, especially among APA voters in urban areas and of foreign birth. According to reports released by these civil rights organizations (e.g., Shinagawa 1995, 1997; Feng and Tang 1997; Feng, Ichinose, and Patraporn 1999; and the newsletter *Outlook* of the AALDEF), several reasons account for the higher level of accuracy and representativeness of these community polls. First, bilingual surveyors conducted the polls with questionnaires written in a number of Asian languages. Volunteers were assigned, whenever possible, to communities where they would share the same ethnicity and language with the respondents. Second, interviewers conducted polls in areas with high concentrations of Asian populations or voters and in places experiencing a great influx of new immigrants from Asia. Poll sites were also selected to reflect the broadest possible range of the Asian population in terms of ethnic background, age, immigration generation, English-language ability, and political affiliation. The polls targeted those areas with high concentrations of APA population and of APA voters, areas experiencing a great influx of APA immigration, and areas occupied predominantly by a single Asian ethnic group or mixed APA populations. Third, the sample size of each poll was generally much larger and sampling errors much smaller than the mainstream polls. The 1996 AALDEF general election exit poll surveyed 3,264 Asian voters and was the largest ever of its kind. The 1998 APLAC general election exit poll had 2,100 Asian respondents. Fourth, the polls gathered voter information in multiple regions and in multiple years. The AALDEF, for instance, has been conducting exit polls of Asians in New York City since 1988. These features enabled the sampling of a cross section of Asian voters missed by mainstream media polls and the collecting of highly valuable information across time and place.

However, these exit polls were designed to be completed in less than five minutes, during peak voting hours in the morning and evening, and had the limited goals of surveying the bilingual needs and political preferences of voters. In order to maximize the resulting sample size for each ethnic group, the exit polls used a nonrandom (targeted) site sampling method, which might have threatened the representativeness of the APA population at large. In addition, the nature of exit polls severely restricts the type and number of questions that can be asked of the respondents. Finally, these exit polls share the general omission of the opinions of nonvoters, absentee voters, poll voters not voting in peak hours, or those not residing in targeted sample areas. Absentee voters might have had a different profile than the poll voters in such matters as English-language ability and voting history.[4] To compensate for this omission, a phone poll of absentee voters with APA surnames was conducted within days after the November 1998 election as an addendum to the election-day exit poll (Feng et al. 1999). Figures used in this research are based upon the combined results.

APALC, 1996.   In November 1996, over 900 APA voters in four areas—Koreatown of Los Angeles, San Gabriel Valley (Monterey Park and

Alhambra), South Bay (Carson, Gardena, and Torrance), and Little Saigon of Orange County (Westminster and Garden Grove)—were interviewed as they exited thirty-six polling places. Over half of the respondents chose to use one of the Asian language questionnaires in Chinese, Korean, Vietnamese, Tagalog, and Japanese.

ALC, 1996.   In November 1996, 550 APA voters in San Francisco and Oakland were surveyed in English, Spanish, and Chinese as they exited seventeen polling sites. Over half of the APA respondents used the Chinese-language questionnaire.

APALC, 1998.   In November 1998, about 3,000 voters, close to half of them of APA origin, were polled as they exited forty-five precincts in the fourteen selected areas or cities in Los Angeles County (Chinatown, Koreatown, and Filipinotown of Los Angeles, San Gabriel Valley, and South Bay Region), and Westminster City of Orange County. Poll sites were selected based on the size and density of targeted APA ethnic populations, the presence of APA candidates, and the anticipated relevance to future APA redistricting efforts. Interviewers polled by phone an additional 500 APA absentee voters residing in these areas. Six languages—Chinese, English, Korean, Spanish, Tagalog, and Vietnamese—were used in these surveys.

Notes

Introduction

1. Under most circumstances, my use of the term *Asian Americans* does not intend to cover the distinct experiences of the Pacific Islanders. However, until the 1997 revision of the Statistical Policy Directive No. 15, Race and Ethnic Standards for Federal Statistics and Administrative Reporting, data on the Pacific Islanders have often been lumped together with Asians. One of the two modifications to the 1977 standards for the classification of federal data on race and ethnicity is that the Asian or Pacific Islander category was separated into two categories, "Asian" and "Native Hawaiian or Other Pacific Islander." The federal government's new definition of *Asian* refers to any person having origins in any of the original peoples of the Far East, Southeast Asia, or the Indian subcontinent including, for example, Cambodia, China, India, Japan, Korea, Malaysia, Pakistan, the Philippine Islands, Thailand, and Vietnam. The new standards were used by the Bureau of the Census in the 2000 decennial census. Other federal programs are expected to adopt the standards as soon as possible (no later than January 1, 2003) for use in household surveys, administrative forms and records, and other data collections.

2. The proper classification and labeling of individuals of European, African, Hispanic, and Asian origins is a highly controversial matter. For convenience, this book uses the umbrella terms *Black* and *African American* interchangeably. *Latino* and *Hispanic American*, (*non-Hispanic*) *white* and *European American*, as well as *Asian* and *Asian American* are also used interchangeably. Unless noted otherwise, these racial terms are treated as representing both males and females and the categories are coded as mutually exclusive of each other.

Chapter 1 Charting a Hidden Terrain: Historical Struggles for Inclusion and Justice Prior to the Era of Civil Rights and Electoral Politics

1. Given the dearth of scientifically collected information and analysis, the narrative may tend to be a descriptive one when an inductive approach is often the only way to generalize group norms from the behaviors of individuals who may have been acting in ways apart from what was typical of other members in the community. Nevertheless, findings from this laborious survey should provide new ground for researching and understanding the political behavior of Asians and their relationship to the American political system.

2. According to Tsai (1986), Buddhist missionaries from China might have visited the Palos Verdes Peninsula, just south of the California coast, in the fifth century. Three Chinese seamen were reported stranded in Baltimore in 1785. Several authors also noted that a small number of Chinese merchants, workers, and students arrived in Philadelphia, New York, Connecticut, and Massachusetts as well as Canada and the Hawaiian Islands prior to 1847. For instance, Tchen (1999) notes that the first documented visit of a Chinese to New York occurred in 1808 by a Chinese man who arrived to collect debts owed him by two American merchants. The first Asian woman to achieve notoriety was Afong Moy who, in 1834, was displayed in a Manhattan museum furnished with Chinese artifacts (Tchen 1999).

Another group of Asians who had an early presence on the East Coast were Asian Indians. A small number of them were found in Massachusetts and Pennsylvania in the 1790s. These early immigrants probably married Black women and became part of the Black population (Jensen 1988).

3. For more information on the politics of Chinese exclusion, see Coolidge (1909), Miller (1969), Saxton (1971), Sandmeyer (1973), and Gyory (1998). See Hune (1982) specifically for intensive debates within Congress, between Congress and the White House, and between the governments of the United States and China over a six-year period prior to the adoption of the 1882 Act.

4. For an overview of the various laws and the restrictions they impose, see the chronology appendix in Chan (1991a) and Hing (1993). Also available are general reference materials such as Ng (1995, 1998), Natividad (1996), Baron and Gall (1996), Natividad and Gall (1996), and an interactive multimedia presentation of the Asian American experience in *American Journey* (Research Publications 1997).

5. Executive Order 9066 was signed by President Franklin D. Roosevelt on February 19, 1942, and repealed thirty-four years later by President Gerald R. Ford through the issuing of Presidential Proclamation 4417, which formally revoked the wartime document and apologized for the relocation.

6. *Statutes at Large* 1 (1790), 103.

7. The question of naturalization for Chinese was debated in the Reconstruction era as Congress tried to extend franchise to Blacks. Massachusetts senator Charles Sumner's proposal to include Asians was defeated.

8. *Ozawa v. United States*, 260 U.S. 178 (1922); *United States v. Thind*, 261 U.S. 204 (1923).

9. Page Law of March 3, 1875, 18 Stat. 477.

10. Statutes of California (1852), 84. See Sandmeyer (1973) and Nee and Nee (1986) for a description of the discriminatory measure.

11. *People v. Hall*, 4 Cal. 399, 404 (1854). McClain (1994) notes that the ban did not apply to federal courts. In as early as 1851, the U.S. District Court covering northern California was able to receive Chinese testimony on an unrestricted basis.

12. *Tape v. Hurley*, 66 Cal. 473–474 (1885); *Gong Lum v. Rice*, 275 U.S. 78, 87 (1927).

13. The percentage of foreign-born among the Chinese was 48.1 percent in 1940. Strictly speaking, that percentage of the population should be higher than reported in the Census. According to a note to the author from historian Him Mark Lai, during the exclusion era an unknown but highly significant number of Chinese born in China had entered the United States by claiming either to have been born in the United States or to be the offspring of a U.S. citizen. These immigrants were counted as natives in the census. The claims of U.S. birth or relationship were difficult to verify, particularly after the 1906 San Francisco earthquake when fire destroyed all birth and other records in the city, and the U.S. immigration officials adopted harsh interrogative means to try to discredit the claims. These skirmishes with the U.S. system might have delayed the political adaptation of Chinese Americans (Kitano and Daniels 1995).

14. The JACL attacked individuals like Minoru Yasui of Portland, Oregon, who attempted to test the evacuation in the courts, and those who resisted the draft in 1944 and 1945 on grounds of conscience. Daniels (1988) commented that the JACL position of acquiescence was not unique in the history of American minority group leadership. Neither was the unwillingness of JACL leaders to tolerate a diversity of opinion and tactics.

15. For instance, in order to eliminate one level of judicial review and shorten the time an exclusion case would take to reach the Supreme Court, the Chinese counsel often chose to begin proceedings in the circuit court instead of the district court (McClain 1994).

16. *Ekiu Nishimura v. United States*, 142 U.S. 651 (1892).

17. *Toyota v. United States*, 268 U.S. 402 (1925). This case decided that, unlike Filipinos, WWI veterans of Japanese nativity could not be eligible for U.S. citizenship. The right for Japanese and other Asian veterans to petition for naturalization was not granted until the passage of the Nye-Lea bill of 1935.

18. Slocum had his own citizenship revoked by the U.S. Immigration Service in 1923 because of his nonwhite race, despite the Act of 1862 and Section 2166 of a 1901 act permitting citizenship to any aliens honorably discharged. He campaigned tirelessly in Congress as a lobbyist for JACL to rally support for the passage of the Nye-Lea bill of 1935.

19. In Missouri, the case involved *Petition of Easurk Emsen Charr*, 273 F. 207 (1921). In California, the case was *In re En Sk Song*, 271 F. 23 (1921).

20. *In re Bautista*, 245 F. 765 (1917). Other cases were reported in Melendy (1977, 264 n7, n8).

21. *Sun Cheong-Kee v. United States*, 70 U.S. L. Ed. 72 (1865).

22. *Yick Wo v. Hopkins*, 118 U.S. 356 (1886).

23. *Wong Wai v. Williamson*, 103 F. 1,5 (C.C.N.D. Cal. 1900).

24. *Jew Ho v. Williamson*, 103 F. 10, 16–17 (C.C.N.D. Cal. 1900).

25. In 1920, that number was 1.64 percent, owned or leased (Chuman 1976).

26. *Suwa v. Johnson*, 54 Cal. 119 (1921). Johnson, an owner and lessor of agricultural land to Japanese immigrants was to void his lease with Suma. The appeals court ruled in favor of Suma.

27. *Estate of Tetsubumi Yano* 118 Cal., 645 (1922).
28. *Oyama v. California,* 332 U.S. 633; 68 Sup. Ct. 269 (1948).
29. 66 Cal. 473 (1885).
30. *Wong Him v. Callahan,* 119 F. 381 (C.C.N.D. Cal. 1902).
31. 275 U.S. 78, 87 (1927).
32. *Baldwin v. Franks,* 120 U.S. 678 (1887).
33. Korean immigration to the United States was suppressed by Japanese government after 1905 so as to protect the position of Japanese workers in Hawaii.
34. *Hirabayashi v. United States,* 320 U.S. 81 (1943); *Yasui v. United States,* 320 U.S. 115; 63 SC. 1392 (1943); *Korematsu v. United States,* 323 U.S. 214 (1944).
35. *Ex parte Mitsuye Endo,* 323 U.S. 283 (1944).

Chapter 2   Constructing a Community That (Almost) Cannot Be: Contemporary Movements Toward Liberation and Empowerment— After 1965

1. Both Asian Indians (misnamed as Hindus) and Koreans had their own categories in the censuses between 1920 and 1940. Because of their small numbers, Koreans were relegated into the "Other" category in the censuses of 1950 and 1960. Between 1950 and 1970, Asian Indians were also relegated to the "Other" category, but they were subsequently reclassified as whites. These changes reflect both the demographic marginality of the two population groups among Asians created by the serial labor migration practices, immigration exclusion, and anti-miscegenation policies as well as the inconsistent and arbitrary nature of the counting of nonwhites in the U.S. censuses (Lott 1997).

2. An important reason for the sharp rise in the number of ethnic origins, other than the legal, economic, and political reasons delineated in the next section, is the change in census enumeration of Asians. A 100 percent enumeration of all Asians in America was not possible until the 1990 Census when an "Asian or Pacific Islander" banner was created under the race question and a write-in category for "Other Asian or Pacific Islander" was added to the response list of the new banner in the census short form asked of all households (Lott 1997).

3. Sen. Mitch McConnell (R-KY) and Rep. Charles Canady (R-FL) introduced H.R.1909/S.950 or the so-called "Civil Rights Act of 1997" to eliminate all federal affirmative action programs and activities. In the 105th Congress, Rep. Bob Stump (R-AZ) introduced H.R.622, a bill to declare English the official language of the government of the United States. It would prohibit any bilingual agent of the government to communicate and conduct business in any language other than English. Similar bills were introduced by Rep. Peter King (R-NY), Rep. Randy Cunningham (R-CA), and Sen. Richard Shelby (R-AL).

4. One was a foreman at an automobile factory who lost his job soon after the incident. The other was a laid-off worker at the time of the killing (Espiritu 1992).

5. Scholars differ on the definition of "interest groups" and it has been used

interchangeably with pressure groups, organized interests, special interests, political groups, the lobby, and so on. For this study, interest groups are simply membership- or nonmembership-based organizations or institutions that engage in activities to influence government policy (Petracca 1992; Rozell and Wilcox 1999).

6. A clear exception is the USPAACC, which is a strong advocate of conservative values and policies. Although this orientation is more an exception than the norm among the capital crowd of Asian American groups, the formation of panethnic groups with such orientation is another area of departure from the initial phase of the movement. The extent to which organizations like USPAACC present a threat to the validity of the panethnic concept is a question that warrants further research.

7. However, I argue in Chapter 4 that shared grievances against a common enemy may not necessarily provide sufficient incentive for building coalitions.

8. Although there appeared to be a 10 percent drop in 1997, the NAPALC audit commented that the decline was overstated and that anti-Asian incidents increased significantly in California and New Jersey, the nation's first and fifth largest states in terms of the Asian and Pacific Islander population (1998).

9. The bill was later rejected during negotiations with the House. In June 2000, a similar bill was passed by the Senate under a new name, the Local Law Enforcement Enhancement Act of 2000. The bill (S. Admt. 3473) provides up to $100,000 in grant money to state, local, and American Indian law enforcement officials who incur extraordinary expenses from investigating and prosecuting hate crimes.

10. This ratio is not much different from that reported in Takeda (1997) who found that 17.7 percent of students at Columbia, 17 percent of students at Northwestern, and 10.5 percent of students at Princeton during the 1994–95 academic year were Asian.

11. Unless indicated otherwise, information on student activism comes from a variety of Internet resources including press releases and e-mail exchanges posted to the Association for Asian American Studies Community List and website publications of student organizations.

12. The official title of John Huang, one of the most infamous Asian Americans charged with illegal conduct, was Vice Chair of the Finance Committee of the Democratic National Committee in the 1996 Clinton/Gore reelection campaign. It was the first time in the party's history that an APA was given a leadership role commensurate with the group's financial contributions.

13. The discrimination experienced by petitioners includes "treating Americans of Asian descent as foreigners, using racial stereotypes, making unfounded presumptions and generalizations based on ethnicity or alienage, ascribing criminal behavior or tendencies to an entire race of people in order to explain alleged illegal acts by a few, employing double standards in examining the conduct of Asians and Asian Pacific Americans far more critically than comparable and even more egregious conduct by others, and catering to xenopho-

bic fears by dramatizing claims of Asian Pacific American involvement in international conspiracies to corrupt American elections without specific proof" (Chen and Minami 1998, 358–59).

14. On August 3, 2000, President Clinton exercised his executive authority to recess appoint Lee, naming him Assistant Attorney General for Civil Rights and bypassing the stalled Senate confirmation process.

15. This is a classic metaphor in political science to describe the symbiotic relationship existing among interest groups, legislators, and agency bureaucrats, especially in the policy domains of agriculture, public works, and defense.

16. The power of full committees and their chairs was lost to subcommittees and the seniority system was undermined, whereas resources for individual members of Congress expanded, the number of staff exploded, and their performance was professionalized. This trend of decentralization (and re-centralization after the 1995 Republican reforms) was accompanied by the opening up of committee meetings and an increase in voting and amendment activity on the floor. All of these enhanced opportunities for interest group influence and congressional dependency on interest groups for information, expertise, and political support (Sheppard 1985; Evans and Oleszek 1997).

17. These reforms ban corporations, unions, and other groups from contributing money from their treasuries to federal candidates or party accounts that are used to finance federal election campaigns, place ceilings on the amounts individuals can give to candidates and parties in federal election, and require the disclosure of money spent in congressional elections. However, they allow corporations, trade associations, unions, and other groups to create campaign committees (Shaiko 1998).

18. PACs may contribute up to $5,000 per candidate per election and give directly to party committees and other PACs. Members of each group may also contribute as individuals to candidates, parties, and other PACs. In addition, PACs can spend unlimited amounts of money, through independent expenditures, to inform voters of the candidate's issue positions. Finally, PACs can make unlimited "soft money" contributions to state and national parties to help in party building (Petracca 1992).

Chapter 3   Participation in Electoral Politics: Evolving Patterns in Hawaii and Mainland States

1. The two cases involved are *Achi v. Kapiolani Estate* 1 U.S. D.C. HI 86 and *United States v. Ching Tai Sai* 1 U.S. D.C. HI 118.

2. Doubts about the loyalty of the territorial population and the novel nature of the application for admission from an overseas territory were two other major reasons. However, Hawaii had the support of the American public. Statehood bills passed the House in 1947, 1950, and 1953, but the Senate refused to concur until 1959 (Daniels 1988).

3. Dalip Singh Saund (D-CA) was the first Asian American congressman. He was elected, however, from a district that was predominantly white.

4. Unless indicated otherwise, the primary source of information on congresspersons serving in the 106th Congress (1999–2001) came from their respective websites published by the House (http://www.house.gov) and the Senate (http://www.senate.gov). It is supplemented by information contained in the Asian Pacific American Institute for Congressional Studies website (http://www.apaics.org) as well as by news coverage found in the Ethnic Newswatch, an electronic full-text database of the newspapers and magazines of the nonwhite press in America between 1991 and 1999.

5. These delegates from the Pacific Islands are included not only because of their close identification with fellow Asians in Congress, by law, these delegates do not have the privilege to vote on the floor, but can participate in House debates, serve on committees, and possess the powers and privileges of committee members. Their ability to influence was significantly boosted between 1993 and 1995, when the House Democrats changed the rules to allow delegates to participate in many key floor votes (Tarr and O'Connor 1999). Like other congresspersons, the delegates' priorities are to articulate and advance the unique needs and concerns of their constituents. However, as delegates of small population groups, they actively pursue political alliances by working extensively and cooperatively with others to promote environmental concerns, economic interests, educational opportunities and other common civil rights issues affecting Asian Americans, Pacific Islanders, and other peoples of color. Their presence and affinity with other Asian Americans on the Hill enhance the visibility and clout of Asian Americans by extending the notion of Asian America to cover the Pacific Islands whenever such a union is warranted or needed. Their support of pan-Asian causes has often been reciprocated with special legislation and allocations proposed by the Asian delegation from Hawaii. As an illustration of the solidarity between the Pacific Islanders and other Asians in Congress, Underwood was elected chair of the Congressional Asian Pacific Caucus (CAPC), a bicameral, panethnic coalition founded in 1994 by congressional members of Asian and other origins dedicated to advancing issues affecting Asian Pacific Americans.

6. It may be worth noting that the battle to appropriate was almost as intense as the fight for passage of the redress bill for several reasons. First, new restrictions set by the Gramm-Rudman-Hollings Act on the federal deficit made competition for federal monies more fierce than ever. Second, support for redress in the 101st Congress had weakened because of changeovers in House leadership. Third, funds set aside in the 1989 entitlement package were found to be insufficient to cover all of the eligible recipients, and a new legislation was needed.

7. Saiki entered the redress fight late and, as a freshman representative with few connections and a political and gender identity different from other Nikkei members, was not able to play a pivotal role in getting redress passed.

8. Hayakawa, a Canadian Sansei, actively denounced the redress movement and defended the incarceration order. He ran for the U.S. Senate as a political newcomer in 1976 and won by riding a tide of popularity resulting from his

rowdy handling of tumultuous student strikers in December 1968, when he leapt onto a sound truck and ripped out the public address system's wires before a crowd of 1,500 protestors. Kim, the nation's first Korean-born congressman, was one of the three congressmen from California who proposed amendments to curb illegal immigration in 1994. In an amendment to a housing program reauthorization bill, he proposed prohibiting illegal immigrants from receiving disaster assistance from the Federal Emergency Management Agency for longer than seven days. After limiting its application to crisis situations not declared as a national disaster by the president, his amendment passed on a 220–176 vote (Gimpel and Edwards 1999).

9. For instance, only Senator Akaka spoke on record to protest media and government stereotyping against Asian Americans during the campaign finance hearings. Except for sponsoring a concurrent resolution in the House highlighting the contributions of Asian Americans, none made any public attempt to help restore the liberty of and justice for Dr. Wen Ho Lee, a Chinese American citizen who was denied bail and held in solitary confinement after being charged with fifty-nine counts of mishandling nuclear data in December 1999.

10. The three-term representative shocked his supporters in July 1997 when he pleaded guilty to campaign finance violations after a four-year investigation. What troubled observers most was his apparent failure to differentiate between a personal account and that of the company he owned, which he had used to fund his campaigns. The other was the reluctance to admit wrongdoing in accepting donations from foreign corporations based in Korea (Lam 1996). He lost his reelection bid in the GOP primary in June 1998 after he was sentenced to house arrest and was unable to campaign in person because of the conviction.

11. In Idaho, for example, it was not until 1962 that a statute in the constitution amended in 1949 banning Chinese or persons of Mongolian descent not born in the United States from voting, serving as jurors, or holding any civil office was appealed. Congressman Compton White cited the outstanding military records of Nisei as the major reason for its repeal (Hosakawa 1969).

12. The aggregate number reported here is the total count of all individuals listed in the *Almanac*, which includes all elected and appointed officials at federal, state, and local levels of government as well as all state-executive agency members. Adding all individuals appointed to major commissions anywhere in the nation to this count, the total number of Asian Americans holding elective or appointive positions in the mid- to late 1990s could be as high as 2,000, according to an estimate made by the editors in a personal correspondence with the author in October 1999.

13. Despite the best of intentions and efforts, the editors of the *Almanac* acknowledged that it was unlikely to have a complete record of all Asian Pacific American elected and appointed officials because of limitations associated with the surname identification approach and the reliance on knowledgeable individuals and selected printed resources in the collection of data (Nakanishi and Lai 1998).

14. Naomi Matsusow, a Caucasian woman elected to the Assembly in 1992, was listed in the *Almanac* as an Asian, perhaps because of her marriage to a Japanese American.

15. This list is based on Cho's (1999a) research using the Federal Election Commission Data and reported in Tables 1A and 1B. The list included only those who raised at least $50,000 or received at least 40 percent of votes in a contested election.

16. There are a few exceptions to this rule. In cities such as New York and Chicago, noncitizen parents of children enrolled in public schools were allowed to vote in school board elections. In Takoma Park, Maryland, noncitizens were able to vote in local elections (Raskin 1993).

17. Between 1848 and 1922, about twenty states in the Midwest, West, and South extended, at some point, voting rights to aliens who had declared their intention to become citizens (Kleppner 1987).

18. Chinese assistance is provided in three California counties (Alameda, Los Angeles, and San Francisco) and three New York counties (Kings, New York, and Queens). Japanese assistance is provided in Los Angeles County and Honolulu County. Vietnamese assistance is provided in two counties of Southern California (Los Angeles and Orange). Los Angeles County also provides Tagalog assistance, and three counties in Hawaii (Honolulu, Kauai, and Maui) offer Ilocano assistance.

Chapter 4   How Can We All Get Along? Cross-Racial Coalition-Building Possibilities and Barriers

1. Whiteness here refers to a privileged position in the society produced by the contending forces of capitalism and republicanism, which can theoretically be occupied by individuals or groups of any skin color or bloodline but has realistically been occupied mostly by European immigrant groups (Jacobson 1998). Like any other racialized identity, whiteness exists as a contested terrain and its meanings vary over time and space (Omi and Winant 1994; Haney Lopez 1996; Lipsitz 1998).

2. Much of the Southwest was Mexico until the annexation of Texas in 1845 and the annexation of Arizona, California, Colorado, New Mexico, Nevada, Kansas, Oklahoma, Utah, and Wyoming in the 1848 Treaty of Guadalupe Hidalgo.

3. Puerto Ricans residing on the island are subject to military draft but cannot vote in U.S. presidential elections.

4. Given that the 1992 disturbances in Los Angeles probably marked one of the low points in race relations, the finding of this improvement might be, in part, an artifact of the time frame. I thank Andrew Aoki for pointing this out.

5. Details about this measure indexing group-based participation using the LASUI dataset are described in Chapter 5.

6. The appropriateness of using mainstream indicators such as political partisanship and ideology to gauge the opinions of Asians may be a subject of

debate. However, we need more research addressing the meanings of these terms to Asians before we can assess the degree of bias associated with these measures.

7. The assessment of local level voting patterns is based on the APALC 1998 exit poll results reported in Feng, Ichinose, and Patraporn (1999). In the fifty-third state assembly district race, a Democrat, George Nakano, received 85 percent of the Asian vote, 81 percent of the Latino vote, and 50 percent of the white vote. In the sixtieth district race, a Democrat, Ben Wong, received 61 percent of votes among Asians, 42 percent among Latinos, and 23 percent among whites.

8. When an Asian Democrat male ran against a white Republican male in the 1993 Los Angeles mayoral race, a *Los Angeles Times* exit poll showed that Michael Woo received higher support from Blacks (86 percent) and Latinos (57 percent) than from whites (33 percent).

9. This is the same question used in table 5.3, except that the racial term *Asian* may be replaced with *Black, Latino,* or *white.*

Chapter 5   What Ties That Bind? Comparing Political Attitudes and Behavior Across Major Asian American Groups

1. The on-air exchange took place on May 23, 1999, between Joe Klein of *Newsweek* and William Safire of the *New York Times.*

2. The measure of homeownership is used as a surrogate indicator of one's class status. Information on this from a more direct measure, family income, is not as useful because of the large number of missing cases.

3. For models predicting registration (N=4,028), the model chi-square improves from 94.15 for the restricted model to 698.06 for the full model. For models predicting turnout among the registered (N=2,199), the model chi-square improves from 46.51 for the restricted model to 198.11 for the full model.

4. The adjusted R square jumps from 0.04 for the restricted model to 0.19 for the full model, meaning that 19 percent of the variation in the dependent variable is being explained away by ethnicity and control variables.

Chapter 6   Linking Race, Ethnicity, Class, and Gender: Asian American Women and Political Participation

1. The size of the logistic regression coefficient for an Asian male changes from -0.57 to -0.88 in 1990, from -0.67 to -1.07 in 1992, from -0.68 to -0.75 in 1994, and from -0.53 to -0.60 in 1996, but from -0.85 to -0.79 in 1998. All coefficients are significant at $p \leq 0.005$.

Appendix   Researching Asian American Political Behavior with Sample Surveys: A Methodological Report

1. This is assessed according to author's analysis of the voter supplement files complied by the Census Bureau in the November elections of 1990 to 1998 and reported in Chapter 3.

2. According to the California Secretary of State's office, 20 percent of registered voters used absentee ballots in the 1996 general elections, a number that has risen significantly since 1990. To address this phenomenon in California, VNS conducted telephone surveys of absentee voters the week before the general elections. About 25 percent of Asian respondents in 1996 and 15 percent of them in 1998 were interviewed by phone.

3. Major components of the redesign include a new questionnaire, computer-assisted method of data collection, and new population controls based on the 1990 census. See CPS-94 Technical Documentation, Attachment 5 "Revisions to the CPS" for details.

4. However, in the author's analysis of the 139 Asian voters, 26 percent were absentee voters. In the VNS-CA data for 1996, they showed no statistical differences between the two types of voters in age, education, income, presidential vote, political party identification, ideology, and the vote on Proposition 209.

References

Abramson, Paul John Aldrich, and David Rohde. 1994. *Change and Continuity in the 1992 Elections*. Washington, D.C.: Congressional Quarterly Press.
———. 1998. *Change and Continuity in the 1996 Elections*. Washington, D.C.: Congressional Quarterly Press.
Acuna, Rodolfo F. 1996. *Anything but Mexican: Chicanos in Contemporary Los Angeles*. New York: Verso.
Akamine, Ruth. 1993. "Class, Ethnicity, and the Transformation of Hawaii's Sugar Workers, 1920–1946." Pp. 175–195 in *The Politics of Immigrant Workers: Labor Activism and Migration in the World Economy Since 1830*, ed. Camille Guerin-Gonzales and Carl Strikwerda. New York: Holmes & Meier.
Almaguer, Tomas. 1984. "Racial Domination and Class Conflict in Capitalist Agriculture: The Oxnard Sugar Beet Workers' Strike of 1903." *Labor History* 21:325–50.
———. 1994. *Racial Fault Lines: The Historical Origins of White Supremacy in California*. Berkeley: University of California Press.
Alozie, Nicholas O. 1992. "The Election of Asians to City Councils." *Social Science Quarterly* 73:90–99.
American Enterprise Institute for Public Policy Research. 1980–present. *Vital Statistics on Congress*. Washington, D.C.: Author.
Amott, Teresa, and Julie Matthaei. 1991. *Race, Gender, and Work: A Multicultural Economic History of Women in the United States*. Boston: South End Press.
Ancheta, Angelo N. 1998. *Race, Rights, and the Asian American Experience*. New Brunswick, N.J.: Rutgers University Press.
Anderson, Benedict. 1983. *Imagined Communities*. London: Verso.
Anthony, J. Garner. 1955. *Hawaii under Army Rule*. Stanford, Calif.: Stanford University Press.
Arinaga, Esther K., and Rene E. Ojiri. 1992. "Patsy Takemoto Mink." Pp. 251–80 in *Called from Within: Early Women Lawyers of Hawaii*, ed. Mari Matsuda. Honolulu: University of Hawaii Press.
Ariyoshi, Koji. 1976. "Plantation Struggles in Hawaii." Pp. 380–92 in *Counterpoint: Perspectives on Asian America*, ed. Emma Gee. Los Angeles: UCLA Asian American Studies Center.
Armentrout Ma, L. Eve. 1990. *Revolutionaries, Monarchists, and Chinatowns: Chinese Politics in the Americas and the 1911 Revolution*. Honolulu: University of Hawaii Press.
Arvizu, John, and F. Chris Garcia. 1996. "Latino Voting Participation: Explaining and Differentiating Latino Voting Turnout." *Hispanic Journal of Behavioral Sciences* 18:104–28.

Babbie, Earl. 1989. *The Practice of Social Research*. 5th ed. Belmont, Calif.: Wadsworth.

Bailey, Paul. 1971. *City in the Sun: The Japanese Concentration Camp at Poston, Arizona*. Los Angeles: Westernlore Press.

Baron, Deborah G., and Susan B. Gall. eds. 1996. *Asian American Chronology*. New York: U.X.L.

Baxter, Sandra, and Majorie Lansing. 1983. *Women and Politics: The Visible Minority*. Ann Arbor: University of Michigan Press.

Bell, David. 1985. "The Triumph of Asian Americans." *The New Republic* (July 15–22) 193:24–31.

Bell, Roger. 1984. *Last Among Equals: Hawaiian Statehood and American Politics*. Honolulu: University of Hawaii Press.

Blalock, Hubert M., Jr. 1967. *Toward a Theory of Minority-Group Relations*. New York: Wiley.

————. 1982. *Race and Ethnic Relations*. Englewood Cliffs, N.J.: Prentice-Hall.

Bobo, Lawrence, and Franklin D. Gilliam, Jr. 1990. "Race, Sociopolitical Participation, and Black Empowerment." *American Political Science Review* 84: 377–93.

Bobo, Lawrence, James Johnson, Melvin Oliver, Reynolds Farley, Barry Bluestone, Irene Browne, Sheldon Danziger, Gary Green, Harry Holzer, Maria Krysan, Michael Massagli, and Camille Zubrinsky Charles. 1998. Multi-City Study of Urban Inequality, 1992–1994: Atlanta, Boston, Detroit, and Los Angeles: Household Survey Data [computer file]. 2d ICPSR version. Atlanta: Mathematica; Boston: University of Massachusetts, Survey Research Laboratory; Ann Arbor, Mich: University of Michigan, Detroit Area Study and Institute for Social Research, Survey Research Center; Los Angeles: University of California, Survey Research Program [producers]. Inter-university Consortium for Political and Social Research [distributor].

Bonacich, Edna. 1972. "A Theory of Ethnic Antagonism: The Split Labor Market." *American Sociological Review* 37:547–59.

————. 1984. "Some Basic Facts: Patterns of Asian Immigration and Exclusion." Pp. 60–77 in *Labor Immigration Under Capitalism: Asian Workers in the United States Before World War II*, eds. Lucie Cheng and Edna Bonacich. Berkeley: University of California Press.

Bonner, Arthur. 1997. *Alas! What Brought Thee Hither? The Chinese in New York 1800–1950*. Cranbury, N.J.: Associated University Presses.

Boylan, Dan. 1992. "Blood Runs Thick: Ethnicity as a Factor in Hawaii's Politics." Pp. 67–80 in *Politics and Public Policy in Hawaii*, ed. by Zachary Smith and Richard Pratt. Albany: State University of New York Press.

Briggs, Vernon, Jr. 1992. *Mass Immigration and the National Interest*. Armonk, N.Y.: M.E. Sharpe.

Browning, Rufus P., Dale Rogers Marshall, and David H. Tabb. 1986. *Protest Is Not Enough*. Berkeley: University of California Press.

Brownstone, David M. 1988. *The Chinese-American Heritage*. New York: Facts on File.

Cabezas, Amado, Larry Shinagawa, and Gary Kawaguchi. 1986–87. "New Inquiries into the Labor Force: Pilipino Americans in California." *Amerasia Journal* 13 (1): 1–21.

Cain, Bruce E., Roderick Kiewiet, and Carole Uhlaner. 1991. "The Acquisition of Partisanship Among Latinos and Asian Americans." *American Journal of Political Science* 35:390–422.

Carmichael, Stokely, and Charles Hamilton. 1967. *Black Power: The Politics of Liberation in America*. New York: Random House.

Carroll, Susan. 1988. "Women's Autonomy and the Gender Gap." Pp. 236–57 in *The Politics of the Gender Gap: The Social Construction of Political Influence*, ed. C.M. Mueller. Newbury Park, Calif.: Sage.

Chan, Sucheng. 1991a. *Asian Americans: An Interpretive History*. Boston: Twayne Publishers.

———. 1991b. *Asian Californians*. San Francisco: MTL/Boyd & Fraser.

———. 1991c. "The Exclusion of Chinese Women, 1870–1943." Pp. 94–146 in *Entry Denied: Exclusion and the Chinese Community in America, 1882–1943*, ed. Sucheng Chan. Philadelphia: Temple University Press.

Chang, Edward, and Jeannette Diaz-Veizades. 1998. *Ethnic Peace in the American City: Building Community in Los Angeles and Beyond*. New York: New York University Press.

Chavez, John R. 1989. "Aztlan, Cibola and Frontier New Spain." In *Aztlan: Essays on the Chicano Homeland*, ed. Rudolfo Anaya and Francisco Lomeli. Albuquerque: University of New Mexico Press.

Chavez, Leo. 1997. "Immigration Reform and Nativism: The Nationalist Response to the Transnational Challenge." Pp. 61–77 in *Immigrants Out! The New Nativism and the Anti-immigrant Impulse in the United States*, ed. Juan Perea. New York: New York University Press.

Chen, Edward, and Dale Minami. 1998. "Petition for Hearing." *Asian Law Journal* 5:357–82.

Chen, Hsuan Julia. 1941. The Chinese Community in New York, 1920–1940. Ph.D. diss., American University.

Cheng, Lucie. 1984. "Free, Indentured, Enslaved: Chinese Prostitutes in Nineteenth-Century America." Pp. 402–34 in *Labor Immigration Under Capitalism: Asian Workers in the United States Before World War II*, ed. Lucie Cheng and Edna Bonacich. Berkeley: University of California Press.

Cheng, Lucie, and Edna Bonacich, eds. 1984. *Labor Immigration Under Capitalism: Asian Workers in the United States Before World War II*. Berkeley: University of California Press.

Cheng, Lucie, and Yen Espiritu. 1989. "Korean Business in Black and Hispanic Neighborhoods: A Study of Intergroup Relations." *Sociological Perspectives* 32:521–34.

Chin, Gabriel J. 1996. "The Civil Rights Revolution Comes to Immigration Law: A New Look at the Immigration and Nationality Act of 1965." *North Carolina Law Review* 75:273–345.

Chinese Equal Rights League. 1892. *Appeal of the Chinese Equal Rights League to the People of the United States for Equality of Manhood*. New York: Chinese Equal Rights League.

Chinn, Thomas, H. Mark Lai, and Philip P. Choy. 1969. *A History of the Chinese in California: A Syllabus*. San Francisco: Chinese Historical Society of America.

Cho, Wendy Tam. 1999a. Expanding the Logic Behind Campaign Contributions:

Lessons from Asian American Campaign Contributors. Paper delivered at the Annual Meeting of the American Political Science Association, 2–5 September, Hilton Atlanta and Towers and Atlanta Marriott Marquis, Atlanta, Georgia.

———. 1999b. "Naturalization, Socialization, and Participation: Immigrants and (Non-) Voting." *Journal of Politics* 61:1140–55.

Chow, Esther Ngan-Ling. 1987. "The Development of Feminist Consciousness Among Asian American Women." *Gender and Society* 1 (3): 284–99.

———. 1996. "Introduction: Transforming Knowledgment: Race, Class, and Gender." Pp. xix-xxvi in *Race, Class, & Gender: Common Bonds, Different Voices*, ed. Esther Chow, Doris Wilkinson, and Maxine Baca Zinn. Thousand Oaks, Calif.: Sage.

Choy, Bong-youn. 1979. *Koreans in America*. Chicago: Nelson-Hall.

Chu, Judy. 1989. "Asian Pacific American Women in Mainstream Politics." Pp. 405–21 in *Making Waves: An Anthology of Writings By and About Asian American Women*. Boston: Beacon Press.

Chu, Judy, and Susie Ling. 1984. "Chinese Women at Work." Pp. 65–90 in *Linking Our Lives*. Los Angeles: Chinese Historical Society of Southern California.

Chuman, Frank F. 1976. *The Bamboo People: The Law and Japanese Americans*. Del Mar, Calif.: Publisher's Inc.

Chung, Sue Fawn. 1998. "Fighting for Their American Rights: A History of the Chinese American Citizens Alliance." Pp. 95–126 in *Claiming America: Constructing Chinese American Identities During the Exclusion Era*, ed. Scott Wong and Sucheng Chan. Philadelphia: Temple University Press.

Clar, Reva, and William M. Kramer. 1988. "Chinese-Jewish Relations in the Far West: 1850–1950." *Western States Jewish History* 21:12–35, 116–121.

Cohen, Lucy M. 1984. *The Chinese in the Post–Civil War South: A People Without a History*. Baton Rouge: Louisiana State University Press.

Congressional Quarterly, Inc. 1965. *Politics in America, 1945–1964*. Washington, D.C.: Congressional Quarterly Press.

———. 1965–present. *Politics in America*.Washington D.C.: Congressional Quarterly Press.

Conway, M. Margaret. 1991. *Political Participation in the United States*. 2d ed. Washington, D.C.: Congressional Quarterly Press.

Conway, M. Margaret, Gertrude Steuernagel, and David Ahern. 1997. *Women and Political Participation*. Washington, D.C.: Congressional Quarterly Press.

Coolidge, Mary R. 1909. *Chinese Immigration*. New York: H. Holt & Co.

Cooper, George, and Gavan Daws. 1985. *Land and Power in Hawaii*. Honolulu: Benchmark Books.

Cordova, Fred. 1983. *Filipinos: Forgotten Asian Americans*. Seattle: Demonstration Project for Asian Americans.

Cornell, Stephen. 1988. *The Return of the Native: American Indian Political Resurgence*. New York: Oxford University Press.

Dang, Janet. 1999. "Calls Intensify for Stiffer Hate Crime Law." *Asianweek* 20 (46): 9.

Daniels, Roger. 1962. *The Politics of Prejudice: The Anti-Japanese Movement in California and the Struggle for Japanese Exclusion*. Berkeley: University of California Press.

————. 1971. *Concentration Camps USA: Japanese Americans and World War II.* Hinsdale, Ill.: Dryden Press.

————. 1988. *Asian America: Chinese and Japanese in the United States since 1850.* Seattle: University of Washington Press.

————. 1990. *Coming to America: A History of Immigration and Ethnicity in American Life.* New York: HarperCollins.

Dao, James. 1999. "Immigrant Diversity Slows Traditional Political Climb." *New York Times* (28 December).

Davidson, Chandler. 1994. "The Recent Evolution of Voting Rights Law Affecting Racial and Language Minorities." Pp. 21–37 in *Quiet Revolution in the South: The Impact of the Voting Rights Act, 1965–1990,* ed. Chandler Davidson and Bernard Grofman. Princeton, N.J.: Princeton University Press.

Davison, Sue. 1994. *A Heart in Politics: Jeannette Rankin and Patsy Mink.* Seattle: Seal Press.

Daws, Gavan. 1968. *Shoal of Time.* New York: Macmillan.

Delgado, Gary. 1996. "How the Empress Gets Her Clothes: Asian Immigrant Women Fight Fashion Designer Jessica McClintock." Pp. 81–94 in *Beyond Identity Politics: Emerging Social Justice Movements in Communities of Color,* ed. John Anner. Boston: South End Press.

Dennis, Jack. 1991. "The Study of Electoral Behavior." Pp. 51–89 in *Political Science.* Vol. 3, ed. William Crotty. Evanston, Ill.: Northwestern University Press.

De Witt, Howard. 1976. *Anti-Filipino Movements in California: A History, Bibliography and Study Guide.* San Francisco: R & E Research Associates.

————. 1980. *Violence in the Field: California Filipino Farm Labor Unionization During the Great Depression.* Saratoga, Calif.: Century Twenty One Publishing.

Dirlik, Arif. 1998. "The Asia-Pacific in Asian-American Perspective." Pp. 283–308 in *What Is in a Rim? Critical Perspectives on the Pacific Region Idea,* 2d ed., ed. Arif Dirlik. Lanham, Md.: Rowman and Littlefield.

————. 1999. "Asians on the Rim: Transnational Capital and Local Community in the Making of Contemporary Asian America." Pp. 29–60 in *Across the Pacific: Asian Americans and Globalization,* ed. Evelyn Hu-DeHart. Philadelphia: Temple University Press.

Drinnon, Richard. 1987. *Keeper of Concentration Camps: Dillon S. Myer and American Racism.* Berkeley: University of California Press.

Eisinger, Peter K. 1976. *Patterns of Interracial Politics.* New York: Academic Press.

Erie, Steven P., and Harold Brackman. 1993. *Paths to Political Incorporation for Latinos and Asian Pacifics in California.* University of California: The California Policy Seminar.

Espina, Marina E. 1988. *Filipinos in Louisiana.* New Orleans: Laborde.

Espiritu, Yen Le. 1992. *Asian American Panethnicity.* Philadelphia: Temple University Press.

————. 1997. *Asian American Women and Men: Labor, Laws, and Love.* Thousand Oaks, Calif.: Sage.

————, ed. 1995. *Filipino American Lives.* Philadelphia: Temple University Press.

Espiritu, Yen Le, and Paul Ong. 1994. "Class Constraints on Racial Solidarity among Asian Americans." Pp. 295–322 in *The New Asian Immigration in Los*

Angeles and Global Restructuring, ed. Paul Ong, Edna Bonacich, and Lucie Cheng. Philadelphia: Temple University Press.

Esser, Dominique, Kevin Fitzpatrick, Mohammed Kazem, Biju Mathew, and Rizwan Raja. 1999. "Reorganizing Organizing: Immigrant Labor in North America: Interview with New York Taxi Workers' Alliance." *Amerasia Journal* 25 (3): 171–81.

Euchner, Charles. 1996. *Extraordinary Politics*. Boulder, Colo.: Westview Press.

Evans, C. Lawrence, and Walter J. Oleszek. 1997. "Congressional Tsunami? The Politics of Committee Reform." Pp. 193–211 in *Congress Reconsidered*, 6th ed., ed. Lawrence C. Dodd and Bruce I. Oppenheimer. Washington, D.C.: Congressional Quarterly.

Feagin, Joe. 1991. "The Continuing Significance of Race: Antiblack Discrimination in Public Places." *American Sociological Review* 56:101–16.

———. 1997. "Old Poison in New Bottles: The Deep Roots of Modern Nativism." Pp. 13–43 in *Immigrants Out! The New Nativism and the Anti-immigrant Impulse in the United States*, ed. Juan Perea. New York: New York University Press.

Feagin, Joe R., and Clairece Feagin. 1999. *Racial and Ethnic Relations*. 6th ed. Upper Saddle River, N.J.: Prentice Hall.

Feng, Kathay, Daniel Ichinose, and Rita Paraporn. 1999. *November 1998 Southern California Voter Survey Report*. Los Angeles: Asian Pacific American Legal Center.

Feng, Kathay, and Bonnie Tang. 1997. *1996 Southern California Asian Pacific American Exit Poll Report: An Analysis of APA Voter Behavior and Opinions*. Los Angeles and Washington, D.C.: Asian Pacific American Legal Center and National Asian Pacific American Legal Consortium.

Flanigan, William H., and Nancy H. Zingale. 1994. *Political Behavior of the American Electorate*. 8th ed. Washington, D.C.: Congressional Quarterly.

Foner, Philip S. 1947. *History of the Labor Movement in the United States*. Vol. 3. New York: International.

Foner, Philip S., and Daniel Rosenberg, eds. 1993. *Racism, Dissent, and Asian Americans from 1850 to the Present: A Documentary History*. Westport, Conn.: Greenwood Press.

Franks, Joel. 1993. "Chinese Shoemaker Protest in 19th Century San Francisco." Pp. 305–8 in *Asian Americans in the United States*. Vol. 1, ed. Alexander Yamato, Soo-Young Chin, Wendy L. Ng, and Joel Franks. Dubuque, Iowa: Kendall/Hunt.

Friday, Chris. 1994. *Organizing Asian American Labor: The Pacific Coast Canned-Salmon Industry, 1870–1942*. Philadelphia: Temple University Press.

———. 1995. "Asian American Labor and Historical Interpretation." *Labor History* 36:524–46.

Fuchs, Lawrence H. 1961. *Hawaii Pono: A Social History*. New York: Harcourt, Brace & World.

———. 1990. *The American Kaleidoscope: Race, Ethnicity, and the Civic Culture*. Hanover, Conn.: Wesleyan University Press.

Fugita, Stephen, and David O'Brien. 1978. "Economics, Ideology, and Ethnicity: The Struggle Between the United Farm Workers and the Nisei Farmers League." *Social Problems* 25:146–56.

Garza, Rodolfo de la, Angelo Falcon, F. Chris Garcia, and John A. Garcia. 1992. "Latino National Political Survey," 1989–1990 [Computer file]. Philadelphia: Temple University, Institute for Social Research [producer]. Ann Arbor, Mich.: Inter-university Consortium for Political and Social Research [distributor].

Gee, Emma. 1982. "Issei Women." Pp. 66–74 in *Asian and Pacific American Experiences: Women's Perspectives*, ed. Nobuya Tsuchida. Minneapolis, Minn.: Asian/Pacific American Learning Resource Center.

Geron, Tomio. 1996. "APA Activism, New York Style: The Confrontational Tactics of the Coalition on Anti-Asian Violence Are Controversial, but Effective." *Asianweek* 17 (32): 13.

Gimpel, James G., and James R. Edwards, Jr. 1999. *The Congressional Politics of Immigration Reform*. Needham Heights, Mass.: Allyn & Bacon.

Glenn, Evelyn Nakano. 1985. "Racial Ethnic Women's Labor: The Intersection of Race, Gender and Class Oppression." *Review of Radical Political Economics* 17:86–108.

———. 1986. *Issei, Nisei, War Bride: Three Generations of Japanese American Women in Domestic Service*. Philadelphia: Temple University Press.

Goldman, Sheldon, and Elliot Slotnick. 1997. "Clinton's First Term Judiciary: Many Bridges and Cross." *Judicature* 80:269.

Gonzalez, Gilbert G. 1999. "The 1993 Los Angeles County Farm Workers Strike." Pp. 111–40 in *Latino Social Movements: Historical and Theoretical Perspectives*, ed. Rodolfo D. Torres and George Katsiaficas. New York: Routledge.

Gorelick, Sherry. 1996. "Contradictions of Feminist Methodology." Pp. 385–401 in *Race, Class, & Gender: Common Bonds, Different Voices*, ed. Esther Chow, Doris Wilkinson, and Maxine Baca Zinn. Thousand Oaks, Calif.: Sage.

Gupta, Anu. 1998. "At the Crossroads: College Activism and Its Impact on Asian American Identity Formation." Pp. 127–45 in *A Part, Yet Apart: South Asians in Asian America*, ed. Lavina Shankar and Rajini Srikanth. Philadelphia: Temple University Press.

Gutierrez, David. 1995. *Walls and Mirrors: Mexican Americans, Mexican Immigrants, and the Politics of Ethnicity*. Berkeley: University of California Press.

Gyory, Andrew. 1998. *Closing the Gate: Race, Politics, and the Chinese Exclusion Act*. Chapel Hill: The University of North Carolina Press.

Haas, Michael. 1992. *Institutional Racism: The Case of Hawaii*. Westport, Conn.: Praeger.

Haines, David. 1996. "Patterns in Refugee Resettlement and Adaptation." Pp. 28–59 in *Refugees in America in the 1990s*, ed. David Haines. Westport, Conn.: Greenwood Press.

Haney Lopez, Ian. 1996. *White by Law: The Legal Construction of Race*. New York: New York University Press.

Harris, Davis. 1994. "The 1990 Census Count of American Indians: What Do the Numbers Really Mean?" *Social Science Quarterly* 75:580–93.

Hata, Donald T., Jr. 1978. *"Undesirables": Early Immigrants and the Anti-Japanese Movement in San Francisco, 1892–1893.* New York: Arno Press.

Hatamiya, Leslie T. 1993. *Righting a Wrong: Japanese Americans and the Passage of the Civil Liberties Act of 1988.* Stanford, Calif.: Stanford University Press.

Heclo, Hugh. 1978. "Issue Networks and the Executive Establishment." In *The New American Political System*, ed. Anthony King. Washington, D.C.: American Enterprise Institute.

Hellwig, David. 1977. "Afro-American Reactions to the Japanese and the Anti-Japanese Movement, 1906–1924." *Phylon* 38:93–104.

———. 1979. "Black Reactions to Chinese Immigration and the Anti-Chinese Movement: 1850–1910." *Amerasia* 6 (2): 25–44.

Helweg, Arthur, and Usha Helweg. 1990. *An Immigrant Success Story: East Indians in America.* Philadelphia: University of Pennsylvania Press.

Hendrick, Irving G. 1977. *The Education of Non-whites in California, 1849–1970.* San Francisco: R & E Research Associates.

Hess, Gary. 1974. "The Forgotten Asian Americans: The East Indian Community in the United States." *Pacific Historical Review* 43:576–96.

Hing, Bill Ong. 1993. *Making and Remaking Asian America Through Immigration Policy 1850–1990.* Stanford, Calif.: Stanford University Press.

Hington, Benjamin, and Raymond E. Wolfinger. 1998. "Estimating the Effects of the National Voter Registration Act of 1993." *Political Behavior* 20:79–104.

Hoexter, Corinne K. 1976. *From Canton to California: The Epic of Immigration.* New York: Four Winds Press.

Hong, Peter Y. 1998. "The Changing Face of Higher Education; Trends: Asian Americans' Numbers and Influence Now Mark All Segments of College Life." *Los Angeles Times* (14 July).

Horton, John. 1995. *The Politics of Diversity: Immigration, Resistance, and Change in Monterey Park, California.* Philadelphia: Temple University Press.

Hosakawa, Bill. 1969. *Nisei: The Quiet Americans, the Story of a People.* New York: Morrow.

———. 1982. *JACL: In Quest of Justice.* New York: Morrow.

Hu-DeHart, Evelyn, ed. 1999. *Across the Pacific: Asian Americans and Globalization.* Philadelphia: Temple University Press.

Hum, Tarry, and Michela Zonta. 2000. "Residential Patterns of Asian Pacific Americans." Pp. 191–242 in *Transforming Race Relations*, ed. Paul Ong. Los Angeles: LEAP Asian Pacific American Public Policy Institute and UCLA Asian American Studies Center.

Hune, Shirley. 1982. "Politics of Chinese Exclusion: Legislative Executive Conflict 1876–1882." *Amerasia Journal* 9 (1): 5–27.

———. 1996. "Mind, Body, and Soul: Why American Higher Education Needs Asian American Programs." *Asianweek* 18 (3): 13.

———. 2000. "Doing Gender with a Feminist Gaze: Toward a Historical Reconstruction of Asian America." Pp. 413–30 in *Contemporary Asian America: A*

Multidisciplinary Reader, ed. Min Zhou and James V. Gatewood. New York: New York University Press.

Hurh, Won M., and Kwang C. Kim. 1984. "Adhesive Sociocultural Adaptation of Korean Immigrants in the U.S.: An Alternative Strategy of Minority Adaptation." *International Migration Review* 18:188–217.

Ichioka, Yuji. 1979. "Asian Immigrant Coal Miners and the United Mine Workers of America: Race and Class at Rock Springs, Wyoming, 1907." *Amerasia Journal* 6 (2): 1–23.

————. 1988. *The Issei: The World of the First Generation Japanese Immigrants, 1885–1924.* New York: The Free Press.

————. 1990. "Japanese Immigrant Nationalism: The Issei and the Sino-Japanese War, 1937–1941." *California History* 69:260–74.

Inouye, Daniel K. 1967. *Journey to Washington.* Englewood Cliffs, N.J.: Prentice Hall.

Irons, Peter. 1983. *Justice at War: The Story of the Japanese American Internment Cases.* New York: Oxford University Press.

Jackson, James S. 1993. National Black Election Panel Study, 1984 and 1988 [Computer file]. Conducted by University of Michigan, Research Center for Group Dynamics. ICPSR, ed. Ann Arbor, Mich.: Inter-university Consortium for Political and Social Research [producer and distributor].

Jacobson, Matthew F. 1998. *Whiteness of a Different Color: European Immigrants and the Alchemy of Race.* Cambridge, Mass.: Harvard University Press.

Jaimes, M. Annette. 1994. "Liberating Race." Pp. 365–72 in *The State of Asian America: Activism and Resistance in the 1990s,* ed. Karin Aguilar-San Juan. Boston: South End Press.

Jamieson, Kathleen H. 1992. *Packaging the Presidency: A History and Criticism of Presidential Campaign Advertising.* 2d ed. New York: Oxford University Press.

Jaynes, Gerald, and Robin Williams, Jr. 1989. *A Common Destiny: Blacks and American Society.* Washington, D.C.: National Academy Press.

Jen, Gish. 2000. "Wen Ho Lee, Still Not So Very Free." *New York Times* (15 September).

Jennings, James, and Francisco Chapman. 1998. "Puerto Ricans and the Community Control Movement: An Interview with Luis Fuentes." Pp. 280–95 in *The Puerto Rican Movement: Voices from the Diaspora,* ed. Andres Torres and Jose E. Velazquez. Philadelphia: Temple University Press.

Jennings, Jerry T. 1993. *Voting and Registration in the Election of November 1992.* Washington, D.C.: U.S. Government Printing Office.

Jensen, Joan M. 1988. *Passage from India: Asian Indian Immigration in North America.* New Haven, Conn.: Yale University Press.

Jer, Darren. 1994. "One for All?" *A. Magazine* (31 October).

Jiobu, Robert M. 1996. "Recent Asian Pacific Immigrants: The Demographic Background." Pp. 35–57 in *The State of Asian Pacific America: Reframing the Immigration Debate: A Public Policy Report,* ed. Bill Ong Hing and Ronald Lee. Los Angeles: LEAP Asian Pacific American Public Policy Institute and UCLA Asian American Studies Center.

Jo, Moon H. 1984. "The Putative Political Complacency of Asian Americans." *Political Psychology* 5:583–685.

Jo, Moon H., and Daniel Mast. 1993. "Changing Images of Asian Americans." *International Journal of Politics, Culture and Society* 6:417–41.

Johnson, Kevin. 1997a. "Racial Hierarchy, Asian Americans and Latinos as 'Foreigners,' and Social Change: Is Law the Way to Go?" *Oregon Law Review* 76:347–68.

———. 1998. "Race, Immigration Laws, and Domestic Race Relations: A 'Magic Mirror' into the Heart of Darkness." *Indiana Law Journal* 73:1111–59.

Kang, K. Connie. 1997. "Asian American Needs Are Focus of New Group." *Los Angeles Times* (24 August).

Kantowicz, Edward T. "Voting and Parties." Pp. 29–68 in *The Politics of Ethnicity,* ed. Michael Walzer, Edward Kantowicz, John Higham, and Mona Harrignton. Cambridge, Mass.: Harvard University Press.

Kearney, Reginald. 1998. *African American Views of the Japanese: Solidarity or Sedition?* Albany: State University of New York Press.

Kent, Noel J. 1983. *Hawaii: Islands Under the Influence.* New York: Monthly Review Press.

Kibria, Nazli. 1990. "Power, Patriarchy, and Gender Conflict in the Vietnamese Immigrant Community." *Gender and Society* 4 (1): 9–24.

Kim, Elaine H., Lilia V. Villanueva, and Asian Women United of California, eds. 1997. *Making More Waves: New Writing by Asian American Women.* Boston: Beacon.

Kim, Hyung-chan, ed. 1992. *Asian Americans and the Supreme Court: A Documentary History.* Westport, Conn.: Greenwood Press.

———. 1994. *A Legal History of Asian Americans, 1790–1990.* Westport, Conn.: Greenwood Press.

———, ed. 1996. *Asian Americans and Congress: A Documentary History.* Westport, Conn.: Greenwood Press.

Kim, Hyun Sook. 1995. "Theorizing Marginality: Violence Against Korean Women." Pp. 217–32 in *Privileging Positions: The Sites of Asian American Studies,* ed. Gary Okihiro, Marilyn Alquizola, and Dorothy Fujita Rory. Pullman: Washington State University Press.

Kitano, Harry. 1969. *Japanese Americans: The Evolution of a Subculture.* Englewood Cliffs, N.J.: Prentice-Hall.

Kitano, Harry L., and Roger Daniels. 1995. *Asian Americans: Emerging Minorities.* 2d ed. Englewood Cliffs, N.J.: Prentice-Hall.

Kleppner, Paul. 1987. *Continuity and Change in Electoral Politics, 1893–1928.* Westport, Conn.: Greenwood.

Kochiyama, Yuri. 1994. "The Impact of Malcolm X on Asian American Politics and Activism." Pp. 129–41 in *Blacks, Latinos, and Asians in Urban America: Status and Prospects for Politics and Activism,* ed. James Jennings. Westport, Conn.: Praeger.

Kubota, Akira. 1980. "Japanese Americans in Local Politics: The Case of Gardena." Pp. 30–35 in *Political Participation of Asian Americans: Problems and*

Strategies, ed. Yung-hwan Jo. Chicago: Pacific/Asian American Mental Health Research Center.

Kwong, Peter. 1979. *Chinatown, New York: Labor and Politics, 1930–1950.* New York: Monthly Review Press.

———. 1987. *The New Chinatown.* New York: Hill & Wang.

Lai, Him Mark. 1976. "China Politics and the U.S. Chinese Communities." Pp. 152–159 in *Counterpoint: Perspectives on Asian America,* ed. Emma Gee. Los Angeles: UCLA Asian American Studies Center.

———. 1992. *From Overseas Chinese to Chinese Americans* [In Chinese]. Hong Kong: Joint.

Lal, Brij V. 1993. "'Nonresistance' on Fiji Plantations: The Fiji Indian Experience, 1879–1920." Pp. 187–216 in *Plantation Workers: Resistance and Accommodation,* ed. Brij Lal, Doug Munro, and Edward Beechert. Honolulu: University of Hawaii Press.

Lam, Karen. 1996. "The Man Outside." *A. Magazine* (August/September).

Lavilla, Stacy. 1998. "Counting on Multiracialism: The Risks and Rewards of the New Census Plan for Racial Identity." *Asianweek* 19 (20): 11.

Lee, Edmund. 1998. "Unity Now, Sensitivity Later?" *A. Magazine* (April/May).

Lee, Marjorie. 1984. "Building Community." Pp. 91–102 in *Linking Our Lives.* Los Angeles: Chinese Historical Society of Southern California.

Lee, Robert G. 1996. "The Hidden World of Asian Immigrant Radicalism." Pp. 256–288 in *The Immigrant Left in the United States,* ed. Paul Buhle and Dan Georgakas. Albany: State University of New York Press.

Lee, Rose Hum. 1978. *The Growth and Decline of Chinese Communities in the Rocky Mountain Region.* New York: Arno Press.

Lee, Siew Hua. 1999. "U.S. Asians Seek Political Clout." *The Straits Times* (Singapore) (29 August).

Leighton, Alexander. 1945. *The Governing of Men: General Principles and Recommendations Based on Experiences at a Japanese Relocation Camp.* Princeton, N.J.: Princeton University Press.

Lesser, Jeff H. 1985–86. "Always 'Outsiders': Asians, Naturalization, and the Supreme Court." *Amerasia Journal* 12 (1): 83–100.

Leung, Vitus, and Don Mar. 1991. "1990 Census Outreach to Asian and Pacific Americans in the San Francisco Metropolitan Area." *Asian American Policy Review* 2:3–15.

Levine, Michael L. 1996. *African Americans and Civil Rights: From 1619 to the Present.* Phoenix, Ariz.: Oryx Press.

Lien, Pei-te. 1994. "Ethnicity and Political Participation: A Comparison Between Asian and Mexican Americans." *Political Behavior* 16:237–64.

———. 1997a. *The Political Participation of Asian Americans: Voting Behavior in Southern California.* New York: Garland Publishing.

———. 1997b. "Ethnicity and Political Adaptation: Comparing Filipinos, Koreans, and the Vietnamese in Southern California." Paper presented at the Annual Meeting of Association of Asian American Studies, 15–17 April, Seattle, Washington.

―――. 1998a. "Who Gives? With What Agenda? And Why? Chinese Americans and Political Contributions." Paper presented at the Annual Meeting of the Association for Asian American Studies, 24–27 June, Honolulu, Hawaii.

―――. 1998b. "Does the Gender Gap in Political Attitudes and Behavior Vary Across Racial Groups? Comparing Asians to Whites, Blacks, and Latinos." *Political Research Quarterly* 51:869–94.

―――. 1999. "What Ties That Bind? Comparing Patterns of Political Opinion Across Major Asian American Groups." Paper presented at the Annual Meeting of the American Political Science Association, 2–5 September, Atlanta, Georgia.

―――. 2000. "Who Votes in Multiracial America? An Analysis of Voting and Registration by Race and Ethnicity, 1990–96." Pp. 199–224 in *Black Politics in Multiracial America,* ed. Yvette Alex-Assensoh and Lawrence Hanks. New York: New York University Press.

―――. Forthcoming. "Residential Context, Interracial Contact, Intergroup Conflict, and the Perceived Anti-Asian Vote in Southern California." *Journal of Asian American Studies.*

Liestman, Daniel. 1999. "Horizontal Inter-ethnic Relations: Chinese and American Indians in the Nineteenth-Century American West." *Western Historical Quarterly* 30:327–49.

Lim, Christina, and Sheldon Lim. 1993. "In the Shadow of the Tiger: The 407th Air Service Squadron." Pp. 25–74 in *Chinese America: History and Perspectives.* San Francisco: Chinese Historical Society of America.

Lim, Gerard. 1994. "David Valderrama Bids for Reelection to Maryland's State Legislature." *Asianweek* 15 (46): 11.

Lin, Jan. 1998. *Reconstructing Chinatown: Ethnic Enclave, Global Change.* Minneapolis: University of Minnesota Press.

Lin, Margaretta Wan Ling, and Cheng Imm Tan. 1994. "Holding Up More Than Half the Heavens: Domestic Violence in Our Communities, A Call for Justice." Pp. 321–34 in *The State of Asian America: Activism and Resistance in the 1990s,* ed. Karin Aguilar-San Juan. Boston: South End Press.

Ling, Huping.1998. *Surviving on the Gold Mountain: A History of Chinese American Women and Their Lives.* Albany: State University of New York.

Ling, Susie. 1989. "The Mountain Movers: Asian American Women's Movement in Los Angeles." *Amerasia Journal* 15 (1): 51–67.

Lipsitz, George. 1998. *The Possessive Investment in Whiteness: How White People Profit from Identity Politics.* Philadelphia: Temple University Press.

Litt, Edgar. 1970. *Beyond Pluralism: Ethnic Politics in America.* Glenview, Ill.: Scott, Foreman and Co.

Liu, John, and Lucie Cheng. 1994. "Pacific Rim Development and the Duality of Post-1965 Asian Immigration to the United States." Pp. 74–99 in *The New Asian Immigration in Los Angeles and Global Restructuring,* ed. Paul Ong, Edna Bonacich, and Lucie Cheng. Philadelphia: Temple University Press.

Locke, Gary. 1998. "The One-Hundred Year Journey: From Houseboy to the Governor's Office." Pp. 1–6 in *National Asian Pacific American Political Alma-*

nac 1998–99, ed. Don Nakanishi and James Lai. Los Angeles: UCLA Asian American Studies Center.

Loewen, James. 1971. *The Mississippi Chinese: Between Black and White.* Cambridge, Mass.: Harvard University Press.

Lopez, David, and Yen Espiritu. 1990. "Panethnicity in the United States: A Theoretical Framework." *Ethnic and Racial Studies* 13 (2): 198–224.

Lott, Juanita T. 1997. *Asian Americans: From Racial Category to Multiple Identities.* Walnut Creek, Calif.: Alta Mira Press.

Low, Victor. 1982. *The Unimpressible Race: A Century of Educational Struggle by the Chinese in San Francisco.* San Francisco: East/West.

Lowe, Lisa. 1996. *Immigrant Acts: On Asian American Cultural Politics.* Durham, N.C.: Duke University Press.

Lowry, Thomas, and Edward Milligan. 1999. "Chinese in the Civil War." *North and South: The Magazine of Civil War Conflict* 2 (4): 35–41.

Lyman, Stanford M. 1974. *Chinese Americans.* New York: Random House.

Lyu, Kingsley. 1977. "Korean Nationalist Activities in Hawaii and the Continental United States, 1900–1945, Part I (1910–1919)." *Amerasia Journal* 4 (1): 23–90.

———. 1977. "Korean Nationalist Activities in Hawaii and the Continental United States, 1900–1945, Part II (1920–1945)." *Amerasia Journal* 4 (2): 53–100.

Maehara, G. Akito. 1995. "Asian Americans Studies and Coalition Building." Pp. 209–20 in *Multiethnic Coalition Building in Los Angeles: A Two-Day Symposium, Nov. 19–20, 1993*, ed. Eui-Young Yu and Edward Chang. Claremont, Calif.: Regina Books.

Maki, Mitchell T., Harry H. R. Kitano, and S. Megan Berthold. 1999. *Achieving the Impossible Dream: How Japanese Americans Obtained Redress.* Urbana and Chicago: University of Illinois Press.

Mansbridge, Jane. 1985. "Myth and Reality: The ERA and the Gender Gap in the 1980 Election." *Public Opinion Quarterly* 49:164–78.

Mar, Don. 1999. "Regional Differences in Asian American Earnings Discrimination: Japanese, Chinese, and Filipino American Earnings in California and Hawaii." *Amerasia Journal* 25 (2): 67–93.

Marquez, Romeo. 1999. "Diginity Beyond Dollars and Cents for Filipino Veterans." *San Diego Union-Tribune* (29 September).

Martinez, George A. 1998. "Essay: African-Americans, Latinos, and the Construction of Race: Toward an Epistemic Coalition." *Chicano-Latino Law Review* 19:213–22.

Massey, Douglas S., and Nancy Denton. 1993. *American Apartheid.* Cambridge, Mass.: Harvard University Press.

Matsuda, Mari. 1996. *Where Is Your Body?* Boston: Beacon Press.

Matsumoto, Valerie. 1984. "Japanese American Women During World War II." *Frontiers* 8:6–14.

Mazumdar, Sucheta. 1989. "General Introduction: A Woman-Centered Perspective on Asian American History." Pp. 1–22 in *Making Waves: An Anthology of Writings by and about Asian American Women*, ed. Asian Women United of California. Boston: Beacon Press.

McAdam, Doug. 1983. "Tactical Innovation and the Pace of Insurgency." *American Sociological Review* 48:735–54.

McClain, Charles. 1994. *In Search of Equality: The Chinese Struggle Against Discrimination in Nineteenth-Century America.* Berkeley: University of California Press.

McClain, Charles, and Laurene Wu McClain. 1991. "The Chinese Contribution to the Development of American Law." Pp. 3–24 in *Entry Denied: Exclusion and the Chinese Community in America, 1882–1943,* ed. Sucheng Chan. Philadelphia: Temple University Press.

McClain, Paula, and Albert K. Karnig. 1990. "Black and Hispanic Socioeconomic and Political Competition." *American Political Science Review* 84:535–45.

McClain, Paula, and Joseph Stewart, Jr. 1999. *"Can We All Get Along?" Racial and Ethnic Minorities in American Politics.* 2d ed. Boulder, Colo.: Westview Press.

McKee, Delber. 1986. "The Chinese Boycott of 1905–1906 Reconsidered: The Role of Chinese Americans." *Pacific Historical Review* 55 (2): 165–191.

Meier, Kenneth J., and Joseph Stewart, Jr. 1991. "Cooperation and Conflict in Multiracial School Districts." *Journal of Politics* 53:1123–33.

Melendy, H. Brett. 1977. *Asians in America: Filipinos, Koreans, and East Indians.* Boston: Twayne Publishers.

———. 1984. *Chinese and Japanese Americans.* New York: Hippocrene Books.

Miller, Stuart C. 1969. *The Unwelcome Immigrant: The American Image of the Chinese, 1785-1882.* Berkeley and Los Angeles, Calif.: University of California Press.

Min, Pyong Gap. 1986–87. "Filipino and Korean Immigrants in Small Business: A Comparative Analysis." *Amerasia Journal* 13 (1): 53–71.

Morales, Iris. 1998. "Palante, Siempre Palante! The Young Lords." Pp. 210–27 in *The Puerto Rican Movement: Voices From the Diaspora,* ed. Andres Torres and Jose E. Velazquez. Philadelphia: Temple University Press.

Morris, Glenn T. 1996. "Coalitions and Alliances: The Case of Indigenous Resistance to the Columbian Quincentenary." Pp. 215–32 in *The Politics of Minority Coalitions: Race, Ethnicity, and Shared Uncertainties,* ed. Wilbur Rich. Westport, Conn.: Praeger.

Morris, Lorenzo, and Linda F. Williams. 1989. "The Coalition at the End of the Rainbow: The 1984 Jackson Campaign." Pp. 227–48 in *Jesse Jackson's 1984 Presidential Campaign: Challenge and Change in American Politics,* ed. Lucius Barker and Ronald Waters. Urbana: University of Illinois Press.

Muller, Thomas. 1997. "Nativism in the Mid-1990s: Why Now?" Pp. 105–18 in *Immigrants Out! The New Nativism and the Anti-immigrant Impulse in the United States,* ed. Juan Perea. New York: New York University Press.

Murayama, Yuzo. 1984. "Contractors, Collusion, and Competition: Japanese Immigrant Railroad Laborers in the Pacific Northwest, 1898–1911." *Explorations in Economic History* 21:290–305.

Nagasawa, Richard. 1986. *Summer Wind: The Story of an Immigrant Chinese Politicians.* Tucson, Ariz.: Westernlore Press.

Nagel, Joanne. 1982. "The Political Mobilization of Native Americans." *Social Science Journal* 19:37–45.

———. 1994. "Constructing Ethnicity: Creating and Recreating Ethnic Identity and Culture." *Social Problems* 41 (1): 152–76.

———. 1996. *American Indian Ethnic Renewal: Red Power and the Resurgence of Identity and Culture*. New York: Oxford University Press.

Nakanishi, Don T. 1986. "Asian American Politics: An Agenda for Research." *Amerasia Journal* 12 (2): 1–27.

———. 1991. "The Next Swing Vote? Asian Pacific Americans and California Politics." Pp. 25–54 in *Racial and Ethnic Politics in California*, ed. Byran O. Jackson and Michael B. Preston. Berkeley, Calif.: IGS Press.

———. 1996. "The Growing Impact of Asian Pacific Americans in American Politics." Pp. 7–9 in *1996 National Asian Pacific American Political Almanac*, ed. Don Nakanishi and James Lai, Los Angeles: UCLA Asian American Studies Center.

———. 1998a. "When Numbers Do Not Add Up: Asian Pacific Americans and California Politics." Pp. 3–43 in *Racial and Ethnic Politics in California*. Vol. 2, ed. Michael Preston, Bruce Cain, and Sandra Bass. Berkeley, Calif.: IGS Press.

———. 1998b. "When the 'Spin' is Out of Control: Asian Pacific Americans After the November 1996 Elections." Pp. 8–11 in *National Asian Pacific American Political Almanac 1998–99*, ed. Don Nakanishi and James Loi. Los Angeles: UCLA Asian American Studies Center.

Nakanishi, Don, and James Lai, eds. 1998. *National Asian Pacific American Political Almanac 1998–99*. Los Angeles: UCLA Asian American Studies Center.

Nash, Phil Tajitsu. 1998a. "State of Politics-1998: An Analysis of APA Participation." *AsianWeek* 19 (39): 10.

———. 1998b. "Washington Journal: How We All Won." *AsianWeek* 20 (11): 9.

National Asian Pacific American Legal Consortium. 1997. *Report on Status of Bilingual Assistance to Asian Pacific American Voters Under Section 203 of the Voting Rights Act*. Washington, D.C.: National Asian Pacific American Legal Consortium.

———. 1998. *Audit of Violence Against Asian Pacific Americas, 1997: Fifth Annual Report*. Washington, D.C.: National Asian Pacific American Legal Consortium.

National Journal. 1972–present. *The Almanac of American Politics*. Washington, D.C.: Author.

Natividad, Irene. 1996. *Reference Library of Asian America*. Detroit, Mich.: Gale Research.

Natividad, Irene, and Susan B. Gall, eds. 1996. *Asian American Almanac*. Detroit, Mich: U.X.L.

Nee, Victor G., and Brett de Bary Nee. 1986. *Longtime Californ': A Documentary Study of an American Chinatown*. Stanford, Calif.: Stanford University Press.

Ng, Franklin, ed. 1995. *The Asian American Encyclopedia*. New York: Cavendish.

———. ed. 1998. *Asians in America Series*. 6 vols. New York: Garland.

Nichioka, Joyce, and Janet Dang. 1999. "David Wu in the House! The Pacific Northwest's Mr. Nice Guy Goes to Washington." *Asianweek* 20 (46): 13.

O'Connor, Karen, and Larry Sabato. 1996. *American Government: Roots and Reform.* 2d ed. Needham Heights, Mass.: Allyn and Bacon.

Okihiro, Gary Y. 1973. "Japanese Resistance in America's Concentration Camps: A Re-evaluation." *Amerasia Journal* 2 (2): 20–34.

———. 1991. *Cane Fires: The Anti-Japanese Movement in Hawaii, 1865–1945.* Philadelphia: Temple University Press.

———. 1994. *Margins and Mainstream.* Seattle: University of Washington Press.

Okumura, Jonathan Y. 1997. "Filipino-Americans: The Marginalized Minority." Pp. 177–94 in *Cultural Diversity in the United States,* ed. Larry Naylor. Westport, Conn.: Bergin & Garvey.

Oliver, Melvin, and David Grant. 1995. "Making Space for Multiethnic Coalitions: The Prospects for Coalition Politics in Los Angeles." Pp. 1–34 in *Multiethnic Coalition Building in Los Angeles: A Two-Day Symposium, Nov. 19–20, 1993,* ed. Eui-Young Yu and Edward Chang. Claremont, Calif.: Regina Books.

Olzak, Susan. 1983. "Contemporary Ethnic Mobilization." *Annual Review of Sociology* 9:355–74.

———. 1992. *The Dynamics of Ethnic Competition and Conflict.* Stanford, Calif.: Stanford University Press.

Omatsu, Glenn. 1994. "The 'Four Prisons' and the Movement of Liberation: Asian American Activism from the 1960s to the 1990s." Pp. 19–67 in *The State of Asian America: Activism and Resistance in the 1990s,* ed. Karin Aguilar-San Juan. Boston: South End Press.

Omi, Michael, and Howard Winant. 1994. *Racial Formation in the United States.* 2d ed. New York: Routledge.

———. 1996. "Contesting the Meaning of Race in the Post-Civil Rights Movement Era." Pp. 470–78 in *Origins and Destinies: Immigration, Race, and Ethnicity in America,* ed. Silvia Pedraza and Ruben Rumbaut. Belmont, Calif.: Wadsworth.

Ong, Paul, and Tania Azores. 1991. "Reapportionment and Redistricting in a Nutshell." Los Angeles: LEAP Asian Pacific American Public Policy Institute.

Ong, Paul, and Suzanne Hee. 1994. "Economic Diversity." Pp. 31–56 in *The State of Asian Pacific America: Economic Diversity, Issues and Policies.* Los Angeles: LEAP Asian Pacific American Public Policy Institute and UCLA Asian American Studies Center.

Ong, Paul, and Don Nakanishi. 1996. "Becoming Citizens, Becoming Voters: The Naturalization and Political Participation of Asian Pacific Immigrants." Pp. 275–305 in *Reframing the Immigration Debate,* ed. Bill Ong Hing and Ronald Lee. Los Angeles: LEAP Asian Pacific American Public Policy Institute and UCLA Asian American Studies Center.

Ortiz, Vilma. 1994. "Women of Color: A Demographic Overview." Pp. 13–40 in *Women of Color in U.S. Society,* ed. Maxine Baca Zinn and Bonnie Thornton Dill. Philadelphia: Temple University Press.

Padilla, Felix M. 1985. *Latino Ethnic Consciousness.* Notre Dame, Ind.: University of Notre Dame Press.

Park, Eunice. 1999. "Indiana Town Unites Against Hate Shooting." *Asianweek* 20 (49): 8.

Park, Robert. 1950. *Race and Culture*. Glencoe, Ill.: Free Press.

Parrenas, Rhacel S. 1998. " 'White Trash' Meets the 'Little Brown Monkeys': The Taxi Dance Hall as a Site of Interracial and Gender Alliances Between White Working Class Women and Filipino Immigrant Men in the 1920s and 30s." *Amerasia Journal* 24 (2): 115–34.

Parrillo, Vincent N. 1982. "Asian Americans in American Politics." Pp. 89–109 in *America's Ethnic Politics*, ed. Joseph Roucek and Bernard Eisenberg. Westport, Conn.: Greenwood Press.

Passel, Jeffrey. 1990. Effects of Population Estimates on Voter Participation Rates. In *Studies in the Measurement of Voter Turnout*, ed. U.S. Bureau of the Census. From Current Population Reports, Population Characteristics Series P-23 no. 168. Washington, D.C.: U.S. GPO.

Passel, Jeffrey S., and Barry Edmonston. 1994. "Immigration and Race: Recent Trends in Immigration to the United States." Pp. 31–71 in *Immigration and Ethnicity: The Integration of America's Newest Arrivals*, ed. Barry Edmonston and Jeffrey Passel. Washington, D.C.: Urban Institute Press.

Pegues, Juliana. 1997. "Strategies from the Field: Organizing the Asian American Feminist Movement." Pp. 3–16 in *Dragon Ladies: Asian American Feminists Breathe Fire*, ed. Sonia Shah. Boston: South End Press.

Petersen, William. 1966. "Success Story, Japanese American Style." *New York Times Magazine* (9 January).

Petersilia, Joan, and Allan Abrahamse. 1994. "A Profile of Those Arrested." Pp. 135–48 in *The Los Angeles Riots: Lessons for the Urban Future*, ed. Mark Baldassare. Boulder, Colo.: Westview Press.

Petracca, Mark P., ed. 1992. *The Politics of Interests: Interest Groups Transformed*. Boulder, Colo.: Westview Press.

Phan, Peter. 1993. "Familiar Strangers: The Fourteenth Air Service Group Case Study of Chinese American Identity During World War II." Pp. 75–107 in *Chinese America: History and Perspectives*. San Francisco: Chinese Historical Society of America.

Picache, Beverly R. 1992. "Velma Veloria Wins Primary for Washington State Legislature: Gears Up for November Elections." *Asianweek* 14 (8): 17.

Pido, Antonio J. A. 1986. *The Pilipinos in America: Macro/Micro Dimensions of Immigration and Integration*. New York: Center for Migration Studies.

Pinderhughes, Dianne M. 1995. "The Role of African American Political Organizations in the Mobilization of Voters." Pp. 35–52 in *From Exclusion to Inclusion: The Long Struggle for African American Political Power*, ed. Ralph C. Gomes and Linda Faye Williams. Westport, Conn.: Praeger.

Poole, Keith, and Harmon Zeigler. 1985. *Women, Public Opinion and Politics*. New York: Longman.

Portes, Alejandro, and Ruben G. Rumbaut. 1996. *Immigrant America: A Portrait*. 2d ed. Berkeley, Calif.: University of California Press.

Raskin, Jamin. 1993. "Legal Aliens, Local Citizens." *University of Pennsylvania Law Review* 141:1391–470.

Regalado, James. 1994. "Community Coalition-Building." Pp. 205–36 in *The Los Angeles Riots: Lessons for the Urban Future*, ed. Mark Baldassare. Boulder, Colo.: Westview Press.

Reimers, David M. 1992. *Still the Golden Door: The Third World Comes to America.* 2d ed. New York: Columbia University Press.

———. 1998. *Unwelcome Strangers: American Identity and the Turn against Immigration.* New York: Columbia University Press.

Research Publications. 1997. *American Journey: Asian American Experience* [interactive multimedia]. Woodbridge, Conn.: Primary Source Media.

Revilla, Linda. 1998. "Filipino American Identity." Pp. 95–111 in *Filipino Americans: Transformation and Identity*, ed. Maria Root. Thousand Oaks, Calif.: Sage.

Rich, Wilbur, ed. 1996. *The Politics of Minority Coalitions: Race, Ethnicity, and Shared Uncertainties.* Westport, Conn.: Praeger.

Riggs, Fred W. 1950. *Pressures on Congress: A Study of the Repeal of Chinese Exclusion.* New York: King's Crown Press.

Rosenstone, Steven J., and John M. Hansen. 1993. *Mobilization, Participation, and Democracy in America.* New York: Macmillan.

Routledge, Paul James. 1992. *The Vietnamese Experience in America.* Bloomington: Indiana University Press.

Rozell, Mark J., and Clyde Wilcox. 1999. *Interest Groups in American Campaigns: The New Face of Electioneering.* Washington, D.C.: Congressional Quarterly Press.

Ruiz, Vicki. 1987. *Cannery Women, Cannery Lives: Mexican Women, Unionization, and the California Food Processing Industry, 1930–1950.* Albuquerque: University of New Mexico.

———. 1998. *From Out of the Shadows: Mexican Women in Twentieth-Century America.* New York: Oxford University Press.

Rumbaut, Ruben. 1996. "A Legacy of War: Refugees from Vietnam, Laos, and Cambodia." Pp. 319–33 in *Origins and Destinies: Immigration, Race, and Ethnicity in America*, ed. Silvia Pedraza and Ruben Rumbaut. Belmont, Calif.: Wadsworth.

Saito, Leland. 1998. *Race and Politics: Asian Americans, Latinos, and Whites in a Los Angeles Suburb.* Urbana: University of Illinois Press.

Saito, Leland, and Edward Park. 2000. "Multiracial Collaborations and Coalitions." Pp. 435–74 in *Transforming Race Relations*, ed. Paul Ong. Los Angeles: LEAP Asian Pacific American Public Policy Institute and UCLA Asian American Studies Center.

Saito, Natsu T. 1997. "Alien and Non-Alien Alike: Citizenship, 'Foreignness,' and Racial Hierarchy in American Law." *Oregon Law Review* 76:261–345.

Salisbury, Robert H., John P. Heinz, Robert L. Nelson, and Edward O. Laumann. 1992. "Triangles, Networks, and Hollow Cores: The Complex Geometry of Washington Interest Representation." Pp. 130–149 in *The Politics of Interests: Interest Groups Transformed*, ed. Mark Petracca. Boulder, Colo.: Westview Press.

Salyer, Lucy E. 1995. *Laws Harsh as Tigers: Chinese Immigrants and the Shaping of Modern Immigration Law.* Chapel Hill: University of North Carolina Press.

Sandmeyer, Elmer C. 1973 [1939]. *The Anti-Chinese Movement in California.* Urbana: University of Illinois Press.

Sapiro, Virginia. 1983. *The Political Integration of Women.* Urbana: University of Illinois Press.

Saxton, Alexander. 1971. *The Indispensable Enemy: Labor and the Anti-Chinese Movement in California.* Berkeley: University of California Press.

————. 1990. *The Rise and Fall of the White Republic.* New York: Verso.

Schattschneider, E. E. 1960. *The Semi-Sovereign People.* New York: Holt, Rinehart & Winston.

Schmidley, Diane, and Campbell Gibson. 1999. *Profile of the Foreign-Born Population in the United States.* U.S. Census Bureau, Current Population Reports, Series P23–195. Washington, D.C.: U.S. GPO.

Scholzman, Kay, Nancy Burns, and Sidney Verba. 1994. "Gender and the Pathways to Participation: The Role of Resources." *Journal of Politics* 56:963–87.

Scholzman, Kay, Nancy Burns, Sidney Verba, and Jesse Donahue. 1995. "Gender and Citizen Participation: Is There a Different Voice?" *American Journal of Political Science* 39:267–93.

Schonberger, Howard. 1990. "Dilemmas of Loyalty: Japanese Americans and the Psychological Warfare Campaigns of the Office of Strategic Services, 1943–45." *Amerasia Journal* 16 (1): 20–38.

Schuman, Howard, Charlotte Steech, Lawrence Bobo, and Maria Krysan. 1997. *Racial Attitudes in America: Trends and Interpretations.* Cambridge, Mass.: Harvard University Press.

Sehgal, Renu, and Jeff Yang. 1992. "A Movement of Parts: Asian American Activism, 10 Years after Vincent Chin." *A. Magazine* (3 April).

Seltzer, Richard A., Jody Newman, and Melissa Leighton. 1997. *Sex as a Political Variable: Women as Candidates and Voters in U.S. Elections.* Boulder, Colo.: Rienner.

Shaffer, Robert. 1998. "Cracks in the Consensus: Defending the Rights of Japanese Americans During World War II." *Radical History Review* 72:84–120.

————. 1999. "Opposition to Internment: Defending Japanese American Rights during World War II." *The Historian* 61:597–619.

Shah, Purvi. 1997. "Redefining the Home: How Community Elites Silence Feminist Activism." Pp. 46–56 in *Dragon Ladies: Asian American Feminists Breathe Fire,* ed. Sonia Shah. Boston: South End Press.

Shah, Sonia. 1997. "Introduction: Slaying the Dragon Lady: Toward an Asian American Feminism." Pp. xii–xxi in *Dragon Ladies: Asian American Feminists Breathe Fire,* ed. Sonia Shah. Boston: South End Press.

Shaiko, Ronald G. 1998. "Lobbying in Washington: A Contemporary Perspective." Pp. 3–18 in *The Interest Group Connection: Electioneering, Lobbying, and Policymaking in Washington,* ed. Paul Herrnson, Ronald Shaiko, and Clyde Wilcox. Chatham, N.J.: Chatham House.

Shankman, Arnold. 1982. *Ambivalent Friends: Afro-Americans View the Immigrant.* Westport, Conn.: Greenwood Press.

Shapiro, Robert, and Harpreet Mahajan. 1986. "Gender Differences in Policy Preferences: A Summary of Trends from the 1960s to the 1980s." *Public Opinion Quarterly* 50:42–61.

Sharma, Miriam. 1984. "The Philippines: A Case of Migration to Hawaii, 1906–1946. Pp. 337–58 in *Labor Immigration Under Capitalism: Asian Workers in the United States Before World War II,* ed. Lucie Cheng and Edna Bonacich. Berkeley: University of California Press.

Sheppard, Burton D. 1985. *Rethinking Congressional Reform: The Reform Roots of the Special Interest Congress.* Cambridge, Mass.: Schenkman.

Shinagawa, Larry H. 1995. *Asian Pacific American Electoral Participation: Three Region Study.* Washington, D.C.: National Asian Pacific American Legal Consortium.

———. 1996. "The Impact of Immigration on the Demography of Asian Pacific Americans." Pp. 59–126 in *The State of Asian Pacific America: Reframing the Immigration Debate: A Public Policy Report,* ed. Bill Ong Hing and Ronald Lee. Los Angeles: LEAP Asian Pacific American Public Policy Institute and UCLA Asian American Studies Center.

———. 1997. *1996 San Francisco Bay Area Exit Poll Report: An Analysis of APA Voter Demographics, Behavior, and Political Participation.* San Francisco: Asian Law Caucus and National Asian Pacific American Legal Consortium.

Shinagawa, Larry H., and Gin Yong Pang. 1996. "Asian American Panethnicity and Intermarriage." *Amerasia* 22 (2): 127–52.

Shingles, Richard D. 1981. "Black Consciousness and Political Participation: The Missing Link." *American Political Science Review* 75:76–91.

Sitkoff, Harvard. 1993. *The Struggle for Black Equality, 1954–1992.* New York: Hill and Wang.

Smith, Rogers M. 1997. *Civic Ideals: Conflicting Visions of Citizenship in U.S. History.* New Haven, Conn.: Yale University Press.

Sonenshein, Raphael. 1993. *Politics in Black and White: Race and Power in Los Angeles.* Princeton, N.J.: Princeton University Press.

Song, Alfred. 1980. "The Asian American in Politics." Pp. 16–20 in *Political Participation of Asian Americans: Problems and Strategies,* ed. Yung-hwan Jo. Chicago: Pacific/Asian American Mental Health Research Center.

Sowell, Thomas. 1983. *The Economics and Politics of Race.* New York: Quill.

———. 1994. *Race and Culture: A World View.* New York: Basic.

Sterngold, James. 1999. "For Asian-Americans, a New Political Resolve." *New York Times* (22 September).

———. 2000. "Nuclear Scientist Set Free After Plea in Secrets Case." *New York Times* (14 September).

Stimson, Grace H. 1955. *Rise of the Labor Movement in Los Angeles.* Los Angeles: University of California Press.

Sung, Betty Lee. 1974. *The Story of the Chinese in America.* New York: Collier Books.

Suro, Roberto. 1996. *Watching America's Door: The Immigration Backlash and the New Policy Debate*. New York: Twentieth Century Fund Press.

Takagi, Dana. 1992. *The Retreat from Race: Asian American Admissions and Racial Politics*. New Brunswick, N.J.: Rutgers University Press.

Takahashi, Jere. 1997. *Nisei/Sansei: Shifting Japanese American Identities and Politics*. Philadelphia: Temple University Press.

Takaki, Ronald. 1983. *Pau Hana: Plantation Life and Labor in Hawaii 1835–1920*. Honolulu: University of Hawaii Press.

———. 1989. *Strangers from a Different Shore*. Boston: Little, Brown.

———. 1990. "They Also Came: The Migration of Chinese and Japanese Women to Hawaii and the Continental United States." Pp. 3–19 in *Chinese America: History and Perspectives*. San Francisco: Chinese Historical Society of America.

Takeda, Okiyoshi. 1997. "The Multi-Dimensionality of the Racial/Ethnic Identities of Asian American College Students: Evidence from Research at Princeton University" [in Japanese]. *The American Review* 31:193–206.

Takezawa, Yasuko I. 1995. *Breaking the Silence: Redress and Japanese American Ethnicity*. Ithaca, N.Y.: Cornell University Press.

Tam, Wendy. 1995. "Asians—A Monolithic Voting Bloc?" *Political Behavior* 17:223–49.

Tarr, David, and Ann O'Connor, eds. 1999. *Congress A to Z*. 3d ed. Washington, D.C.: Congressional Quarterly Press.

Tate, Katherine. 1993. *From Protest to Politics: The New Black Voters in American Elections*. New York: Harvard University Press.

———. 1998. National Black Election Study, 1996 [computer file]. ICPSR version. Columbus: Ohio: Ohio State University [producer], 1997. Ann Arbor, Mich.: Inter-university Consortium for Political and Social Research [distributor].

Taylor, Quintard. 1991. "Blacks and Asians in a White City: Japanese Americans and African Americans in Seattle, 1890–1940." *Western Historical Quarterly* 22:401–29.

Tchen, John Kuo Wei. 1999. *New York before Chinatown: Orientalism and the Shaping of American Culture, 1776–1882*. Baltimore: Johns Hopkins University Press.

Teixeira, Ruy A. 1992. *The Disappearing American Voter*. Washington, D.C.: Brookings.

Thornton, Michael, and Robert Taylor. 1988. "Intergroup Attitudes: Black American Perceptions of Asian Americans." *Ethnic and Racial Studies* 11:474–88.

Tien, Chang-Lin. 1996. "Affirming Affirmative Action." Pp. 19–20 in *Perspectives on Affirmative Action*, ed. Gena A. Lew. Los Angeles: LEAP Asian Pacific American Public Policy Institute.

Tong, Benson. 1994. *Unsubmissive Women: Chinese Prostitutes in Nineteenth-Century San Francisco*. Norman: University of Oklahoma Press.

Truman, David B. 1951. *The Governing Process: Political Interests and Public Opinion*. New York: Knopf.

Tsai, Shih-shan. 1983. *China and the Overseas Chinese in the United States, 1868–1911*. Fayetteville, Ark.: University of Arkansas Press.

Tsai, Shih-Shan Henry. 1986. *The Chinese Experience in America*. Bloomington: Indiana University Press.

Tsang, Daniel C. 1993. "UCI Settles 35-day Student Hunger Strike: Protesters Claim Victory for Ethnic Studies." *Asianweek* 14 (44): 12.

Umemoto, Karen. 1989. " 'On Strike!' San Francisco State College Strike, 1968–69: The Roots of Asian American Studies." *Amerasia Journal* 15 (1): 3–41.

U.S. Bureau of the Census. 1943. *Sixteenth Census of the U.S.: 1940. Population. 2nd Series. Characteristics of the Population. United States Summary*. Washington, D.C.: U.S. GPO.

———. 1953. *U.S. Census of Population: 1950. IV, 3B, Special Reports. Nonwhite Population by Race*. Washington, D.C.: U.S. GPO.

———. 1963. *U.S. Census of Population: 1960. Subject Reports. Nonwhite Population by Race. Final Report*. PC(2)-1C. Washington, D.C.: U.S. GPO.

———. 1964. *U.S. Census of Population: 1960. Characteristics of the Population: U.S. Summary*. PC(1)-C. Washington, D.C.: U.S. GPO.

———. 1973. *1970 Census of Population: Detailed Characteristics. U.S. Summary*. Washington, D.C.: U.S. GPO.

———. 1992. *Current Population Survey: Voter Supplement File, 1990*. ICPSR version. Washington, DC: U.S. Department of Commerce, Bureau of the Census [producer], 1990. Ann Arbor, MI: Inter-university Consortium for Political and Social Research [distributor].

———. 1993a. *1990 Census of Population. General Population Characteristics: United States*. Washington, D.C.: U.S. GPO.

———. 1993b. *1990 Census of Population. Social and Economic Characteristics: United States*. Washington, D.C.: U.S. GPO.

———. *1990 Census of Population. Asians and Pacific Islanders in the United States*. Washington, D.C.: U.S. GPO.

———. 1995. *1992 Census of Governments: Popularly Elected Officials*. GC92(1)-2. Washington, D.C.: U.S. GPO.

———. 1997a. *Current Population Survey: Voter Supplement File, 1992* [Computer file]. ICPSR version. Washington, DC: U.S. Department of Commerce, Bureau of the Census [producer], 1992. Ann Arbor, MI: Inter-university Consortium for Political and Social Research [distributor].

———. 1997b. *Current Population Survey: Voter Supplement File, 1994.* [Computer file]. 2nd ICSPR version. Washington, DC: U.S. Department of Commerce, Bureau of the Census [producer], 1994. Ann Arbor, MI: Inter-university Consortium for Political and Social Research [distributor].

———. 1997c. *Current Population Survey: Voter Supplement File, 1996* [Computer file]. ICPSR version. Washington, DC: U.S. Department of Commerce, Bureau of the Census [producer], 1997. Ann Arbor, MI: Inter-university Consortium for Political and Social Research [distributor].

———. 1998. *Money Income in the United States: 1997*. Current Population Reports, P60–200. Washington, D.C.: U.S. GPO.

———. 1999a. "Resident Population Estimates of the United States by Sex, Race, and Hispanic Origin: April 1, 1990, to July 1, 1999." Population Division, Population Estimates Program. Internet Release Date: 27 August.

————. 1999b. "States Ranked by Asian and Pacific Islander Population in 1998." Population Estimates Program, Population Division. ST-98–24. Internet Release Date: 15 September.

————. 1999c. *Current Population Survey: Voter Supplement File, 1998* [Computer file]. ICPSR version. Washington, D.C.: U.S. Department of Commerce, Bureau of the Census [producer], 1999. Ann Arbor, MI: Inter-university Consortium for Political and Social Research [distributor], 1999.

U.S. Immigration and Naturalization Service. 1992. *Annual Report Immigration and Naturalization Service*. Washington, D.C.: U.S. GPO.

U.S. National Telecommunications and Information Administration. 1999. *Falling through the Net: Defining the Digital Divide: A Report on the Telecommunications and Information Technology Gap in America*. Washington, D.C.: U.S. Department of Commerce.

U.S. Office of Personnel Management. 1999. *The Fact Book: Federal Civilian Workforce Statistics*. Washington, D.C.: U.S. GPO.

Verba, Sidney, and Norman H. Nie. 1972. *Participation in America*. New York: Harper & Row.

Verba, Sidney, Kay Lehman Schlozman, Henry E. Brady, and Norman Nie. 1995a. American Citizen Participation Study, 1990 [Computer file]. ICPSR version. Chicago: University of Chicago, National Opinion Research Center (NORC) [producer]. Ann Arbor, Mich.: Inter-university Consortium for Political and Social Research [distributor].

Verba, Sidney, Kay Schlozman, and Henry Brady. 1995b. *Voice and Equality: Civic Voluntarism in American Politics*. Cambridge: Harvard University Press.

Vigil, Maurilio E. 1987. *Hispanics in American Politics: The Search for Political Power*. Lanham, Md.: University Press of America.

Voter News Service. 1997. Voter News Service General Election Exit Polls, 1996 [Computer file]. ICPSR version. New York: Voter News Service [producer], 1996. Ann Arbor, Mich.: Inter-university Consortium for Political and Social Research [distributor].

————. 1999. Voter News Service General Election Exit Polls, 1998 [Computer file]. ICPSR version. New York: Voter News Service [producer], 1998. Ann Arbor, MI: Inter-university Consortium for Political and Social Research [distributor].

Walton, Hanes, Jr. 1997. *African American Power and Politics*. New York: Columbia University Press.

Wang, Ling-chi. 1996. "Exclusion and Fragmentation in Ethnic Politics: Chinese Americans in Urban Politics." Pp. 128–42 in *The Politics of Minority Coalitions: Race, Ethnicity, and Shared Uncertainties*, ed. Wilbur Rich. Westport, Conn.: Praeger.

————. 1998. "Race, Class, Citizenship, and Extraterritoriality: Asian Americans and the 1996 Campaign Finance Scandal." *Amerasia Journal* 24 (1): 1–21.

Washington Post, Kaiser Foundation, and Harvard University. 1995. Race Poll. [Computer file]. Chilton Research Services [producers]. Roper Center for Public Opinion Research [distributor].

Watts, Jerry G. 1996. "Blacks and Coalition Politics: A Theoretical Reconceptualization." Pp. 35–51 in *The Politics of Minority Coalitions: Race, Ethnicity, and Shared Uncertainties,* ed. Wilbur Rich. Westport, Conn.: Praeger.

Weglyn, Michi. 1976. *Years of Infamy: The Untold Story of America's Concentration Camps.* New York: Morrow.

Wei, William. 1993. *The Asian American Movement.* Philadelphia: Temple University Press.

———. 1995. "Forward Movement." *Asianweek* 17 (17): 13.

Welch, Susan, and Lee Sigelman. 1989. "A Black Gender Gap?" *Social Science Quarterly* 70:120–33.

———. 1992. "A Gender Gap Among Hispanics? A Comparison with Blacks and Anglos." *Western Political Quarterly* 45:181–99.

Wiener, Jon. 1989. "Reagan's Children: Racial Hatred on Campus." *The Nation,* (27 February).

Wilson, William J. 1987. *The Truly Disadvantaged: The Inner City, the Underclass, and Public Policy.* Chicago: University of Chicago Press.

Wirls, Daniel. 1986. "Reinterpreting the Gender Gap." *Public Opinion Quarterly* 50:316–30.

Wollenberg, Charles M. 1995. " 'Yellow Peril' in the Schools (I and II)." Pp. 1–29 in *The Asian American Educational Experience,* ed. Don Nakanishi and Tina Nishida. Lanham, Md.: Rowman and Littlefield.

Wong, Kent Scott. 1994. "Building an Asian Pacific Labor Alliance: A New Chapter in Our History." Pp. 335–49 in *The State of Asian America: Activism and Resistance in the 1990s,* ed. Karin Aguilar-San Juan. Boston: South End Press.

Wong, Kent Scott, and Sucheng Chan, eds. 1998. *Claiming America: Constructing Chinese American Identities during the Exclusion Era.* Philadelphia: Temple University Press.

Wong, Paul. 1972. "The Emergence of the Asian American Movement." *Bridge* 2 (1): 33–39.

Woo, Deborah. 1985. "The Socioeconomic Status of Asian American Women in the Labor Force: An Alternative View." *Sociological Perspectives* 28:307–38.

———. 1989. "The Gap Between Striving and Achieving: The Case of Asian American Women." Pp. 185–94 in *Making Waves: An Anthology of Writings by and about Asian American Women,* ed. Asian Women United of California. Boston: Beacon Press.

Wu, Frank. 1997a. "Damned if We Don't." *A. Magazine* (February/March).

———. 1997b. "Fundraising Investigation Targets APAs." *Asianweek* 18 (29): 8.

———. 1997c. "Have You No Decency? An Analysis of Racial Aspects of Media Coverage on the John Huang Matter." *Asian American Policy Review* VII:1–37.

Xu, Wu, and Ann Leffler. 1992. "Gender and Race Effects on Occupational Prestige, Segregation, and Earnings." *Gender and Society* 6:376–92.

Yamamoto, Eric K. 1997. "Conflict and Complicity: Justice among Communities of Color." *Harvard Latino Law Review* 2: 495–501.

———. 1999. *Interracial Justice: Conflict and Reconciliation in Post–Civil Rights America.* New York: New York University Press.

Yanagisako, Sylvia. 1995. "Transforming Orientalism: Gender, Nationality, and Class in Asian American Studies." Pp. 275–98 in *Naturalizing Power: Essays in Feminist Cultural Analysis*, ed. Sylvia Yanagisako and C. Delaney. New York: Routledge.

Yang, Eun Sik. 1984. "Korean Women of America: From Subordination to Partnership, 1903–1930." *Amerasia Journal* 11 (2): 1–28.

Yang, Jeff. 1993. "The Power of Two: An Interview with Bob and Doris Matsui." *A. Magazine* (15 December).

Yang, Philip Q. 1995. *Post-1965 Immigration to the United States: Structural Determinants*. Westport, Conn.: Praeger.

Yip, Athena. 1996. "APAs for AAS: Fighting for Their Right to Study." *Asianweek* 18 (3): 14.

Yoneda, Karl. 1971. "100 Years of Japanese Labor History in the USA." Pp. 150–58 in *Roots: An Asian American Reader*, ed. Amy Tachiki, Eddie Wong, Franklin Odo, and Buck Wong. Los Angeles: UCLA Asian American Studies Center.

———. 1983. *Ganbatte: Sixty-Year Struggle of a Kibei Worker*. Los Angeles: UCLA Asian American Studies Center.

Yoon, In-Jin. 1997. *On My Own: Korean Businesses and Race Relations in America*. Chicago: The University of Chicago Press.

Yoshikawa, Yoko. 1994. "The Heat Is on *Miss Saigon* Coalition: Organizing across Race and Sexuality." Pp. 275–94 in *The State of Asian America: Activism and Resistance in the 1990s*, ed. Karin Aguilar-San Juan. Boston: South End Press.

Yu, Renqiu. 1992. *To Save China, To Save Ourselves: The Chinese Hand Laundry Alliance of New York*. Philadelphia: Temple University Press.

———. 1998. "Exercise Your Sacred Rights: The Experience of New York's Chinese Laundrymen in Practicing Democracy." Pp. 64–91 in *Claiming America: Constructing Chinese American Identities During the Exclusion Era*, ed. K. Scott Wong and Sucheng Chan. Philadelphia: Temple University Press.

Yung, Judy. 1986. *Chinese American Women: A Pictorial History*. Seattle: University of Washington Press.

———. 1995. *Unbound Feet: A Social History of Chinese Women in San Francisco*. Berkeley: University of California Press.

Zhang, Qingsong. 1998. "The Origins of the Chinese Americanization Movement: Wong Chin Foo and the Chinese Equal Rights League." Pp. 41–63 in *Claiming America: Constructing Chinese American Identities During the Exclusion Era*, ed. K. Scott Wong and Sucheng Chan. Philadelphia: Temple University Press.

Zia, Helen, and Susan Gall, eds. 1995. *Notable Asian Americans*. Detroit, Mich.: Gale Research.

Index

283